SECOND EDITION

Introduction to
LEADERSHIP

To Laurel, Scott, Lisa, and Madison

SECOND EDITION

Introduction to
LEADERSHIP
CONCEPTS AND PRACTICE

Peter G. Northouse
Western Michigan University

Los Angeles | London | New Delhi
Singapore | Washington DC

Los Angeles | London | New Delhi
Singapore | Washington DC

FOR INFORMATION:

SAGE Publications, Inc.
2455 Teller Road
Thousand Oaks, California 91320
E-mail: order@sagepub.com

SAGE Publications Ltd.
1 Oliver's Yard
55 City Road
London EC1Y 1SP
United Kingdom

SAGE Publications India Pvt. Ltd.
B 1/I 1 Mohan Cooperative Industrial Area
Mathura Road, New Delhi 110 044
India

SAGE Publications Asia-Pacific Pte. Ltd.
33 Pekin Street #02-01
Far East Square
Singapore 048763

Acquisitions Editor: Lisa Cuevas Shaw
Development Editor: Julie Nemer
Editorial Assistant: MaryAnn Vail
Production Editor: Eric Garner
Copy Editor: Melinda Masson
Typesetter: C&M Digitals (P) Ltd.
Proofreader: Susan Schon
Indexer: Molly Hall
Cover Designer: Gail Buschman
Marketing Manager: Helen Salmon
Permissions Editor: Karen Ehrmann

Printed in the United States of America

Library of Congress Cataloging-in-Publication Data

Northouse, Peter Guy.

Introduction to leadership : concepts and practice / Peter G. Northouse. — 2nd ed.

p. cm.
Includes bibliographical references and index.

ISBN 978-1-4129-8952-7 (pbk.)

1. Leadership. I. Title.

HM1261.N667 2012 303.3′4—dc22 2011001687

This book is printed on acid-free paper.

11 12 13 14 15 10 9 8 7 6 5 4 3

Contents

Preface

Leadership is a popular topic today. The public is fascinated by who leaders are and what leaders do. People want to know what accounts for good leadership and how to become good leaders. Despite this strong interest in leadership, there are very few books that clearly describe the complexities of practicing leadership. I have written *Introduction to Leadership: Concepts and Practice* to fill this void.

Each chapter describes a fundamental principle of leadership and how it relates to becoming an effective leader. These fundamentals are illustrated through examples and case studies. The text comprises 11 chapters: **Chapter 1, "Being a Leader,"** analyzes how different definitions of leadership have an impact on the practice of leadership. **Chapter 2, "Recognizing Your Traits,"** examines the leadership traits of a select group of historical and contemporary figures and the leadership traits found to be important in social science research. **Chapter 3, "Recognizing Your Philosophy and Style of Leadership,"** explores how a person's view of people, work, and human nature forms a personal philosophy of leadership and how this relates to three commonly observed styles of leadership: authoritarian, democratic, and laissez-faire. **Chapter 4, "Attending to Tasks and Relationships,"** describes how leaders can integrate and optimize task and relationship behaviors in their leadership role. **Chapter 5, "Developing Leadership Skills,"** considers three types of leadership skills: administrative, interpersonal, and conceptual. **Chapter 6, "Creating a Vision,"** explores the characteristics of a vision and how a vision is expressed and implemented. **Chapter 7, "Setting the Tone,"** focuses on how important it is for leaders who are running groups or organizations to provide structure, clarify norms, build cohesiveness, and promote standards of excellence. **Chapter 8, "Listening to Out-Group Members,"** explores the nature of out-groups, their impact, and ways leaders should respond to out-group members. **Chapter 9,**

"Handling Conflict," addresses the question of how we can manage conflict and produce positive change. **Chapter 10, "Overcoming Obstacles,"** addresses seven obstacles that subordinates may face and how a leader can help to overcome these. **Chapter 11, "Addressing Ethics in Leadership,"** explores six factors that are related directly to ethical leadership: character, actions, goals, honesty, power, and values.

► SPECIAL FEATURES

Introduction to Leadership: Concepts and Practice is designed to help the reader understand how to become a better leader. While the book is grounded in leadership theory, it describes the basics of leadership in an understandable and user-friendly way. Each chapter focuses on a fundamental aspect of leadership, discusses how it can be applied in real leadership situations, and ends with a case study to illustrate the leadership concepts discussed in the chapter. At the end of each case, thought-provoking questions are provided to help the reader analyze the case using ideas presented in the chapter.

Perhaps the most notable features of this book are the three *interactive components* included in every chapter, which give the reader the means to explore leadership concepts and real-world applications:

- **Questionnaires** help the reader determine his or her own leadership style and preferences.

- **Observational Exercises** guide the reader in examining behaviors of leaders from his or her life experiences.

- **Reflection and Action Worksheets** stimulate the reader to reflect on his or her leadership style and identify actions to take to become more effective.

Each chapter begins with a directive to the reader to complete the questionnaire (located at the end of the chapter) before reading the chapter's content. By completing the questionnaire first, the reader will be more aware of how the chapter's content specifically applies to his or her leadership tendencies.

AUDIENCE ◄

A practice-oriented book, *Introduction to Leadership: Concepts and Practice* is written in a user-friendly style appropriate for introductory leadership courses across disciplines. Specifically, it is well suited for programs in leadership studies and leadership courses in schools of agriculture, allied health, business, management, communication, education, engineering, military science, public administration, nursing, political science, social work, and religion. In addition, this book is appropriate for programs in continuing education, corporate training, executive development, in-service training, and government training. It is also useful for student extracurricular activities.

ACKNOWLEDGMENTS ◄

I would like to express my appreciation to many individuals who directly or indirectly played a role in the development of this book. First, I would like to thank the many people at SAGE Publications, in particular my editor, Lisa Cuevas Shaw, who has strongly supported this project and provided exemplary leadership throughout the revision process. As always, I am especially thankful for the efforts of MaryAnn Vail, whose time, energy, and commitment contributed significantly to the quality of the project and ensured its success. In addition, I would like to thank Julie Nemer and Eve Oettinger for their special efforts in developing the book and its ancillaries. For their work during the production of the book, I would like to thank copy editor Melinda Masson and production editor Eric Garner. In their own unique ways, each of these people made valuable contributions that enhanced the overall quality of the book. Collectively, they are an extraordinary team that demonstrates the very highest standards of excellence in all that they do.

For comprehensive reviews of the manuscript, I would like to thank the following reviewers:

Maureen Baldwin, *Saint Ambrose University*

Barry L. Boyd, *Texas A&M University*

Linda L. Brennan, *Mercer University*

Tom Butkiewicz, *University of Redlands*

Patricia Cane, *Klamath Community College*

James R. "Chip" Coldren, Jr., *Governors State University*

Barbara Collins, *Cabrini College*

Don Green, *Lincoln Christian University*

Jean Gabriel Jolivet, *Southwestern College*

Ruth Klein, *Le Moyne College*

Joseph W. T. Pugh, *Immaculata University*

Bronte H. Reynolds, *California State University, Northridge*

Louis Rubino, *California State University, Northridge*

Pearl Sims, *Peabody College of Vanderbilt University*

Amy Wilson, *University at Buffalo*

Critiques by these reviewers were invaluable in helping to focus my thinking and writing during the revision process.

For her outstanding work in developing creative instructor's materials for this edition, I am grateful to Isolde Anderson.

A special acknowledgment goes to Marie Lee, for her exceptional editing and support throughout this project. Her insights and contributions have added considerably to the quality of this edition.

Finally, I would like to thank my colleagues and students in the School of Communication at Western Michigan University for their continued encouragement and interest in this project.

About the Author

 **Peter G. Northouse,** PhD, is professor of communication in the School of Communication at Western Michigan University. For more than 20 years, he has taught undergraduate and graduate courses in leadership, interpersonal communication, and organizational communication. In addition to publications in professional journals, he is the author of *Leadership: Theory and Practice* (now in its fifth edition) and coauthor of *Health Communication: Strategies for Health Professionals* (now in its third edition). His scholarly and curricular interests include models of leadership, leadership assessment, ethical leadership, and leadership and group dynamics. He has worked as a consultant in a variety of areas, including leadership development, leadership education, conflict management, and health communication. He holds a doctorate in speech communication from the University of Denver, and master's and bachelor's degrees in communication education from Michigan State University.

1

Before you begin reading . . .

Complete the *Conceptualizing Leadership Questionnaire*, which you will find on pp. 11–12. As you read the chapter, consider your results on the questionnaire.

1

Being a Leader

This book is about *what it takes to be a leader.* Everyone, at some time in life, is asked to be a leader, whether to lead a classroom discussion, coach a children's soccer team, or direct a fund-raising campaign. Many situations require leadership. A leader may have a high profile (e.g., an elected public official) or a low profile (e.g., a volunteer leader in Big Brothers Big Sisters), but in every situation there are leadership demands placed on the individual who is the leader. Being a leader is challenging, exciting, and rewarding, and carries with it many responsibilities. This chapter discusses different ways of looking at leadership and their impacts on what it means to be a leader.

DEFINING LEADERSHIP ◄

At the outset, it is important to address a basic question: *What is leadership?* Scholars who study leadership have struggled with this question for many decades and have written a great deal about the nature of leadership (Antonakis, Cianciolo, & Sternberg, 2004; Bass, 1990; Conger & Riggio, 2007). (See Box 1.1.) In leadership literature, more than 100 different definitions of leadership have been identified (Rost, 1991). Despite these many definitions, a number of concepts are recognized by most people as accurately reflecting what it is to be a leader.

Video Link 1.1
Watch people talk about their definitions of leaderhship.

Box 1.1 The Evolution of Leadership

Leadership has long intrigued humankind and has been the topic of extensive literature for centuries. The earliest writings include philosophies of leadership such as Machiavelli's *The Prince* (1531), and biographies of great leaders. With the development of the social sciences during the 20th century, inquiry into leadership became prolific. Studies on leadership have emerged from every discipline "that has had some interest in the subject of leadership: anthropology, business administration, educational administration, history, military science, nursing administration, organizational behavior, philosophy, political science, public administration, psychology, sociology, and theology" (Rost, 1991, p. 45).

As a result, there are many approaches to leadership. Not unlike fashion, approaches to leadership have evolved, changed focus and direction, and built upon one another during the past century. To understand this evolution a brief historical view can be helpful:

Trait Approach

The early **trait approach** theories were called **"Great Man" theories** because they focused on identifying the innate qualities and characteristics possessed by great social, political, and military leaders such as Catherine the Great, Mohandas Gandhi, Abraham Lincoln, Moses, and Joan of Arc. Studies of leadership traits were especially strong from 1900 to the early 1940s and enjoyed a renewed emphasis beginning in the 1970s as researchers began to examine visionary and charismatic leadership. In the 1980s, researchers linked leadership to the *"Big Five" personality factors* while interest in *emotional intelligence* as a trait gained favor in the 1990s.

Behavior Approach

In the late 1930s, leadership research began to focus on behavior—what leaders do and how they act. Groundbreaking studies by researchers at The Ohio State University and the University of Michigan in the 1940s and 1950s analyzed how leaders acted in small group situations. **Behavior approach** theories hit their heyday in the early 1960s with Blake and Moulton's (1964) work exploring how managers use **task behaviors** and **relationship behaviors** in the organizational setting.

Situational Approach

The premise of this approach is that different situations demand different kinds of leadership. Serious examination of **situational approach** theories began in the late 1960s by Hersey and Blanchard and Reddin. Situational approaches continued to be refined and revised from the 1970s through the 1990s (Vecchio, 1987). One of these, **path-goal theory**, examines how leaders use employee motivation to enhance performance and satisfaction. Another approach, **contingency theory**, focuses on the match between the leader's style and specific situational variables.

Relational Approach

In the 1990s, researchers began examining the nature of relations between leaders and followers. This research ultimately evolved into the *Leader-Member Exchange (LMX) Theory.* LMX Theory predicts that high-quality relations generate more positive leader outcomes than lower-quality relations. Research in the **relational approach** of leadership continues to generate moderate interest today.

"New Leadership" Approach

When these approaches began appearing in the mid-1980s—three decades ago—they were, and continue to be, called "new leadership" approaches (Bryman, 1992). Beginning in 1985 with the work of Bass and his associates, leadership studies generated *visionary* or *charismatic leadership* theories. From these approaches developed **transformational leadership theory**, which describes leadership as a process that changes people and organizations.

Emerging Leadership Approaches

A diverse range of approaches to leadership are emerging during the 21st century. Currently, **authentic leadership** that looks at the authenticity of leaders and their leadership is enjoying strong interest. Similarly, the **spiritual leadership** approach examines how leaders use values, a sense of "calling," and membership to motivate followers. **Servant leadership** emphasizes the "caring principle" with leaders as "servants" who focus on their followers' needs in order to help these followers become more autonomous, knowledgeable, and like servants themselves. *Gender-based studies* have gained much momentum as women continue to become more dominant in the workforce, especially on a global level. The shrinking of the world through technology has also been illuminated through the study of *cultural and global approaches* to leadership.

This historical timeline is not intended to represent these approaches as being separate and distinct eras, only to disappear from the picture when a new theory appears. Instead, many of these theories occur concurrently, building upon one another (see Figure 1.1). Even when a certain approach's period of popularity has waned, the theory continues to influence further study and the development of new leadership approaches.

Encyclopedia Link 1.1
Read more on contemporary leadership theories.

Video Link 1.2
Watch more about changes in leadership.

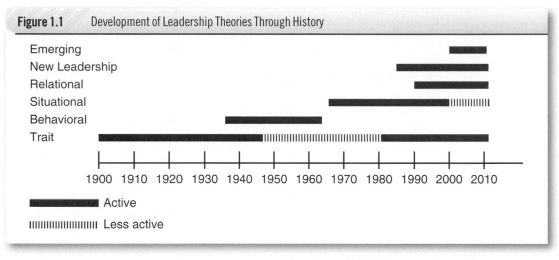

Figure 1.1   Development of Leadership Theories Through History

Source: Adapted from Antonakis, J., Cianciolo, A. T., & Sternberg, R. J. (Eds.). (2004). *The nature of leadership.* Thousand Oaks, CA: Sage, p. 7.

"LEADERSHIP IS A TRAIT"

First, leadership is thought of as a *trait.* A **trait** is a distinguishing quality of an individual, which is often inherited. Defining leadership as a trait means that each individual brings to the table certain qualities that influence the way he or she leads. Some leaders are confident, some are decisive, and still others are outgoing and sociable. Saying that leadership is a trait places a great deal of emphasis on the leader and on the leader's special gifts. It follows the often-expressed belief "leaders are born, not made." Some argue that focusing on traits makes leadership an elitist enterprise because it implies that only a few people with special talents will lead. Although there may be some truth to this argument, it can also be argued that all of us are born with a wide array of unique traits and that many of these traits can have a positive impact on our leadership. It also may be possible to modify or change some traits.

Encyclopedia Link 1.2
Read more about traits and leadership.

Through the years, researchers have identified a multitude of traits that are associated with leadership. In Chapter 2 we will discuss many of these. Although there are many important leadership traits, what is most important for leaders is having the required traits that a particular situation demands. For example, a chaotic emergency room at a hospital requires a leader who is insightful and decisive and can bring calm to the situation. Conversely, a high school classroom in which students are bored demands a teacher who is inspiring and creative.

Effective leadership results when the leader engages the right traits in the right place at the right time.

"LEADERSHIP IS AN ABILITY"

In addition to being thought of as a trait, leadership is conceptualized as an ability. A person who has leadership **ability** is *able* to be a leader—that is, has the capacity to lead. While the term *ability* frequently refers to a natural capacity, ability can be acquired. For example, some people are naturally good at public speaking, while others rehearse to become comfortable speaking in public. Similarly, some people have the natural physical ability to excel in a sport, while others develop their athletic capacity through exercise and practice. In leadership, some people have the natural ability to lead, while others develop their leadership abilities through hard work and practice.

An example of leadership as ability is the legendary University of California at Los Angeles basketball coach John Wooden, whose teams won seven consecutive National Collegiate Athletic Association titles. Described first as a teacher and then as a coach, Wooden implemented four laws of learning into his coaching: explanation, demonstration, imitation, and repetition. His goal was to teach players how to do the right thing instinctively under great pressure. Less visible or well known, but also an example of leadership as ability, is the unheralded but highly effective restaurant manager who, through years of experience and learning, is able to create a successful, award-winning restaurant. In both of these examples, it is the individuals' abilities that create outstanding leadership.

"LEADERSHIP IS A SKILL"

Third, leadership is a *skill*. Conceptualized as a **skill**, leadership is a *competency* developed to accomplish a task effectively. Skilled leaders are competent people who know the means and methods for carrying out their responsibilities. For example, a skilled leader in a fund-raising campaign knows every step and procedure in the fund-raising process and is able to use this knowledge to run an effective campaign. In short, skilled leaders are competent—they know what they need to do, and they know how to do it.

Describing leadership as a skill makes leadership available to everyone because skills are competencies that people can learn or develop. Even without natural leadership ability, people can improve their leadership with practice, instruction, and feedback from others. Viewed as a skill, leadership can be studied and learned. If you are capable of learning from experience, you can acquire leadership.

"LEADERSHIP IS A BEHAVIOR"

Leadership is also a *behavior*. It is *what leaders do* when they are in a leadership role. The behavioral dimension is concerned with how leaders act toward others in various situations. Unlike traits, abilities, and skills, leadership behaviors are observable. When someone leads, we see that person's leadership behavior.

Video Link 1.3
See a definition of leadership.

Research on leadership has shown that leaders engage primarily in two kinds of general behaviors: **task behaviors** and **process behaviors**. Task behaviors are used by leaders to get the job done (e.g., a leader prepares an agenda for a meeting). Process behaviors are used by leaders to help people feel comfortable with other group members and at ease in the situations in which they find themselves (e.g., a leader helps individuals in a group to feel included). Since leadership requires both task and process behaviors, the challenge for leaders is to know the best way to combine them in their efforts to reach a goal.

"LEADERSHIP IS A RELATIONSHIP"

Another, and somewhat unusual, way to think about leadership is as a *relationship*. From this perspective, leadership is centered on the communication between leaders and followers rather than on the unique qualities of the leader. Thought of as a relationship, leadership becomes a process of collaboration that occurs between leaders and followers (Rost, 1991). A leader affects and is affected by followers, and both leader and followers are affected in turn by the situation that surrounds them. This approach emphasizes that leadership is not a linear one-way event, but rather an interactive event. In traditional leadership, authority is often top down; in the interactive type of

Video Link 1.4
Watch a leader speak about collaboration.

leadership, authority and influence are shared. When leadership is defined in this manner, it becomes available to everyone. It is not restricted to the formally designated leader in a group.

Thinking of leadership as a relationship suggests that leaders must include followers and their interests in the process of leadership. A leader needs to be fully aware of the followers and the followers' interests, ideas, positions, attitudes, and motivations. In addition, this approach has an ethical overtone because it stresses the need for leaders to work with followers to achieve their mutual purposes. Stressing mutuality lessens the possibility that leaders might act toward followers in ways that are forced or unethical. It also increases the possibility that leaders and followers will work together toward a common good (Rost, 1991).

"LEADERSHIP IS AN INFLUENCE PROCESS"

A final way of thinking about leadership is as an influence process. This is the perspective that will be emphasized in this book.

> ***Leadership*** *is a process whereby an individual influences a group of individuals to achieve a common goal.*

Video Link 1.5
Watch a leader speak about influence.

Defining leadership as an influence process means that it is not a trait or an ability that resides in the leader, but rather an interactive event that occurs between the leader and the followers. Influence is central to the process of leadership because leaders affect followers. Leaders direct their energies toward influencing individuals to achieve something together. Stressing common goals gives leadership an ethical dimension because it lessens the possibility that leaders might act toward followers in ways that use coercion or are unethical.

▶ GLOBAL LEADERSHIP ATTRIBUTES

Journal Link 1.1
Read about global leadership competencies.

We probably all wonder at the differences in leadership around the world. Why do some countries gravitate toward the distributed leadership of a democracy, while others seem content with the hierarchical leadership of a monarchy or dictatorship? The definition and concepts of leadership outlined in this chapter are from an American perspective. If you were to travel to nations across the world, you would no doubt encounter different views of leadership specific to those ethnic and political cultures.

In 2004, Robert House led a group of 160 researchers in an ambitious study to increase our understanding of the impact culture has on leadership effectiveness. The GLOBE (Global Leadership and Organizational Behavior Effectiveness) studies drew on the input of 17,000 people in 62 countries in determining how leadership varies across the world. Among the many findings generated by the GLOBE studies was the identification of positive and negative leadership characteristics that are universally accepted worldwide (see Table 1.1).

Table 1.1	Universal Leadership Attributes	
Positive Leader Attributes		
Trustworthy	Just	Honest
Foresighted	Plans ahead	Encouraging
Positive	Dynamic	Motivator
Builds confidence	Motivational	Dependable
Intelligent	Decisive	Effective bargainer
Win-win problem solver	Communicative	Informed
Administratively skilled	Coordinator	Team builder
Excellence oriented		
Negative Leader Attributes		
Loner	Asocial	Noncooperative
Irritable	Nonexplicit	Egocentric
Ruthless	Dictatorial	

Source: Adapted from House, R. J., Hanges, P. J., Javidan, M., Dorfman, P. W., & Gupta, V. (Eds.). (2004). *Culture, leadership, and organizations: The GLOBE study of 62 societies.* Thousand Oaks, CA: Sage, pp. 677–678. Reprinted with permission.

To summarize, the meaning of leadership is complex and includes many dimensions. For some people, leadership is a *trait* or an *ability,* for others it is a *skill* or a *behavior,* and for still others it is a *relationship* or *process.* In reality, leadership probably includes components of all of these dimensions. Each dimension explains a facet of leadership.

Journal Link 1.2
Read more about dimensions and leadership.

In considering these various definitions of leadership and based on your Conceptualizing Leadership Questionnaire results, which dimension seems closest to how you think of leadership? How would you define leadership? Answers to these questions are important because *how you think* about leadership will strongly influence *how you practice* leadership.

► PRACTICING LEADERSHIP

There is a strong demand for effective leadership in society today. This demand exists at the local and community levels, as well as at the national level, in this country and abroad. People feel the need for leadership in all aspects of their lives. They want leaders in their personal lives, at school, in the work setting, and even in their spiritual lives. Everywhere you turn, people are expressing a need for strong leadership.

When people ask for leadership in a particular situation, it is not always clear exactly what they want. For the most part, however, they want effective leadership. Effective leadership is intended influence that creates change for the greater good. Leadership uses positive means to achieve positive outcomes. Furthermore, people want leaders who listen to and understand their needs and who can relate to their circumstances. The challenge for each of us is to be prepared to lead when we are asked to be the leader.

CASE STUDY

The following case study describes the leadership of a very successful high school swimming coach. The questions at the end of the case will help you analyze the case using ideas from the different conceptual perspectives provided in the chapter.

King of the Hill

Denny Hill's career as a high school swimming coach didn't start out well. The seniors on his team quit in the first season because he required them to come to all the workouts. The team only won three meets the whole season. That was 40 years ago. Since that time, the high school chemistry teacher's success as a swimming coach has been extraordinary; his winnings include more than 900 boys' and girls' dual meets and a phenomenal 31 state titles.

Denny is noted for creating a team effort out of what is usually considered an individual sport. He begins every season with a team sleepover, followed by "Hell Week," a two-week grueling regimen in which team members swim at least 5 miles a workout and 10 miles a day. Denny sees "Hell Week" as pivotal: "When the kids are in the same boat—kind of like boot camp—there is a certain bonding of them all doing it together" (McCabe, 2003, p. 8D).

Denny sees his team as an aquatic family. "Kids want boundaries at this age," he says, "so I make the rules very clear to them. They also want to feel safe."

And while Denny makes his swimmers train, train, train, he doesn't exclude anyone. Even if a swimmer doesn't show state title–winning potential, Denny still treats him or her as a full-fledged member of the team.

Denny passes the mantle of leadership onto his team members, as well. Seniors are expected to be the mature leaders who inform the freshmen of the team goals and expectations. Juniors are to be role models, while sophomores serve as quiet leaders who are still learning but have a foundation in the team culture. Even the freshmen members have a job: They are required to pay attention to the coaches and other team members as they learn the team's culture and what's expected.

Denny, described as adept at "reading kids," is known for his ability to relate to his swimmers. A good listener, he holds a 20-minute team meeting each Monday where every member has the opportunity to present a rose or a complaint to anyone on the team including the coaches. He is tough on swimmers and makes them work, but when they need support he is always there to put an arm around them. His assistant and wife Liz says, "He knows if you yell all the time, they tune you out, and he knows if you're nice all the time, you're not going to get everything out of them" (McCabe, 2003, p. 8D).

One of his former swimmers says Denny's ability to use humor made him a great coach: "He instantly got the team on his side. He'd make a comment or joke that would take the edge off those long distance workouts . . . But he knew his stuff. We worked very, very hard for him" (McCabe, 2003, p. 8D).

Denny's philosophy is similar to that of the famous University of Michigan football coach, Bo Schembechler. "The winning thing isn't everything. Preparing to win is the key. By preparing to win, everything takes care of itself. When you do win, you've done it the right way," Denny says ("Hill Earns 500th Win as Pioneer Boys Swim Coach," 2009).

Questions

1. What leadership *traits* account for Denny Hill's success?

2. How would you describe Denny Hill's leadership *abilities?*

3. Leadership includes administrative skills, interpersonal skills, and conceptual skills. How does Denny Hill stack up on these *skills?*

4. How does Denny Hill integrate task and relationship *behaviors* in his leadership?

5. From a relational perspective, how would you describe Denny Hill's leadership?

6. In what way does Denny Hill's coaching exemplify leadership as an influence process?

Summary

All of us at some time in our lives will be asked to show leadership. When you are asked to be the leader, it will be both demanding and rewarding. How you approach leadership is strongly influenced by your definitions of and beliefs about leadership. Through the years, writers have defined leadership in a multitude of ways. It is a complex, multidimensional process that is often conceptualized in a variety of ways by different people. Some of the most common ways of looking at leadership are as a trait, an ability, a skill, a behavior, a relationship, or a process. The way you think about leadership will influence the way you practice leadership.

Video Link 1.6
Watch a definition of leadership.

 Go to **http://www.sagepub.com/northouseintro2e/** *for additional exercises and study resources. Select Chapter 1, Being a Leader, for chapter-specific activities.*

Glossary Terms

ability   4

authentic leadership   2

behavior approach   2

contingency theory   2

"Great Man" theories   2

leadership   6

path-goal theory   2

process behaviors   5

relational approach   2

relationship behaviors   2

servant leadership   2

situational approach   2

skill   4

spiritual leadership   2

task behaviors   5

trait   3

trait approach   2

transformational leadership theory   2

References

Antonakis, J., Cianciolo, A. T., & Sternberg, R. J. (Eds.). (2004). *The nature of leadership*. Thousand Oaks, CA: Sage.

Bass, B. M. (1990). *Bass and Stogdill's handbook of leadership: A survey of theory and research*. New York: Free Press.

Blake, R. R., & Moulton, J. S. (1964). *The managerial grid*. Houston, TX: Gulf.

Bryman, A. (1992). *Charisma and leadership in organizations*. London: Sage.

Conger, J. A., & Riggio, R. E. (Eds.). (2007). *The practice of leadership: Developing the next generation of leaders*. San Francisco: Jossey-Bass.

Hill earns 500th win as Pioneer boys swim coach. (2009, January 24). *Ann Arbor News* staff report. Retrieved December 10, 2010, from http://highschoolsports.mlive.com/news/article/101769104/hill-earns-500th-win-as-pioneer-boys-swim-coach/

House, R. J., Hanges, P. J., Javidan, M., Dorfman, P. W., & Gupta, V. (2004). *Culture, leadership, and organizations: The GLOBE study of 62 societies*. Thousand Oaks, CA: Sage.

McCabe, M. (2003, June 20). Pioneer coach turns pool of talent into titles. *Detroit Free Press,* p. 8D.

Rost, J. C. (1991). *Leadership for the twenty-first century*. Westport, CO: Praeger.

Vecchio, R. P. (1987). Situational leadership theory: An examination of a prescriptive theory. *Journal of Applied Psychology, 72*(3), 444–451.

1.1   Conceptualizing Leadership Questionnaire

 Visit **www.sagepub.com/northouseintro2e** for downloadable versions of these questionnaires

Purpose

1. To identify how you view leadership
2. To explore your perceptions of different aspects of leadership

Directions

1. Consider for a moment your own impressions of the word *leadership*. Based on your experiences with leaders in your lifetime, what is leadership?
2. Using the scale below, indicate the extent to which you agree or disagree with the following statements about leadership.

Statement	Strongly disagree	Disagree	Neutral	Agree	Strongly agree
1. When I think of leadership, I think of a person with special personality traits.	1	2	3	4	5
2. Much like playing the piano or tennis, leadership is a learned ability.	1	2	3	4	5
3. Leadership requires knowledge and know-how.	1	2	3	4	5
4. Leadership is about what people do rather than who they are.	1	2	3	4	5
5. Followers can influence the leadership process as much as leaders.	1	2	3	4	5
6. Leadership is about the process of influencing others.	1	2	3	4	5
7. Some people are born to be leaders.	1	2	3	4	5
8. Some people have the natural ability to be leaders.	1	2	3	4	5
9. The key to successful leadership is having the right skills.	1	2	3	4	5
10. Leadership is best described by what leaders do.	1	2	3	4	5
11. Leaders and followers share in the leadership process.	1	2	3	4	5
12. Leadership is a series of actions directed toward positive ends.	1	2	3	4	5
13. A person needs to have certain traits to be an effective leader.	1	2	3	4	5
14. Everyone has the capacity to be a leader.	1	2	3	4	5
15. Effective leaders are competent in their roles.	1	2	3	4	5
16. The essence of leadership is performing tasks and dealing with people.	1	2	3	4	5

Statement	Strongly disagree	Disagree	Neutral	Agree	Strongly agree
17. Leadership is about the common purposes of leaders and followers.	1	2	3	4	5
18. Leadership does not rely on the leader alone but is a process involving the leader, followers, and the situation.	1	2	3	4	5
19. People become great leaders because of their traits.	1	2	3	4	5
20. People can develop the ability to lead.	1	2	3	4	5
21. Effective leaders have competence and knowledge.	1	2	3	4	5
22. Leadership is about how leaders work with people to accomplish goals.	1	2	3	4	5
23. Effective leadership is best explained by the leader-follower relationship.	1	2	3	4	5
24. Leaders influence and are influenced by followers.	1	2	3	4	5

Scoring

1. Sum scores on items 1, 7, 13, and 19 (trait emphasis)

2. Sum scores on items 2, 8, 14, and 20 (ability emphasis)

3. Sum scores on items 3, 9, 15, and 21 (skill emphasis)

4. Sum scores on items 4, 10, 16, and 22 (behavior emphasis)

5. Sum scores on items 5, 11, 17, and 23 (relationship emphasis)

6. Sum scores on items 6, 12, 18, and 24 (process emphasis)

Total Scores

1. Trait emphasis: _____

2. Ability emphasis: _____

3. Skill emphasis: _____

4. Behavior emphasis: _____

5. Relationship emphasis: _____

6. Process emphasis: _____

Scoring Interpretation

The scores you received on this questionnaire provide information about how you define and view leadership. The emphasis you give to the various dimensions of leadership has implications for how you approach the leadership process. For example, if your highest score is *trait emphasis*, it suggests that you emphasize the role of the leader and the leader's special gifts in the leadership process. However, if your highest score is *relationship emphasis*, it indicates that you think leadership is centered on the communication between leaders and followers, rather than on the unique qualities of the leader. By comparing your scores, you can gain an understanding of the aspects of leadership that you find most important and least important. The way you think about leadership will influence how you practice leadership.

1.2   **Observational Exercise**

 Visit **www.sagepub.com/northouseintro2e** for downloadable versions of these questionnaires

Conceptualizing Leadership

Purpose

1. To develop an understanding of the complexity of leadership
2. To become aware of the different ways people define leadership

Directions

1. In this exercise, select five people you know and interview them about leadership.
2. Ask each person to give you his or her definition of leadership, and to describe his or her personal beliefs about effective leadership.
3. Record each person's response on a separate sheet of paper.

    Person #1 (name) _____

    Person #2 (name) _____

    Person #3 (name) _____

    Person #4 (name) _____

    Person #5 (name) _____

Questions

1. What differences did you observe in how these people define leadership?

2. What seems to be the most common definition of leadership?

3. In what ways did people describe leadership differently from the definitions in Chapter 1, "Being a Leader"?

4. Of the people interviewed, whose definition comes closest to your own? Why?

1.3   Reflection and Action Worksheet

 Visit **www.sagepub.com/northouseintro2e** for downloadable versions of these questionnaires

Conceptualizing Leadership

Reflection

1. Each of us has our own unique way of thinking about leadership. What leaders or people have influenced you in your thinking about leadership? Discuss what leadership means to you and give your definition of leadership.

2. What do the scores you received on the Conceptualizing Leadership Questionnaire suggest about your beliefs on leadership? Of the six dimensions on the questionnaire (traits, ability, skills, behavior, relationships, and process), which two are the most similar to your own beliefs? Which two are the least like your own beliefs? Discuss.

3. Do you think leadership is something everyone can learn to do, or do you think it is a natural ability reserved for a few? Explain your answer.

Action

1. Based on the interviews you conducted with others about leadership, how could you incorporate others' ideas about leadership into your own leadership?

2. Treating leadership as a relationship has ethical implications. How could adding the *relationship* approach to your leadership make you a better leader? Discuss.

3. Think about your own leadership. Identify one trait, ability, skill, or behavior that you could develop more fully to become a better leader.

Before you begin reading . . .

Complete the *Leadership Traits Questionnaire*, which you will find on pp. 39–41. As you read the chapter, consider your results on the questionnaire.

Recognizing Your Traits

2

Why are some people leaders while others are not? What makes people become leaders? Do leaders have certain traits? These questions have been of interest for many years. It seems that all of us want to know what characteristics account for effective leadership. This chapter will address the traits you need to be a leader.

Since the early 20th century, hundreds of research studies have been conducted on the traits of leaders. These studies have produced an extensive list of ideal leadership traits (see Antonakis, Cianciolo, & Sternberg, 2004; Bass, 1990). The list of important leadership traits is long, and includes such traits as diligence, trustworthiness, dependability, articulateness, sociability, open-mindedness, intelligence, confidence, self-assurance, and conscientiousness. Because the list is so extensive, it is difficult to identify specifically which traits are essential for leaders. In fact, nearly all of the traits are probably related to effective leadership.

What traits do you need to be a leader? To answer the question, two areas will be addressed in this chapter. First, the lives of several historical and contemporary leaders will be examined with a discussion of the traits that play a role in their leadership. Second, a set of selected traits that appear by all accounts to be strongly related to effective leadership in everyday life will be discussed. Throughout this discussion, the unique ways that certain traits affect the leadership process in one way or another will be emphasized.

▶ HISTORICAL LEADERS: WHAT TRAITS DO THESE LEADERS DISPLAY?

Throughout history, there have been many great leaders. Each of them has led with unique talents and in different circumstances. The following section analyzes the accomplishments and the traits of eight famous leaders. Although there are hundreds of equally distinguished leaders, these eight are highlighted because they represent different kinds of leadership at different points in history. All of these leaders are recognized as being notable leaders: Each has had an impact on many people's lives, and accomplished great things.

The leaders discussed below are George Washington, Harriet Tubman, Eleanor Roosevelt, Winston Churchill, Mother Teresa, Nelson Mandela, Bill Gates, and Oprah Winfrey. As you read about each of them, think about their leadership traits.

GEORGE WASHINGTON (1732–1799)

George Washington is considered to be the founding father of the United States of America. His leadership was pivotal in the development of this country's government. He was truly respected by everyone, from lowly soldiers to feisty public officials. He was a man of great integrity who was a good listener. After the Revolutionary War, Washington was *the* reason that various factions did not splinter into small groups or nations. He became the United States' first president because his leadership was so well suited for the times.

Born into a prosperous Virginia family, he grew up on a large plantation. His father died when he was 11. Washington received formal schooling for 7 years and then worked as a surveyor. He entered the military at the age of 20. During the French and Indian War, Washington learned about the difficulties of battle and experienced both victories and defeats. He served as commander in chief of the Continental Army from 1775 to 1783. His leadership was instrumental in leading the colonies to victory over Great Britain in the Revolutionary War. After the war, he retired to farm for a short period. In 1787, however, his interests in politics and the nation took him to the Constitutional Convention in Philadelphia, where he was chosen to preside over the successful creation of the U.S. Constitution. After the Constitution was ratified, Washington was elected by 100% of the electoral college as the first president of the United States. Washington served two terms as president (1789–1793, 1793–1797); although he had the people's support, he chose not to serve a third term. He retired to Mount Vernon in 1797 and died there from pneumonia at the age of 67. At his funeral, one of his officers, Henry Lee, eulogized him as an American who was "first in war, first in peace, and first in the heart of his countrymen."

Traits and Characteristics

George Washington exhibited many special leadership traits (Brookhiser, 1996; Burns & Dunn, 2004; Fishman, 2001; Higginbotham, 2002). Researchers identify him as a modest man with great moral character who demonstrated integrity, virtuousness, and wisdom in his leadership. Though neither highly educated nor brilliant, he is reported to have read 10 newspapers each day. He was tall, and careful about his appearance. For much of his life he kept a daily record of his work. Although reserved, as a military leader he was brave and tenacious. Rather than use power to his own ends, he gave up his position as commander in chief after the war. Washington provided stability, reason, and order after the American Revolution when the United States was in its formative stages. His evenness made him predictable to the American people, who considered him trustworthy. Above all, Washington was a prudent leader who made sound judgments and provided balance and wisdom to the new government. Washington was a special leader with many unique talents who, as Schwartz (1987, p. 147) has suggested, "was 'great' because he was 'good.'"

HARRIET TUBMAN (C. 1820–1913)

Harriet Tubman was an American abolitionist who played a major role in freeing many people from slavery in the years leading up to the Civil War (1861–1865). She was born as a slave, in Dorchester County, Maryland. At the age of 12, she suffered a severe blow to the head while trying to assist a fellow worker who was being attacked. The wound she received caused intermittent blackouts for the rest of her life. In 1849, Tubman escaped on the

Video Link 2.1
Watch more about Harriet Tubman.

Underground Railroad from Maryland to Philadelphia in the free state of Pennsylvania by traveling at night, using the North Star as her guide. After she gained her own freedom, Tubman became a "conductor" for the Underground Railroad. She subsequently made 13 return trips to the South and rescued as many as 300 other slaves. Tubman was known as "Moses" because she helped "her" people escape to freedom. During the Civil War, she became a spy and soldier for the North (i.e., for the Union Army) and was the first woman in the armed services to carry out a military operation: In 1863, she led the successful Combahee River Raid that freed more than 750 slaves. In her later years, she settled in Auburn, New York, where she established a home for the aged and indigent. When she died in 1913, Tubman was 93 years old.

Traits and Characteristics

A symbol of hope, Harriet Tubman was a remarkable leader (C. Clinton, 2004; Wills, 1994). Even though she was illiterate and suffered from seizures brought on by her early injury, she had a far-reaching impact on many people's lives. Courageously, she fought to end slavery with a single-mindedness of purpose. Her fight was devoid of personal fear. Devoted to her cause, she repeatedly risked her own life to bring freedom to others. She was determined, focused, spiritual, and strong. She was an ordinary woman with no pretentiousness. Although Tubman did little talking, her mission was clear to others. Throughout her leadership, there was the mix of the spiritual and the practical. On the one hand, she believed in divine guidance; on the other, she was very practical and methodical in her approach to tasks. Tubman was a remarkable leader and her accomplishments extraordinary.

ELEANOR ROOSEVELT (1884–1962)

One of the most admired people of the 20th century, Eleanor Roosevelt was an active, eloquent first lady of the United States. Although she was born into a wealthy family, her early years were not easy. Her mother died when she was 8 and her father died 2 years later. Roosevelt was a shy, insecure, and plain child who knew sadness and loneliness. She was educated at an English boarding school. When she was 21, she married her fifth cousin,

Franklin Delano Roosevelt, and subsequently served as first lady during her husband's unprecedented four terms in office, from 1933 until his death in 1945. While in the White House, she was a strong advocate for the rights of African Americans, women, working people, and the poor. Her activist agenda transformed the role of first lady. In that role, Roosevelt traveled extensively, held hundreds of press conferences for women only, and wrote a daily newspaper column. After President Roosevelt died, she served as spokesperson to the United Nations, where she played an instrumental role in drafting the Universal Declaration of Human Rights. For her work in championing universal human rights, President Harry Truman nicknamed her "First Lady of the World." Active to the end, Roosevelt died in 1962 at the age of 78.

Audio Link 2.1
Listen to Eleanor Roosevelt speak.

Traits and Characteristics

Eleanor Roosevelt had many strong leadership qualities (Lash, 1984; Levy & Russett, 1999; MacLeish, 1965). Her greatest talents were her abilities to confront conflicts and to discuss major policy differences in human terms. She was a good listener who stressed the importance of people being able to disagree with one another without fear of reprisals (MacLeish, 1965). She fought hard for her own ideas and what she thought was right. Roosevelt was plain, honest, selfless, tolerant, and courageous. She confronted everything that came her way with a positive attitude. She had a deep sense of humanity and human worth. As Kearns Goodwin (1998) points out, Roosevelt was a remarkable woman for her times. She had an identity of her own apart from her husband's, endured struggles with depression and insecurity, turned her weaknesses into strengths, and became one of the century's most effective advocates for social justice.

WINSTON CHURCHILL (1874–1965)

Winston Churchill was one of the greatest statesmen and orators of the 20th century. In addition, he was a talented painter and prolific writer; he received the Nobel Prize in Literature in 1953. Churchill served in the military during World War I, became prime minister of Great Britain in May 1940, and remained in that office through World War II, until 1945. It was at this time that his masterful leadership was most visible. When the Germans threatened to invade Britain,

Video Link 2.2

Watch more about Winston Churchill.

Churchill stood strong. He made many famous speeches that had far-reaching effects on the morale of the people of Great Britain and the allied forces. On the home front, he was a social reformer. He served a second term as prime minister from 1951 to 1955. He died at the age of 90 in 1965.

Traits and Characteristics

Winston Churchill's leadership was remarkable because it emerged from a man who was average in many respects and who faced challenges in his personal life. In his education, he did not stand out as superior to others. On a societal level, he was a loner who had few friends. On a personal level, he suffered from bouts of depression throughout his life. Despite these characteristics, Churchill emerged as a leader because of his other unique gifts and how he used them (Hayward, 1997; Keegan, 2002; Sandys & Littman, 2003). A voracious reader, Churchill was plain speaking, decisive, detail oriented, and informed (Hayward, 1997). Furthermore, he was very ambitious, but not out of self-interest: He wanted what was right for others, and he wanted the best for Great Britain. His most significant talent was his masterful use of language. In his oratory, the normally plainspoken Churchill used words and imagery in powerful ways that touched the hearts of many and set the moral climate of the war (Keegan, 2002). He had the ability to build hope and inspire others to rise to the challenge. His stoicism and optimism were an inspiration to his people and all of the allied forces (Sandys & Littman, 2003).

MOTHER TERESA (1910–1997)

A Roman Catholic nun considered a saint by many, Mother Teresa received the Nobel Peace Prize in 1979 for her work with the poor and helpless in Calcutta, India and throughout the world. Born in Macedonia, Mother Teresa came from a comfortable background. At the age of 18, she joined the Catholic Sisters of Loreto order and worked for 17 years as a high school teacher in Calcutta. Her awareness of poverty in Calcutta caused her to leave the convent in 1948 to devote herself to working full-time with the poorest of the poor in the slums of the city. In 1950, Mother Teresa founded a new religious order, the Missionaries of Charity, to care for the hungry, homeless, unwanted, and unloved.

Today, there are more than 1 million workers affiliated with the Missionaries of Charity in more than 40 countries. The charity provides help to people who have been hurt by floods, epidemics, famines, and war. The Missionaries of Charity also operate hospitals, schools, orphanages, youth centers, shelters for the sick, and hospices. For her humanitarian work and efforts for peace, Mother Teresa has been recognized with many awards, including the Pope John XXIII Peace Prize (1971), the Nehru Award (1972), the U.S. Presidential Medal of Freedom (1985), and the Congressional Gold Medal (1994). Although she struggled with deteriorating health in her later years, Mother Teresa remained actively involved in her work to the very end. She died at the age of 87 in 1997.

Video Link 2.3

Watch more about Mother Teresa.

Traits and Characteristics

Mother Teresa was a simple woman of small stature who dressed in a plain blue and white sari, and who never owned more than the people she served. Mirroring her appearance, her mission was simple—to care for the poor. From her first year on the streets of Calcutta where she tended to one dying person to her last years when thousands of people were cared for by the Missionaries of Charity, Mother Teresa stayed focused on her goal. She was a true civil servant who was simultaneously determined and fearless, and humble and spiritual. She often listened to the will of God. When criticized for her stand on abortion and women's role in the family, or her approaches to eliminating poverty, Mother Teresa responded with a strong will; she never wavered in her deep-seated human values. Teaching by example with few words, she was a role model for others. Clearly, Mother Teresa was a leader who practiced what she preached (Gonzalez-Balado, 1997; Sebba, 1997; Spink, 1997; Vardey, 1995).

NELSON MANDELA (1918–)

Winner of the Nobel Peace Prize in 1993, Nelson Mandela was the first Black president of South Africa. He is best known for his efforts to end apartheid, a racial system that separated groups of individuals by race and deprived people of color from full citizenship. Mandela was educated in South Africa and opened the first Black law partnership in 1942. During the 1950s, he became a leader of the African National Congress (ANC), which was engaged in resisting South Africa's apartheid policies. Influenced by Mohandas Gandhi, Mandela was committed to nonviolent resistance. He shifted to supporting violent tactics, however, when the government refused to change its apartheid policies. In 1964, Mandela received a life sentence for plotting to overthrow the government by violence.

Mandela spent 27 years in prison, during which his reputation grew; during his imprisonment, he became a symbolic figure for the antiapartheid movement. Upon his release, Mandela immersed himself in his life's work—to bring peace to South Africa's Black majority and give them and all marginalized South Africans the right to vote. For his role in negotiations to abolish apartheid, Mandela received the Nobel Peace Prize. As president of South Africa from 1994 to 1999, Mandela oversaw the transition from minority rule and apartheid to freedom and democracy for all. Since leaving office, Mandela has continued to be an advocate for peace and justice throughout the world.

Traits and Characteristics

Nelson Mandela is a leader with many admirable qualities (Asmal, Chidester, & Wilmot, 2003; Hadland, 2003; Joseph, 2003). Foremost, he is a man of conscience who is self-reflective and deeply moral. Throughout his long imprisonment, Mandela steadfastly held to his principles and to his unwavering vision for a South Africa where all people would be treated with fairness and justice. He is focused and disciplined. When given the chance to leave prison early in exchange for denouncing violence, he chose to remain incarcerated rather than give up his beliefs. His spirit never failed. When he was finally released from prison, Mandela was not angry or vindictive. Even in conflict situations, Mandela is a consensus builder. In addition, he is courageous, patient, humble, and compassionate. As former U.S. president Bill Clinton has written, Mandela's legacy is this: "Under a burden of oppression he saw through difference, discrimination and destruction to embrace our common humanity" (W. J. Clinton, 2003). Overall, Mandela is a virtuous leader who believes in what is right and good.

BILL GATES (1954–)

For many years, William (Bill) H. Gates III, cofounder and chair of Microsoft Corporation, the world's largest developer of software for personal computers, was the wealthiest person in the world with assets estimated at more than $70 billion. A self-made man, Gates's interest in computers began at the age of 13 when he and a friend developed their first computer software program. He later attended Harvard University but left without graduating, to focus on software development. He cofounded Microsoft in 1975. Under Gates's leadership, Microsoft developed the well-known Microsoft Disk Operating System (MS-DOS), Windows operating system, and Internet Explorer browser. Microsoft is one of the fastest growing and most profitable companies ever established. From the success of Microsoft, Gates and his wife established the Bill & Melinda Gates Foundation in 2000 to reduce inequities and improve lives around the world. This foundation promotes education, addresses global health issues (such as malaria, HIV/AIDS, and tuberculosis), sponsors libraries, and supports housing and community initiatives in the Pacific Northwest. Beginning in 2006, Gates transitioned away from his day-to-day operating role at Microsoft to spend more time working with his foundation, but he remains as the corporation's chair.

Traits and Characteristics

Bill Gates is both intelligent and visionary. When he cofounded Microsoft, he had a vision about how to meet the technological needs of people in the future, and he hired friends to help him accomplish that vision. Gates is also task oriented and diligent, often working 12 or more hours a day to promote his interest in software product development. Furthermore, Gates is focused and aggressive. When Microsoft was accused by the U.S. government of antitrust violations, Gates appeared before congressional hearings and strongly defended his company. When asked about whether he has a "win at all cost mentality," he answered that you bring people together to work on products and make products better, but there is never a finish line—there are always challenges ahead (Jager & Ortiz, 1997, pp. 151–152). In his personal style, Gates is simple, straightforward, unpretentious, and altruistic: He has demonstrated a strong concern for the poor and underserved.

OPRAH WINFREY (1954–)

An award-winning television talk show host, Oprah Winfrey is one of the most powerful and influential women in the world. Born in rural Mississippi into a dysfunctional family, she was raised by her grandmother until she was 6. Winfrey learned to read at a very early age and skipped two grades in school. Her adolescent years were difficult: While living in inner-city Milwaukee with her mother who worked two jobs, Winfrey was molested by a family member. Despite these experiences, she was an honors student in high school and received national accolades for her oratory ability. She received a full scholarship to Tennessee State University, where she studied communication and worked at a local radio station. Winfrey's work in the media eventually led her to Chicago where she became host of the highly-acclaimed *Oprah Winfrey Show*. She also is an actor, a producer, a book critic, a magazine publisher, and has her own television network (OWN).

Winfrey has many other important accomplishments besides her work as host of a talk show. She also is an actor, a producer, a book critic, and a magazine publisher. In 2007, Winfrey was the highest-paid entertainer in television, earning an annual salary estimated at $260 million. Her total wealth is estimated at more than $1.6 billion. Winfrey is also a highly regarded philanthropist: Her giving has focused on making a difference in the lives of the underprivileged and poor. Winfrey has paid special attention to the needs of people in Africa, raising millions of dollars to help AIDS-affected children there and creating a leadership academy for girls in a small town near Johannesburg, South Africa.

Traits and Characteristics

Oprah Winfrey's remarkable journey from rural poverty to influential world leader can be explained by several of her strengths (Harris & Watson, 2007; Illouz, 2003; McDonald, 2007). Foremost, Winfrey is an excellent communicator. Since she was a little girl reciting Bible passages in church, she has been comfortable in front of an audience. On television, she is able to talk to millions of people and have each person feel as if she is talking directly to him or her. Winfrey is also intelligent and well read, with a strong business sense. She is sincere, determined, and inspirational. Winfrey has a charismatic style of leadership that enables her to connect with people. She is spontaneous and expressive, and has a fearless ability to self-disclose. Because she has "been in the struggle" and survived, she is seen as a role model. Winfrey has overcome many obstacles in her life and encourages others to overcome their struggles, as well. Her message is a message of hope.

In summary, all of these individuals have exhibited exceptional leadership. While each of these leaders is unique, together they share many common characteristics. All are visionary, strong willed, diligent, and inspirational. As purpose-driven leaders, they are role models and symbols of hope. Reflecting on the characteristics of these extraordinary leaders will provide you with a better understanding of the traits that are important for effective leadership. Although you may not aspire to be another Bill Gates or Mother Teresa, you can learn a great deal from these leaders in understanding how your own traits affect your leadership.

Although examining historical and contemporary leadership figures provides a wealth of information, you can also learn by exploring studies of leadership traits based on research conducted by social scientists. The next section discusses the traits that researchers have found to be strongly related to effective leadership in everyday life.

LEADERSHIP STUDIES: WHAT TRAITS DO EFFECTIVE LEADERS EXHIBIT? ◄

From the beginning of the 20th century to the present day, researchers have focused a great deal of attention on the unique characteristics of successful leaders. Thousands of studies have been conducted to identify the traits of effective leaders. The results of these studies have produced a very long list of important leadership traits; each of these traits contributes to the leadership process.

Journal Link 2.1
Read more about the importance of leadership traits.

For example, research studies by several investigators found the following traits to be important: achievement, persistence, insight, initiative, self-confidence, responsibility, cooperativeness, tolerance, influence, sociability, drive, motivation, integrity, confidence, cognitive ability, task knowledge, extraversion, conscientiousness, and openness (Judge, Bono, Ilies, & Gerhardt, 2002; Kirkpatrick & Locke, 1991; Stogdill, 1974). On the international level, House, Hanges, Javidan, Dorfman, and Gupta (2004), in a study of 17,000 managers in 62 different cultures, identified a list of 22 valued traits that were universally endorsed as characteristics of outstanding leadership in these countries. The list, which was outlined in Table 1.1, Chapter 1, "Being a Leader," includes such attributes as being trustworthy, just, honest, encouraging, positive, dynamic, dependable, intelligent, decisive, communicative, informed, and a team builder. As these findings indicate, research studies on leadership traits have identified a wide array of important characteristics of leaders.

However, these research findings raise an important question: If there are so many important leadership traits, which *specific traits* do people need to be successful leaders? While the answer to this question is not crystal clear, the research points to *six key traits: intelligence, confidence, charisma, determination, sociability,* and *integrity.* In the following section, we will discuss each of these traits in turn.

INTELLIGENCE

Intelligence is an important trait related to effective leadership. Intelligence includes having good language skills, perceptual skills, and reasoning ability. This combination of assets makes people good thinkers, and makes them better leaders.

While it is hard for a person to alter his or her IQ (intelligence quotient), there are certain ways for a person to improve intelligence in general. Intelligent leaders are well informed. They are aware of what is going on around them and understand the job that needs to be done. It is important for leaders to obtain information about what their leadership role entails and learn as much as possible about their work environment. This information will help leaders be more knowledgeable and insightful.

For example, a few years ago a friend, Chris, was asked to be the coach of his daughter's middle school soccer team even though he had never played soccer and knew next to nothing about how the game is played. Chris took the job and eventually was a great success, but not without a lot of effort. He spent many hours learning about soccer. He read how-to books, instructors' manuals, and coaching books. In addition, Chris subscribed to several soccer magazines. He talked to other coaches and learned everything he could about playing the game. By the time he had finished the first season, others considered Chris to be a very competent coach. He was smart and learned how to be a successful coach.

Regarding intelligence, few if any of us can expect to be another Albert Einstein. Most of us have average intelligence and know that there are limits to what we can do. Nevertheless, becoming more knowledgeable about our leadership positions gives us the information we need to become better leaders.

CONFIDENCE

Being confident is another important trait of an effective leader. Confident people feel self-assured and believe they can accomplish their goals. Rather than feeling uncertain, they feel strong and secure about their positions. They do not second-guess themselves, but rather move forward on projects with a clear vision. Confident leaders feel a sense of certainty and believe that they are doing the right thing. Clearly,

confidence is a trait that has to do with feeling positive about oneself and one's ability to succeed.

If confidence is a central trait of successful leaders, how can you build your own confidence? First, confidence comes from *understanding* what is required of you. For example, when first learning to drive a car, a student's confidence is low because he or she does not know *what* to do. If an instructor explains the driving process and demonstrates how to drive, the student can gain confidence because he or she now has an understanding of how to drive. Awareness and understanding build confidence. Confidence can also come from having a mentor to show the way and provide constructive feedback. This mentor may be a boss, an experienced coworker, or a significant other from outside the organization. Because mentors act as role models and sounding boards, they provide essential help to learn the dynamics of leadership.

Confidence also comes from *practice*. This is important to point out, because practice is something everyone can do. Consider Tiger Woods, one of the most well-known athletes in the world today. Woods is a very gifted athlete, but he also spends an enormous amount of time practicing golf. His excellent performance and confidence about his game are a result of his practice, as well as his gifts.

In leadership, practice builds confidence because it provides assurance that an aspiring leader can do what needs to be done. Taking on leadership roles, even minor ones on committees or through volunteer activities, provides practice for being a leader. Building one leadership activity on another can increase confidence for more-demanding leadership roles. Those who accept opportunities to practice their leadership will experience increased confidence in their leadership abilities.

CHARISMA

Of all the traits related to effective leadership, charisma gets the most attention. **Charisma** refers to a leader's special magnetic charm and appeal, and can have a huge effect on the leadership process. Charisma is a special personality characteristic that gives a leader the capacity to do extraordinary things. In particular, it gives the leader exceptional powers of influence. A good example of a charismatic leader is former president John F. Kennedy, who motivated the American people with his eloquent oratorical style (see Box 6.1 in Chapter 6, "Creating a

Journal Link 2.2
Read more about charisma.

Vision"). President Kennedy was a gifted, charismatic leader who had an enormous impact on others.

It is not unusual for many of us to feel challenged with regard to charisma because it is not a common personality trait. There are a few select people who are very charismatic, but most of us are not. Since charisma appears in short supply, the question arises: What do leaders do if they are not naturally charismatic?

Based on the writings of leadership scholars, several behaviors characterize charismatic leadership (Conger, 1999; House, 1976; Shamir, House, & Arthur, 1993). First, charismatic leaders serve as a *strong role model* for the values that they desire others to adopt. Mohandas Gandhi advocated nonviolence and was an exemplary role model of civil disobedience; his charisma enabled him to influence others. Second, charismatic leaders *show competence* in every aspect of leadership, so others trust their decisions. Third, charismatic leaders *articulate clear goals* and *strong values*. Martin Luther King Jr.'s "I Have a Dream" speech is an example of this type of charismatic leadership. By articulating his dream, he was able to influence multitudes of people to follow his nonviolent practices. Fourth, charismatic leaders communicate *high expectations* for followers and *show confidence* in their abilities to meet these expectations. Finally, charismatic leaders are an *inspiration* to others. They can excite and motivate others to become involved in real change, as demonstrated by John F. Kennedy and Martin Luther King Jr.

DETERMINATION

Video Link 2.4
Watch more about determination.

Determination is another trait that characterizes effective leaders. Determined leaders are very focused and attentive to tasks. They know *where* they are going and *how* they intend to get there. Determination is the decision to get the job done; it includes characteristics such as initiative, persistence, and drive. People with determination are willing to assert themselves, they are proactive, and they have the capacity to persevere in the face of obstacles. Being determined includes showing dominance at times, especially in situations where others need direction.

We have all heard of determined people who have accomplished spectacular things—the person with cancer who runs a standard 26.2-mile marathon, the blind person who climbs Mount Everest, or the single mom with four kids who graduates from college. A good example of determined leadership is Nelson Mandela, discussed earlier in this chapter. Mandela's single goal was to end apartheid in South Africa. Even though he was imprisoned for many years, he steadfastly held to his principles. He was committed to reaching his goal, and he never wavered from his vision. Mandela was focused and disciplined—a determined leader.

What distinguishes all of these leaders from other people is their determination to get the job done. Of all the traits discussed in this chapter, determination is probably the one trait that is easily acquired by those who lead. All it demands is perseverance. Staying focused on the task, clarifying the goals, articulating the vision, and encouraging others to stay the course are characteristics of determined leaders. Being determined takes discipline and the ability to endure, but having this trait will almost certainly enhance a person's leadership.

SOCIABILITY

Another important trait for leaders is **sociability**. Sociability refers to a leader's capacity to establish pleasant social relationships. People want sociable leaders—leaders with whom they can get along. Leaders who show sociability are friendly, outgoing, courteous, tactful, and diplomatic. They are sensitive to others' needs and show concern for their well-being. Sociable leaders have good interpersonal skills and help to create cooperative relationships within their work environments.

Being sociable comes easier for some than for others. For example, it is easy for extroverted leaders to talk to others and be outgoing, but it is harder for introverted leaders to do so. Similarly, some individuals are naturally "people persons," while others prefer to be alone. Although people vary in the degree to which they are outgoing, it is possible to increase sociability. A sociable leader gets along with coworkers and other people in the work setting. Being friendly, kind, and thoughtful, as well as talking freely with others and giving them support, goes a long way to establish a leader's sociability. Sociable leaders bring positive energy to a group and make the work environment a more enjoyable place.

To illustrate, consider the following example. This scenario occurred in one of the best leadership classes I have had in 40 years of teaching. In this class, there was a student named Anne Fox who was a very sociable leader. Anne was an unusual student who dressed like a student from the 1960s, although it was more than two decades later. Even though she dressed differently than the others, Anne was very caring and was liked by everyone in the class. After the first week of the semester, Anne could name everyone in class; when attendance was taken, she knew instantly who was there and who was not. In class discussions, Anne always contributed good ideas, and her remarks were sensitive of others' points of view. Anne was positive about life, and her attitude was contagious. By her presence, Anne created an atmosphere in which everyone felt unique but also included. She was the glue that held us all together. Anne was not assigned to be the leader in the class, but by the semester's end she emerged as a leader. Her sociable nature enabled her to develop strong relationships and become a leader in the class. By the end of the class, all of us were the beneficiaries of her leadership.

INTEGRITY

Video Link 2.5
Watch more about integrity.

Finally, and perhaps most important, effective leaders have **integrity**. Integrity characterizes leaders who possess the qualities of honesty and trustworthiness. People who adhere to a strong set of principles and take responsibility for their actions are exhibiting integrity. Leaders with integrity inspire confidence in others because they can be trusted to do what they say they are going to do. They are loyal, dependable, and transparent. Basically, integrity makes a leader believable and worthy of our trust.

Grown-ups often tell children, "Never tell a lie." For children, the lesson is "Good children are truthful." For leaders, the lesson is the same: "Good leaders are honest." Dishonesty creates mistrust in others, and dishonest leaders are seen as undependable and unreliable. Honesty helps people to have trust and faith in what leaders have to say and what they stand for. Honesty also enhances a leader's ability to influence others because they have confidence in and believe in their leader.

Integrity demands being open with others and representing reality as fully and completely as possible. However, this is not an easy task: There are times when telling the complete truth can be destructive or counterproductive. The challenge for leaders is to strike a balance between being open and candid and monitoring what is appropriate to disclose in a particular situation. While it is important for leaders to be authentic, it is also essential for them to have integrity in their relationships with others.

Integrity undergirds all aspects of leadership. It is at the core of being a leader. Integrity is a central aspect of a leader's ability to influence. If people do not trust a leader, the leader's influence potential is weakened. In essence, integrity is the bedrock of who a leader is. When a leader's integrity comes into question, his or her potential to lead is lost.

Former president Bill Clinton (1993–2001) is a good example of how integrity is related to leadership. In the late 1990s, he was brought before the U.S. Congress for misrepresenting under oath an affair he had engaged in with a White House intern. For his actions, he was impeached by the U.S. House of Representatives, but then was acquitted by the U.S. Senate. At one point during the long ordeal, the president appeared on national television and, in what is now a famous speech, declared his innocence. Because subsequent hearings provided information suggesting he might have lied during his television speech, many Americans felt Clinton had violated his duty and responsibility as a person, leader, and president. As a result, Clinton's integrity was clearly challenged and the impact of his leadership substantially weakened.

In conclusion, there are many traits related to effective leadership. The six traits discussed above appear to be particularly important in the leadership process. As will be revealed in subsequent chapters, leadership is a very complex process. The traits discussed in this chapter are important, but are only one dimension of a multidimensional process.

CASE STUDY

The following case study describes the career path and traits of a young talented leader. The questions at the end of the case will help you analyze the case using concepts and ideas from the trait approach.

An Emerging Leader

Tim T. portrays his life as a tension between "nature" and "nurture." He sees it this way: He has two sets of DNA, and these two very different sets of characteristics have given him what he needs to be a leader. The first set of DNA, he says, comprises those "God-given genetic talents" that came from the biological parents who abandoned him at birth. The second set comes from the religious and caring Michigan family who adopted him two years later.

Even as a toddler, Tim's nature was to be out in front of people and relating to them. These innate abilities of his have always been very public and people-oriented: from his easy and eloquent speaking

Encyclopedia Link 2.1

Read more about trait approach.

style and teaching skills to singing and acting. "As a baby, I was always an extrovert, and since age 2 or 3, people have told me that I would either be president of the United States, a preacher, or a comedian," he says. "I didn't intentionally work on these abilities; I have just always had them."

His "other strand of DNA" came from his adoptive family whom he describes as gentle, unassuming, and quiet. Tim admits he ran in the "middle of the crowd," while his family members were often silent bystanders standing off in a corner. They did, however, instill in him the strong values of "loving God, loving family, working hard, and giving back" that he embraces today.

Those two sets of characteristics allowed Tim to thrive early. Just out of high school, he was given an opportunity by baseball player Derek Jeter's Turn 2 Foundation to create a new after-school program for second to fifth graders called Proud to Be Me. The goal of the pilot program was to build children's self-esteem and self-concept by providing them with new and diverse experiences. Tim developed it with the goal of giving these children a larger lens of what the world could be, so they would be empowered to see more choices than what they found in their neighborhoods. The Proud to Be Me model was a success and continues to be used for kids in Kalamazoo, Michigan; Tampa, Florida; and New York (Parish, 2002; Turn 2 Foundation, 2010).

"My core belief and approach has been to help others by giving them things that nobody can take away," he says.

At the encouragement of his boss at the Turn 2 Foundation, Tim went back to college. He supported himself working part-time at a bank doing collections, calling people on the phone to try to convince them to make payments on their debts. It wasn't fun, but Tim excelled at it. "I would use my powers of persuasion to get people to make payments, not because it was my job, but because I wanted to help them. These weren't bad people; they just got in over their heads. If they didn't make these payments someone was going to come to their house and take something from them."

It was in this job that Tim realized his talents only worked if there was a purpose. "I tried to sell vacuum cleaners once and couldn't even sell one to my own mama," he says. "Do you know why? Because there was no purpose in it. But yet, I could talk these people who are struggling and hurting into making a payment. That's when I knew that I can't walk on the face of this earth and not help somebody. My persuasion has to have a purpose."

After finishing college, Tim went on to get a master's degree in communication and, at the young age of 28, was hired as executive director of the 88-year-old Douglass Community Association, a private, nonprofit, inner-city social service agency that provides opportunities for youth development, education, healthy living, and leadership. At the center, Tim managed a budget of $1.2 million and 24 people. He spent much of his time out in the larger community raising money and resources and putting out fires. Although Tim enjoyed his role as executive director, he admits he had difficulty handling the day-to-day personnel issues at the agency.

"I was really good at high-level leadership like developing new relationships and new funds for the center, and mobilizing people and resources, but I was horrible at the small stuff," he reflects. "I spent a lot of time managing external human resources, but not paying attention to the needs of internal human resources at the center. When my staff did an assessment of me, they consistently said, 'He does a great job as a leader, but he is our boss and we need him here.'"

To enhance his administrative skills, he took advanced leadership training at the Center for Creative Leadership in North Carolina and Harvard University in Cambridge, Massachusetts. After four years, Tim left the community center to become an associate vice president at Southwest Michigan First, a regional agency focused on catalyzing job creation and economic growth in an area that has been hard hit by job losses. For Tim, it's an opportunity that makes the most of his double set of DNA.

"This is the place where my talent and my passions meet. I can help people. I can sift through problems and take big issues and break them down in ways people understand. I can persuade and motivate people and organizations to grow," he says. "And I am still helping others in ways that people can't take away."

Despite the fact he is "living the dream," Tim still wants to find more ways to help others by creating an independent foundation to help people and kids in need. "My experience has been that it is hard to help hurting people because there is so much bureaucracy and BS tied up in how we do it. I want to help people without strings. If you give someone money to help them, don't give it to them if you need it back. If you're gonna do something for someone, just do it."

In addition, he is writing a book about his own experiences from adoption to the present to help inspire others. "I want to share my story with people who come from places that aren't all that great," he says. "I know I am not Superman and I can't save everybody. But I can just be me and help out in the ways that I can."

Questions

1. What is your reaction to Tim's story?

2. Nature and nurture play a significant role in Tim's leadership journey. From your perspective, which has the greatest impact on Tim? Discuss your answer.

3. Of the six major traits described in the chapter (i.e., intelligence, confidence, charisma, determination, sociability, and integrity) which traits are Tim's strongest, and which traits are his weakest?

4. What characteristics of Tim's leadership would you like to incorporate into your own style of leadership?

Summary

This chapter describes the traits required of a leader. From an examination of a select group of well-known historical and contemporary leaders including George Washington, Winston Churchill, Harriet Tubman, Eleanor Roosevelt, Nelson Mandela, Mother Teresa, Bill Gates, and Oprah Winfrey, it is clear that exemplary leaders exhibit many similar traits. In the main, these leaders were or are visionary, strong willed, diligent, inspirational, purpose driven, and hopeful. These leadership figures provide useful models for understanding the traits that are important and desirable for achieving effective leadership.

Social science research also provides insight into leadership traits. Thousands of leadership studies have been performed to identify the traits of effective leaders; the results of these studies point to a very long list of important leadership traits. From this list, the traits that appear to be especially important for effective leadership are *intelligence, confidence, charisma, determination, sociability,* and *integrity.*

Because leadership is a complex process, there are no simple paths or guarantees to becoming a successful leader. Each individual is unique, and each of us has our own distinct talents for leadership. Those who are naturally strong in the six traits discussed in this chapter will be well equipped for leadership. If you are not strong on all of these traits but are willing to work on them, you can still become an effective leader.

Remember that there are many traits related to effective leadership. By becoming aware of your own traits and how to nourish them, you will be well on your way to becoming a successful leader.

 Go to **http://www.sagepub.com/northouseintro2e/** *for additional exercises and study resources. Select Chapter 2, Recognizing Your Traits, for chapter-specific activities.*

Glossary Terms

charisma 29	integrity 32
confidence 29	intelligence 28
determination 30	sociability 31

References

Antonakis, J., Cianciolo, A. T., & Sternberg, R. J. (Eds.). (2004). *The nature of leadership.* Thousand Oaks, CA: Sage.

Asmal, K., Chidester, D., & Wilmot, J. (2003). *Nelson Mandela: In his own words.* New York: Little, Brown.

Bass, B. M. (1990). *Bass and Stogdill's handbook of leadership: A survey of theory and research.* New York: Free Press.

Brookhiser, R. (1996). *Founding father: Rediscovering George Washington.* New York: Free Press.

Burns, J. M., & Dunn, S. (2004). *George Washington.* New York: Times Books.

Clinton, C. (2004). *Harriet Tubman: The road to freedom.* New York: Little, Brown.

Clinton, W. J. (2003). Foreword. In K. Asmal, D. Chidester, & J. Wilmot (Eds.), *Nelson Mandela: In his own words* (pp. xv–xvi). New York: Little, Brown.

Conger, J. A. (1999). Charismatic and transformational leadership in organizations: An insider's perspective on these developing streams of research. *Leadership Quarterly, 10*(2), 145–170.

Fishman, E. (2001). Washington's leadership: Prudence and the American presidency. In E. Fishman, W. D. Pederson, & R. J. Rozell (Eds.), *George Washington: Foundation of presidential leadership and character* (pp. 125–142). Westport, CT: Praeger.

Gonzalez-Balado, J. L. (1997). *Mother Teresa: Her life, her work, her message.* Liguori, MO: Liguori.

Hadland, A. (2003). Nelson Mandela: A life. In K. Asmal, D. Chidester, & J. Wilmot (Eds.), *Nelson Mandela: In his own words* (pp. xxix–xxxvii). New York: Little, Brown.

Harris, J., & Watson, E. (Eds.). (2007). *The Oprah phenomenon.* Lexington: The University Press of Kentucky.

Hayward, S. F. (1997). *Churchill on leadership: Executive success in the face of adversity.* Rocklin, CA: Prima.

Higginbotham, R. D. (2002). *George Washington: Uniting a nation.* Lanham, MD: Rowman & Littlefield

House, R. J. (1976). A 1976 theory of charismatic leadership. In J. G. Hunt & L. L. Larson (Eds.), *Leadership: The cutting edge* (pp. 189–207). Carbondale: Southern Illinois University Press.

House, R. J., Hanges, P. J., Javidan, M., Dorfman, P. W., & Gupta, V. (2004). *Leadership, culture, and organizations: The GLOBE study of 62 societies.* Thousand Oaks, CA: Sage.

Illouz, E. (2003). *Oprah Winfrey and the glamour of misery.* New York: Columbia University Press.

Jager, R. D., & Ortiz, R. (1997). *In the company of giants: Candid conversations with the visionaries of the digital world.* New York: McGraw-Hill.

Joseph, J. A. (2003). Promoting peace and practicing diplomacy. In K. Asmal, D. Chidester, & J. Wilmot (Eds.), *Nelson Mandela: In his own words* (pp. 499–506). New York: Little, Brown.

Judge, T. A., Bono, J. E., Ilies, R., & Gerhardt, M. W. (2002). Personality and leadership: A qualitative and quantitative review. *Journal of Applied Psychology, 87,* 765–780.

Kearns Goodwin, D. (1998). Eleanor Roosevelt: America's most influential first lady blazed paths for women and led the battle for social justice everywhere. *Time, 151*(14), 122–127.

Keegan, J. (2002). *Winston Churchill*. New York: Viking.

Kirkpatrick, S. A., & Locke, E. A. (1991). Leadership: Do traits matter? *The Executive, 5,* 48–60.

Lash, J. P. (1984). *"Life was meant to be lived": A centenary portrait of Eleanor Roosevelt*. New York: W. W. Norton.

Levy, W. T., & Russett, C. E. (1999). *The extraordinary Mrs. R: A friend remembers Eleanor Roosevelt*. New York: John Wiley & Sons.

MacLeish, A. (1965). *The Eleanor Roosevelt story.* Boston: Houghton Mifflin.

McDonald, K. B. (2007). *Embracing sisterhood: Class, identity, and contemporary black women*. Lanham, MD: Rowman & Littlefield.

Parish, N. B. (2002). *Derek Jeter Turn 2 Foundation*. Retrieved December 13, 2010, from http://iml.jou.ufl.edu/projects/Spring02/Parish/dreamweaver/DEREKJETERPHILANTHROPY.htm

Sandys, C., & Littman, J. (2003). *We shall not fail: The inspiring leadership of Winston Churchill*. New York: Penguin.

Schwartz, B. (1987). *George Washington: The making of an American symbol*. New York: Free Press.

Sebba, A. (1997). *Mother Teresa: Beyond the image*. New York: Doubleday.

Shamir, B., House, R. J., & Arthur, M. B. (1993). The motivational effects of charismatic leadership: A self-concept based theory. *Organization Science, 4*(4), 577–594.

Spink, K. (1997). *Mother Teresa: A complete authorized bibliography*. New York: HarperCollins.

Stogdill, R. M. (1974). *Handbook of leadership: A survey of theory and research*. New York: Free Press.

Turn 2 Foundation. (2010). *Proud to Be Me*. Retrieved December 21, 2010, from http://derekjeter.mlb.com/players/jeter_derek/turn2/proud_douglass.jsp

Vardey, L. (1995). Introduction. In L. Vardey (Ed.), *Mother Teresa: A simple path* (pp. xv–xxxviii). New York: Ballantine.

Wills, G. (1994). *Certain trumpets: The call of leaders*. New York: Simon & Schuster.

2.1   Leadership Traits Questionnaire

 Visit www.sagepub.com/northouseintro2e for downloadable versions of these questionnaires

Purpose

1. To gain an understanding of how traits are used in leadership assessment

2. To obtain an assessment of your own leadership traits

Directions

1. Make five copies of this questionnaire. This questionnaire should be completed by you and *five people* you know (e.g., roommates, coworkers, relatives, friends).

2. Using the following scale, have each individual indicate the degree to which he or she agrees or disagrees with each of the 14 statements below regarding your leadership traits. Do not forget to complete this exercise for yourself.

_____ (name) is

Statements	Strongly disagree	Disagree	Neutral	Agree	Strongly agree
1. Articulate: Communicates effectively with others	1	2	3	4	5
2. Perceptive: Discerning and insightful	1	2	3	4	5
3. Self-confident: Believes in oneself and one's ability	1	2	3	4	5
4. Self-assured: Secure with self, free of doubts	1	2	3	4	5
5. Persistent: Stays fixed on the goals, despite interference	1	2	3	4	5
6. Determined: Takes a firm stand, acts with certainty	1	2	3	4	5
7. Trustworthy: Is authentic, inspires confidence	1	2	3	4	5
8. Dependable: Is consistent and reliable	1	2	3	4	5
9. Friendly: Shows kindness and warmth	1	2	3	4	5
10. Outgoing: Talks freely, gets along well with others	1	2	3	4	5
11. Conscientious: Is thorough, organized, and careful	1	2	3	4	5
12. Diligent: Is industrious, hardworking	1	2	3	4	5
13. Sensitive: Shows tolerance, is tactful and sympathetic	1	2	3	4	5
14. Empathic: Understands others, identifies with others	1	2	3	4	5

Scoring

1. Enter the responses for Raters 1, 2, 3, 4, and 5 in the appropriate columns on the scoring sheet on this page. An example of a completed chart is provided on page 41.

2. For each of the 14 items, compute the average for the five raters and place that number in the "average rating" column.

3. Place your own scores in the "self-rating" column.

Leadership Traits Questionnaire Chart

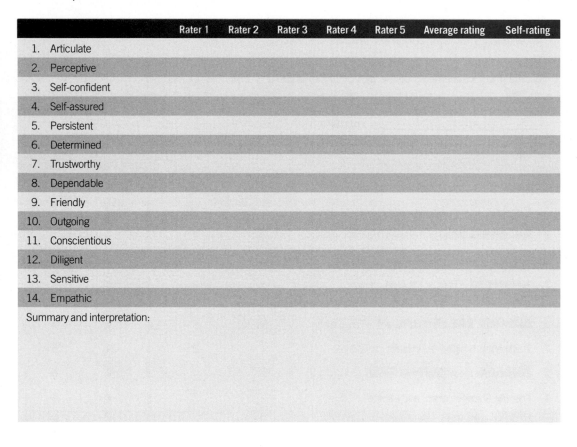

	Rater 1	Rater 2	Rater 3	Rater 4	Rater 5	Average rating	Self-rating
1. Articulate							
2. Perceptive							
3. Self-confident							
4. Self-assured							
5. Persistent							
6. Determined							
7. Trustworthy							
8. Dependable							
9. Friendly							
10. Outgoing							
11. Conscientious							
12. Diligent							
13. Sensitive							
14. Empathic							

Summary and interpretation:

Scoring Interpretation

The scores you received on this questionnaire provide information about how you see yourself and how others see you as a leader. The chart allows you to see where your perceptions are the same as those of others and where they differ. There are no "perfect" scores for this questionnaire. The purpose of the instrument is to provide a way to assess your strengths and weaknesses and to evaluate areas where your perceptions are similar to or different from those of others. While it is confirming when others see you in the same way as you see yourself, it is also beneficial to know when they see you differently. This assessment can help you understand your assets as well as areas in which you may seek to improve.

Example 2.1 Leadership Traits Questionnaire Ratings

	Rater 1	Rater 2	Rater 3	Rater 4	Rater 5	Average rating	Self-rating
1. Articulate	4	4	3	2	4	3.4	4
2. Perceptive	2	5	3	4	4	3.6	5
3. Self-confident	4	4	5	5	4	4.4	4
4. Self-assured	5	5	5	5	5	5	5
5. Persistent	4	4	3	3	3	3.4	3
6. Determined	4	4	4	4	4	4	4
7. Trustworthy	5	5	5	5	5	5	5
8. Dependable	4	5	4	5	4	4.4	4
9. Friendly	5	5	5	5	5	5	5
10. Outgoing	5	4	5	4	5	4.6	4
11. Conscientious	2	3	2	3	3	2.6	4
12. Diligent	3	3	3	3	3	3	4
13. Sensitive	4	4	5	5	5	4.6	3
14. Empathic	5	5	4	5	4	4.6	3

Summary and interpretation: The scorer's self-ratings are higher than the average ratings of others on *articulate, perceptive, conscientious,* and *diligent.* The scorer's self-ratings are lower than the average ratings of others on *self-confident, persistent, dependable, outgoing, sensitive,* and *empathic.* The scorer's self-ratings on *self-assured, determined, trustworthy,* and *friendly* are the same as the average ratings of others.

2.2 Observational Exercise

 Visit **www.sagepub.com/northouseintro2e** for downloadable versions of these questionnaires

Leadership Traits

Purpose

1. To gain an understanding of the role of traits in the leadership process

2. To examine the traits of selected historical and everyday leaders

Directions

1. Based on the descriptions of the historical leaders provided in the chapter, identify the three major leadership traits for each of the leaders listed below.

2. Select and briefly describe two leaders in your own life (e.g., work supervisor, teacher, coach, music director, business owner, community leader). Identify the three major leadership traits of each of these leaders.

Historical leaders	The leader's three major traits		
George Washington	1. _____	2. _____	3. _____
Harriet Tubman	1. _____	2. _____	3. _____
Eleanor Roosevelt	1. _____	2. _____	3. _____
Winston Churchill	1. _____	2. _____	3. _____
Mother Teresa	1. _____	2. _____	3. _____
Nelson Mandela	1. _____	2. _____	3. _____
Bill Gates	1. _____	2. _____	3. _____
Oprah Winfrey	1. _____	2. _____	3. _____

Everyday leaders

Leader #1 _____

Brief description _____

_____

_____

_____

Traits   1. _____ 2. _____ 3. _____

Leader #2 _____

Brief description _____

_____

_____

Traits   1. _____ 2. _____ 3. _____

Questions

1. Based on the leaders you observed, which leadership traits appear to be most important?

2. What differences, if any, did you observe between the historical and everyday leaders' traits?

3. Based on your observations, what one trait would you identify as the definitive leadership trait?

4. Overall, what traits do you think should be used in selecting our society's leaders?

2.3 Reflection and Action Worksheet

 Visit www.sagepub.com/northouseintro2e for downloadable versions of these questionnaires

Leadership Traits

Reflection

1. Based on the scores you received on the Leadership Traits Questionnaire, what are your strongest leadership traits? What are your weakest traits? Discuss.

2. In this chapter, we discussed eight leadership figures. As you read about these leaders, which leaders did you find most appealing? What was it about their leadership that you found remarkable? Discuss.

3. As you reflect on your own leadership traits, do you think some of them are more "you" and authentic than others? Have you always been the kind of leader you are today, or have your traits changed over time? Are you a stronger leader today than you were five years ago? Discuss.

Action

1. If you could model yourself after one or more of the historical leaders we discussed in this chapter, whom would you model yourself after? Identify two of their traits that you could and should incorporate into your own style of leadership.

2. Based on the case study of Tim T., which of his traits could you incorporate into your own leadership? Discuss.

3. Although changing leadership traits is not easy, which of your leadership traits would you like to change? Specifically, what actions do you need to take to change your traits?

4. All of us have problematic traits that inhibit our leadership but are difficult to change. Which single trait distracts from your leadership? Since you cannot easily change this trait, what actions can you take to "work around" this trait? Discuss.

Before you begin reading . . .

Complete the *Leadership Styles Questionnaire*, which you will find on pp. 63–64. As you read the chapter, consider your results on the questionnaire.

Recognizing Your Philosophy and Style of Leadership

3

What is your philosophy of leadership? Are you an in-charge type of leader who closely monitors subordinates? Or are you a laid-back type of leader who gives subordinates a lot of rein? Whether you are one or the other or somewhere in between, it is important to recognize your personal **philosophy of leadership**. This philosophy affects how others respond to you, how they respond to their work, and, in the end, how effective you are as a leader.

Each of us approaches leadership with a unique set of beliefs and attitudes about the nature of people and the nature of work. This is the basis for our *philosophy* of leadership. For example, some think people are basically good and will happily work if given the chance. Others think people are prone to be a bit lazy and need to be nudged to complete their work. These beliefs about people and work have a significant impact on an individual's leadership style. In fact, these beliefs probably come into play in every aspect of a person's leadership.

In this chapter, we will discuss how a person's view of people, work, and human nature forms a personal philosophy of leadership. In addition, this chapter will examine how that philosophy is demonstrated in three of the most commonly observed styles of personal leadership: the authoritarian, democratic, and laissez-faire

Video Link 3.1
Watch more about leadership styles.

styles. We will discuss the nature of these styles and the implications each has for effective leadership performance.

▶ WHAT IS YOUR VIEW OF HUMAN BEHAVIOR AT WORK?

Do you think people like work, or do you think people find work unpleasant? This was one of the central questions addressed by Douglas McGregor in his famous book *The Human Side of Enterprise* (1960). McGregor believed that managers need to understand their core assumptions about human nature and assess how these assumptions relate to their managerial practice.

In particular, McGregor was interested in how managers view the motivations of workers and their attitudes toward work. He believed that understanding these motivations was central to knowing how to become an effective manager. To explain the ways that managers approach workers, McGregor proposed two general theories— Theory X and Theory Y. McGregor believed that by exploring the major assumptions of each of these theories people could develop a better understanding of their own viewpoints on human behavior and the relationship of these viewpoints to their leadership style. Below is a description of both theories. As you read, ask yourself if the assumptions of the theory are consistent or inconsistent with your own attitudes and philosophy of leadership.

Video Link 3.2

Watch more on Theory X and Theory Y managers.

THEORY X

Theory X is made up of three assumptions about human nature and human behavior (see Table 3.1). Taken together, these assumptions represent a philosophy of leadership that many leaders exhibit to one degree or another.

Assumption #1. The average person dislikes work and will avoid it if possible.

This assumption argues that people do not like work; they view it as unpleasant, distasteful, or simply a necessary evil. According to this assumption, if given the chance people would choose not to work. An example of this assumption is the worker who says, "I only go to work to be P-A-I-D. If I didn't need to pay my bills, I would never work." People with this philosophy would avoid work if they could.

Assumption #2. Because people dislike work, they need to be directed, controlled, and sometimes threatened with punishment or reminded of rewards to make them work.

This assumption is derived directly from the first assumption. Since people naturally do not like work, management needs to set up a system of incentives and rewards regarding work that needs to be accomplished because workers are often unwilling or unable to motivate themselves. This assumption says that without external direction and incentives people would be unmotivated to work. An example of this is the high school teacher who persuades students to hand in homework assignments by threatening them with bad grades. The teacher forces students to perform because the teacher thinks that the students are unwilling to do it or incapable of doing it without that force being applied. From the perspective of Theory X, leaders play a significant role in encouraging others to accomplish their work.

Table 3.1	Assumptions of McGregor's Theory X

McGregor's Theory X

- People dislike work.
- People need to be directed and controlled.
- People want security, not responsibility.

Assumption #3. The average person prefers to be directed, wishes to avoid responsibility, has little ambition, and wants security more than choice.

The picture this assumption paints is of workers who want their leaders to take care of them, protect them, and make them feel safe. Because it is too difficult to set their own goals, workers want management to do it for them. This can only happen when managers establish the guidelines for workers. An example of this assumption can be observed at a fast-food restaurant where the employees only have to focus on completing the specific tasks set before them (e.g., cleaning the shake machines or making fries) and are not required to take initiative on their own. In general, many fast-food restaurant workers are not required to accept many challenging responsibilities. Instead, they are told what to do, and how and when to do it. Consistent with this assumption, this example highlights how some workers are not ambitious but want job security above everything else.

So what does it mean if a person's personal leadership style or philosophy is similar to Theory X? It means these leaders have a tendency to view workers as lazy and uninterested in work because they do not value work. As a result, Theory X leaders tend to be directive and controlling. They supervise subordinates closely and are quick to both praise and criticize them as they see fit. At times, these leaders remind workers of their goal (e.g., to be P-A-I-D) or threaten them with punishment to persuade them to accomplish tasks. As the person in charge, a Theory X leader sees his or her leadership role as instrumental in getting the job done. Theory X leaders also believe it is their role to motivate subordinates because these workers have little self-motivation. Because of this belief, these leaders take on the responsibility for their subordinates' actions. From the Theory X perspective, it is clear that subordinates have a *need* for leadership.

THEORY Y

Like Theory X, **Theory Y** is based on several specific assumptions about human nature and behavior (see Table 3.2). Taken together, the assumptions of Theory Y present a distinctly different perspective from the ideas set forth in Theory X. It is a perspective that can be observed to a degree in many leaders today.

Table 3.2	Assumptions of McGregor's Theory Y

McGregor's Theory Y

- People like work.
- People are self-motivated.
- People accept and seek responsibility.

Assumption #1. The average person does not inherently dislike work. Doing work is as natural as play.

Rather than viewing work as a burden or bad, this assumption suggests people see work as satisfying and not as a punishment. It is a natural activity for them. In fact, given the chance people are happy to work. An example of this can be seen in what former president Jimmy Carter has done in his retirement. He has devoted much of his time and energy to constructing homes throughout the United States and around the world with Habitat for Humanity. Certainly, the former president does not need to work: He does so because work is natural for him. All his life, Carter has been used to making a contribution to the well-being of others. Working with Habitat for Humanity is another opportunity for him to contribute. Some people view work as a natural part of their lives.

Assumption #2. People will show responsibility and self-control toward goals to which they are committed.

As opposed to Theory X, which suggests that people need to be supervised and controlled, Theory Y suggests that people can and will make a conscious choice to work on their own.

People can be committed to the objectives of their work. Consider some examples from the sports world. Successful athletes are often highly committed to their goals and usually do not need to be controlled or supervised closely. Coaches design training plans for these athletes, but the athletes do the work themselves. A successful long-distance runner does not need to be pushed to run 60 training miles a week in preparation for a marathon because the runner is already motivated to run long distances. Similarly, an Olympic swimmer does not need to be forced to do daily 3-mile pool workouts at 5:00 a.m. because the swimmer chooses to do this independently of any coach's urging. These athletes are self directed because they are committed to their goals. This is the point of Theory Y. When people can find commitment in their work, they will work without needing leaders to motivate or cajole them. Put another way, when people have a passion for their work, they will do it even without outside direction.

Assumption #3. In the proper environment, the average person learns to accept and seek responsibility.

While Theory X argues that people lack ambition, prefer to be directed, and want security, Theory Y assumes that the average person is inherently resourceful and, if given the chance, will seek to take responsibility. If given the chance, people have the capacity to engage in a wide range of goal setting and creative problem-solving activities. Theory Y argues that, given the opportunity, people will act independently and be productive.

For example, two university students working in the main stacks section of the library were required to complete a checklist whenever they worked to be sure that they correctly carried out various sorting and shelving activities. The checklist was long, cumbersome, and repetitious, however. Frustrated by the checklist, the students took it upon themselves to design an entirely new, streamlined checklist. The new checklist for sorting and shelving was very clear and concise, and was playful in appearance. After reviewing the checklist and giving it a short trial period, management at the library adopted the new checklist and required that it be implemented throughout the entire library. In this example, library management provided an environment where students felt comfortable suggesting a rather major change in how their work was to be completed. In addition, management was willing to accept and adopt a student-initiated work change. It is not unrealistic to imagine that these students will be more confident initiating ideas or taking on new challenges in other work settings in the future.

So if a leader's philosophy of leadership is similar to Theory Y, what does it mean? It means that the leader views people as capable and interested in working. Even though Theory Y leaders may define work requirements, they do not try to control workers. To these leaders, subordinates are not lazy; on the contrary, they naturally want to work. In addition, these leaders do not think they need to try to motivate subordinates or make them work since workers are capable of motivating themselves. Using coercion or external reinforcement schemes is not a part of their leadership repertoire. Theory Y leaders are very attuned to helping subordinates find their passion for what they want to do. These leaders know that when subordinates are committed to their work they are more motivated to do the job. Allowing subordinates to seek and accept responsibilities on their own comes easily for Theory Y leaders. In short, Theory Y leadership means supporting subordinates without the need to direct or control them.

In summary, all of us maintain certain basic beliefs and assumptions about human nature and work; these beliefs are employed in our leadership style. **Leadership style** is defined as the behaviors of leaders, focusing on what leaders do and how they act. This includes leaders' actions toward subordinates in a variety of contexts. Whether a person's philosophy is similar to Theory X or similar to Theory Y, it affects his or her style of leadership. The challenge is to understand the philosophical underpinnings of our own leadership style.

Journal Link 3.1
Read more on Theory X and Theory Y.

The next section shifts the discussion to addressing some of the most commonly observed leadership styles associated with Theory X and Theory Y. The styles we will discuss are authoritarian, democratic, and laissez-faire. While none of these styles emerges directly from Theory X or Theory Y, the authoritarian and democratic styles closely mirror the ideas set forth in these theories, respectively.

▶ STYLES OF LEADERSHIP: AUTHORITARIAN, DEMOCRATIC, AND LAISSEZ-FAIRE

The primary work on styles of leadership was by Lewin, Lippitt, and White (1939), who analyzed the impact of various leadership styles on small group behavior. Using groups of 10-year-old boys who met after school to engage in hobby activities, the researchers analyzed what happened when their adult leaders used one of three styles: authoritarian, democratic, or laissez-faire. The groups of boys experienced the three styles of leadership for 6-week periods each.

The outcome of the study by Lewin and colleagues was a detailed description of the nature of the leadership behaviors used for each of the three styles (White & Lippitt, 1968). They also described the impact each of these three styles had on group members.

Video Link 3.3
Watch more on leadership styles.

The following sections describe and elaborate on their findings and the implications of using each of these leadership styles. Be aware that these styles are not distinct entities (e.g., like personality traits). They overlap each other. That is, a leader can demonstrate more than one style in any given situation. For example, a leader may be authoritarian about some issues and democratic about others, or a leader may be authoritarian at some points during a project and democratic at others. As leaders, we may display aspects of all of these styles.

AUTHORITARIAN LEADERSHIP STYLE

In many ways, **authoritarian leadership** is very similar to Theory X. For example, authoritarian leaders perceive subordinates as needing direction. The authoritarian leader needs to control subordinates and what they do. Authoritarian leaders emphasize that they are in charge, exerting influence and control over group members. They determine tasks and procedures for group members but may remain aloof from participating in group discussions. Authoritarian leaders do not encourage communication among group members; instead, they prefer that communication be directed to them. In evaluating others, authoritarian leaders give praise and criticism freely, but it is given based on their own personal standards rather than based on objective criticism.

Some have argued that authoritarian leadership represents a rather pessimistic, negative, and discouraging view of others. For example, an authoritarian leader might say something like "Because my workers are lazy, I need to tell them what to do." Others would argue that authoritarian leadership is a much-needed form of leadership—it serves a positive purpose, particularly for people who seek security above responsibility. In many contexts, authoritarian leadership is used to give direction, set goals, and structure work. For example, when employees are just learning a new job, authoritarian leadership lets them know the rules and standards for what they are supposed to do. Authoritarian leaders are very efficient and successful in motivating others to accomplish work. In these contexts, authoritarian leadership is very useful.

What are the *outcomes* of authoritarian leadership? Authoritarian leadership has both pluses and minuses. On the positive side, it is efficient and productive. Authoritarian leaders give direction and clarity to people's work and accomplish more in a shorter period. Furthermore, authoritarian leadership is useful in establishing goals and work standards. On the negative side, it fosters dependence, submissiveness, and a loss of individuality. The creativity and personal growth of subordinates may be hindered. It is possible that, over time, subordinates will lose interest in what they are doing and become dissatisfied with their work. If that occurs, authoritarian leadership can create discontent, hostility, and even aggression.

While the negative aspects of authoritarian leadership appear to outweigh the positive, it is not difficult to imagine contexts where authoritarian leadership would be the preferred style of leadership. For example, in a busy hospital emergency room it may be very appropriate for the leader in charge of triaging patients to be authoritarian with various types of emergencies. The same could be true in other contexts, such as the chaperone of a middle school canoe trip, or the coach of a high school team during the state finals basketball tournament. Despite the negatives of authoritarian leadership, this form of leadership is common and necessary in many situations.

Box 3.1 Leadership on the Silver Screen

Leaders, great and terrible and in between, are often the focus of movies. Here are three movies that provide exceptional examples of the leadership styles discussed in this chapter: authoritarian, democratic, and laissez-faire.

Authoritarian
Glory Road (2006)

Glory Road is the story of Don Haskins and the 1965–1966 Texas Western College basketball team that broke race barriers in college sports by winning the 1966 National Collegiate Athletic Association (NCAA) championship with the first all-Black team on the court. As a newly hired coach of an unknown team, Haskins has no chance of recruiting the best White players, so he and his assistant coach head north and find Black players who are happy to have scholarships and a chance to play. These players play a hotshot, Harlem Globetrotters–style basketball. Haskins thinks it is undisciplined and risky, and drills them with his own man-on-man system. He is a merciless taskmaster who imposes strict discipline, including a curfew for players. He kicks one player who refuses to comply off the team.

As a result, there are clashes between coach and players, but Haskins accomplishes team building in the truest sense of the word. Despite the team's success, the Black players are still subjected to hatred and hostility. While on the road, one Black player is beaten in a diner restroom, and the team's motel rooms are trashed and belongings destroyed. Witnessing this abuse further cements the bonds of the White players with their Black teammates. When Coach Haskins announces he plans to play only Black athletes in the final NCAA championship game to make a point, the White players understand the point, and, while disappointed, agree with it.

Haskins represents the authoritarian style of leadership. From the start, he sets the tone as a leader who imposes his work structure and rules on his subordinates, or team members. He discourages their style of basketball in favor of his own, pays close attention to the team members' after hour activities and academics, and punishes them when they deviate from his rules. He is successful in that his direction results in a winning team that overcomes obstacles on and off the court.

Democratic
Invictus (2009)

In this true story, Nelson Mandela, released from prison after 27 years and elected president of South Africa, is determined to unite his country, which has been fractured by generations of apartheid. Taking office during a time of high unemployment, economic stagnation, and rising crime, Mandela gives hope and elation to the Black natives, while White Afrikaners fear for their future.

Mandela sets the tone for his tenure on his first day on the job, when he tells the predominantly White staff of the former president that those who want to can keep their jobs. "Reconciliation starts here," Mandela says.

Mandela turns his sights outward and finds the South African Springboks rugby team. For Afrikaners, the team is a source of intense pride. For Black Africans, the Springboks represent the dark history of apartheid. It is less than a year until the 1995 Rugby World Cup, which is being hosted by South Africa, and the general

consensus is that the Springboks will be knocked out of contention early in the tournament.

Mandela asks the Springboks team captain, François Pienaar, to lead the team to victory in the World Cup, implying that it would bring together their countrymen. But Mandela has more than just extra practice time in mind for the team. Team members conduct "Rugby Coaching Clinics" for children across South Africa, including Black children in impoverished areas. The team is at first resistant, but players soon embrace the clinics as they see their impact on the children and in instilling national pride, regardless of race.

The Springboks persevere and make it to the final match against the undefeated New Zealand team. Across South Africa, crowds of Whites and Blacks convene wherever there is a television to watch the match. In the end, South Africa beats New Zealand, 15-12. After the win, South African streets are booming with elated White and Black South Africans who are cheering for the Springboks in celebration. As Mandela presents the trophy to Pienaar, he thanks the team captain "for what you have done for your country." Pienaar replies, "Thank *you,* sir, for what you have done for our country."

Laissez-Faire
Office Space (1999)

This movie dramatizes the effects of a laissez-faire manager on the morale of the workers at Initech, a high-tech company. The primary leader in the movie, Bill Lumbergh, starts every conversation with an employee with an

(Continued)

(Continued)

"Um . . . yeah . . . ," communicates through endless memos, asks questions but does not wait for answers, gives directives without involving employees, avoids conflicts, and chooses to focus on useless details rather than meaningful processes and outcomes. He provides no feedback on his employees' performances. Rather than actually telling an employee, Milton, he had been fired several years prior, he just moves the hapless man into progressively smaller office spaces and takes away his coveted red stapler.

As a result, Lumbergh's subordinates are unmotivated and hide in their office cubicles to avoid contact. They are unproductive, and resentful of work and management. One employee describes his main work motivation as "to not be hassled." As a result, these dissatisfied employees begin to engage in counterproductive work behaviors, which ultimately become criminal, because they are confident—correctly so—that Lumbergh will never notice. In a great twist of fate, it is the long-suffering Milton who ultimately burns the place down.

Bill Lumbergh's leadership fits the laissez-faire style of leadership because of his lack of interaction with employees. His subordinates barely do the minimum amount of work and do it at their own pace. The direction they receive from Lumbergh is really no direction at all: It focuses on meaningless minutiae, such as the design of cover pages for a weekly report. All admit to dissatisfaction with management and their work environment, and admit that they just show up in order to be P-A-I-D.

DEMOCRATIC LEADERSHIP STYLE

Encyclopedia Link 3.1

Read more on democratic leadership.

The **democratic leadership style** strongly resembles the assumptions of Theory Y. Democratic leaders treat subordinates as fully capable of doing work on their own. Rather than controlling subordinates, democratic leaders *work with* subordinates, trying hard to treat everyone fairly, without putting themselves above subordinates. In essence, they see themselves as guides rather than as directors. They give suggestions to others, but never with any intention of changing them. Helping each subordinate reach personal goals is important to a democratic leader. Democratic leaders do not use "top-down" communication; instead, they speak on the same level as their subordinates. Making sure everyone is heard is a priority. They listen to subordinates in supportive ways and assist them in becoming self-directed. In addition, they promote communication between group members and in certain situations are careful to draw out the less-articulate members of the group. Democratic leaders provide information, guidance, and suggestions, but do so without giving orders and without applying pressure. In their evaluations of subordinates, democratic leaders give objective praise and criticism.

The *outcomes* of democratic leadership are mostly positive. First, democratic leadership results in greater group member satisfaction, commitment, and cohesiveness. Second, under democratic leadership there is more friendliness, mutual praise, and group mindedness.

Subordinates tend to get along with each other and willingly participate in matters of the group, making more "we" statements and fewer "I" statements. Third, democratic leadership results in stronger worker motivation and greater creativity. People are motivated to pursue their own talents under the supportive structure of democratic leadership. Finally, under a democratic leader group members participate more and are more committed to group decisions. The downside of democratic leadership is that it takes more time and commitment from the leader. Work is accomplished, but not as efficiently as if the leader were authoritarian.

LAISSEZ-FAIRE LEADERSHIP STYLE

The **laissez-faire leadership style** is dissimilar to both Theory X and Theory Y. Laissez-faire leaders do not try to control subordinates as Theory X leaders do, and they do not try to nurture and guide subordinates as Theory Y leaders do. Laissez-faire leaders ignore workers and their work motivations. Laissez-faire stands alone as a style of leadership; some have labeled it *nonleadership*. The laissez-faire leader is a nominal leader who engages in minimal influence. As the French phrase implies, *laissez-faire* leadership means the leader takes a "hands off, let it ride" attitude toward followers. These leaders recognize subordinates but are very laid back and make no attempt to influence their activities. Under laissez-faire leadership, subordinates have freedom to do pretty much what they want to do whenever they want to do it. Laissez-faire leaders make no attempt to appraise or regulate the progress of subordinates.

Encyclopedia Link 3.2
Read more on laissez-faire leadership.

Given that laissez-faire leadership involves nominal influence, what are the *effects* of laissez-faire leadership? Laissez-faire leadership will produce primarily negative outcomes. The major effect is that very little is accomplished under a laissez-faire leader. Because people are directionless and at a loss to know what to do, they tend to do nothing. Giving complete freedom results in an atmosphere that most subordinates find chaotic. Subordinates prefer some direction; when left completely on their own they become frustrated. Without a sense of purpose and direction, group members have difficulty finding meaning in their work; they become unmotivated and disheartened. As a result, productivity goes down.

In rare situations, the laissez-faire style will be successful because it allows subordinates complete freedom. In some situations, people will thrive on this freedom. In most situations, though, laissez-faire leadership will be unsuccessful and unproductive.

▶ WHAT IS YOUR STYLE OF LEADERSHIP?

Audio Link 3.1
Listen to more about leadership styles.

Each leader has a unique style of leadership. Some are very demanding and assertive while others are more open and participative. Similarly, some leaders could be called micromanagers, while others could be labeled nondirective leaders. Whatever the case, it is useful and instructive to characterize your leadership regarding the degree to which you are authoritarian, democratic, or laissez-faire.

It is important to note that these styles of leadership are not distinct entities; it is best to think of them as occurring along a continuum, from high leader influence to low leader influence (see Figure 3.1). Leaders who exhibit higher amounts of influence are more authoritarian. Leaders who show a moderate amount of influence are democratic. Those who exhibit little to no influence are laissez-faire. Although we tend to exhibit primarily one style over the others, our personal leadership styles are not fixed and may vary depending on the circumstances.

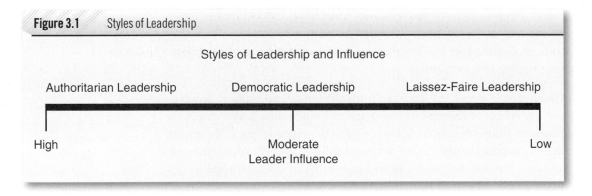

Figure 3.1   Styles of Leadership

Styles of Leadership and Influence

| Authoritarian Leadership | Democratic Leadership | Laissez-Faire Leadership |

| High | Moderate | Low |

Leader Influence

Consider what the results of the Leadership Styles Questionnaire you took at the beginning of this chapter tell you about your leadership style. What is your main style? Are you most comfortable with authoritarian, democratic, or laissez-faire leadership? If you are the kind of leader who likes to structure work, likes to lay out the ground rules for others, likes to closely supervise your subordinates, thinks it is your responsibility to make sure subordinates do their work, wants to be "in charge" or to know what others are doing, and believes strongly that rewarding and punishing subordinates is necessary, then you are *authoritarian*. If you are the kind of leader who seldom gives orders or ultimatums to subordinates, instead trying to work with subordinates and help them figure out how they want to approach a task or complete their work, then you are primarily *democratic*. Helping each subordinate reach his or her own personal goals is important to a democratic leader.

In some rare circumstances, you may find you are showing *laissez-faire leadership*. Although not a preferred style, it is important to be aware when one is being laissez-faire. Laissez-faire leaders take a very low profile to leadership. What subordinates accomplish is up to them. If you believe that your subordinates will thrive on complete freedom, then the laissez-faire style may be the right style for you. However, in most situations laissez-faire leadership hinders success and productivity.

CASE STUDY

The following case study describes the leadership struggles of the editor in chief at a college newspaper. The questions at the end of the case are designed to help you analyze Mary Lewis's philosophy and style of leadership based on concepts presented in the chapter.

Lighten Up, Mary

After working for two years on the weekly student newspaper at her university, Mary Lewis was chosen to be the editor in chief of the publication. Mary was a little apprehensive, but the outgoing editor told her not to worry because the staff operated so well together that the paper ran on autopilot.

Before the school year started, Mary made some changes in how the paper would be run. First, she switched printing companies because she thought it would improve the look of the paper. Second, she decided to have the design and layout of the paper done in-house by the newspaper staff, a task most of them had never done. Third, Mary decided to raise the ad rates to make it easier to cover the cost of the new printer. Mary was certain these changes needed to be made in order to enhance the overall quality of the paper, but she never dreamed she would meet with such resistance.

When the staff met for the first time in the fall and learned of the changes and new layout requirements, they were angry and dismayed. Two of the editors were so mad that they quit. The advertising manager, Sam, was furious that he hadn't been consulted since the decision ultimately affected his sales. Mary told the staff that she was sorry but as the editor in chief she had to, and would continue to, make key editorial decisions without their input.

(Continued)

(Continued)

The fallout of Mary's efforts to make changes was significant. For example, on Layout Night, when the paper is prepared to be sent to the printer the next morning, ads were missing, staff members were writing stories past deadline, and three of the staff members left, saying they had early classes. As a result, Mary and two other staffers had to work all night laying out and editing the paper. When the paper came out on Friday, it had many errors including a misspelled headline on the front page, duplicated stories, and misidentified pictures.

For Mary this was unacceptable and very disappointing. The newspaper had consistently won "College Newspaper of the Year" in its division and had a solid reputation as a well-written and skillfully edited publication. Mary believed as editor in chief the success of the paper lay solely on her shoulders and the only way to ensure that no more mistakes were made was to take total control.

That week's Friday staff meeting was very different from past meetings where the staff critiqued the paper and talked about the next week's stories. Instead, a stern and angry Mary led the meeting, highlighting every mistake in the paper and whose negligence caused each one. She then outlined a long list of new staff rules ranging from stricter deadlines to requiring all staff members to stay on Layout Night until the last page was finished. Knowing that most of them relied on the scholarships they received for working on the paper, she told the staffers they could follow her edicts or lose their jobs. Finally, she introduced two new staff members to replace those who had resigned. In the past, the staff helped interview and make hiring choices; but Mary hired these individuals without anyone else's input. The other staffers secretly called them "Mary-ites."

Over the next two months, the problems for the staff and paper continued. Deadlines were missed, and the layout sessions lasted until the early morning hours. The newspaper staff had always been a tight-knit team with strong friendships, but the current members barely spoke at meetings and had little to do with each other outside the office. Mary felt miserable, the staff was miserable, and, in Mary's opinion, the newspaper was horrible. She planned to take the four-week holiday break to determine if she should continue as editor in chief.

When the staff came to their first meeting of the new year, Mary handed them each a piece of paper with the words "If I were editor in chief, I would . . ." printed at the top. She asked them to type as many endings to the sentence as they wanted and put the answers in her mailbox. Their answers would be anonymous, unless the writers chose to identify themselves. The next week, Mary gave the staff a handout with all the answers she'd received. One said "lighten up and quit being such a dictator" while others made suggestions such as "hire experienced layout staff, even if it means losing a writer." Mary had the staff choose the responses that they thought could be implemented. The staff agreed to earlier deadlines for advertising and for the arts and features pages, and one staff member, Lori, volunteered to oversee the layout and design of the paper because she felt particularly capable in this area.

As hard as it was for her, Mary ceded control of layout to Lori. That week's production went better, and at the next staff meeting, Mary asked them to provide a critique of the new methods. Some members were still silent, but others offered ideas. After four weeks, production of the newspaper was running much more smoothly, and the staff seemed to start enjoying their work.

A month after the first handout, Mary gave the staff a new slip of paper with "As a newspaper staff member, my personal goal is to . . ." After receiving those answers, she met with each staff member to make a plan to achieve his or her goals. For Jeff, the sports editor, it was to win gold in the annual college sportswriting competition. For the photographer, Chris, it was to have a two-page photo spread. Mary assigned the best editor on the staff to work with Jeff to polish his stories. She worked with Sam to set aside two pages free of ads in an upcoming issue for Chris's photo essay on "A Night With the Campus Police."

In May, Mary was chosen to return in the fall as editor in chief, despite the fact that the newspaper lost its coveted "College Newspaper of the Year" status. Mary rehired the staff members who wanted to return, and as a team, they chose others to fill the vacant positions. Each returning staff member became a mentor to a new hire. By the end of the next year, when Mary graduated, the paper had reclaimed its title as "College Newspaper of the Year," and Jeff won first place in the sportswriting category.

Questions

1. Based on the assumptions of Theory X and Theory Y, how would you describe Mary Lewis's philosophy and style of leadership? In what way did Mary's attitudes about her employees affect her leadership?

2. Clearly, Mary Lewis was not a laissez-faire leader. Using as many examples as you can, describe why Mary's style was the antithesis of laissez-faire leadership.

3. In what way did Mary Lewis change her style of leadership at the newspaper? How effective were the changes she made?

4. If you were coaching Mary Lewis on her leadership, what would you tell her?

Summary

All of us have a philosophy of leadership that is based on our beliefs about human nature and work. Some leaders have a philosophy that resembles Theory X: They view workers as unmotivated and needing direction and control. Others have a philosophy similar to Theory Y: They approach workers as self-motivated and capable of working independently without strong direct influence from a leader.

Our philosophy of leadership is played out in our style of leadership. There are three commonly observed styles of leadership: *authoritarian, democratic,* and *laissez-faire.* Similar to Theory X, *authoritarian leaders* perceive subordinates as needing direction, so they exert strong influence and control. Resembling Theory Y, *democratic leaders* view subordinates as capable of self-direction, so they provide counsel and support. *Laissez-faire leaders* leave subordinates to function on their own, providing neither direction nor encouragement.

Effective leadership demands that we understand our philosophy of leadership and how it forms the foundations for our style of leadership. This understanding is the first step to becoming a more informed and competent leader.

 Go to **http://www.sagepub.com/northouseintro2e/** *for additional exercises and study resources. Select Chapter 3, Recognizing Your Philosophy and Style of Leadership, for chapter-specific activities.*

Glossary Terms

authoritarian leadership   53

democratic leadership style   56

laissez-faire leadership style   57

leadership style   52

philosophy of leadership   47

Theory X   48

Theory Y   50

References

Lewin, K., Lippitt, R., & White, R. K. (1939). Patterns of aggressive behavior in experimentally created "social climates." *Journal of Social Psychology, 10,* 271–299.

McGregor, D. (1960). *The human side of enterprise.* New York: McGraw-Hill.

White, R., & Lippitt, R. (1968). Leader behavior and member reaction in three "social climates." In D. Cartwright & A. Zander (Eds.), *Group dynamics* (pp. 318–335). New York: Harper & Row.

3.1   Leadership Styles Questionnaire

 Visit www.sagepub.com/northouseintro2e for downloadable versions of these questionnaires

Purpose

1. To identify your style of leadership
2. To examine how your leadership style relates to other styles of leadership

Directions

1. For each of the statements below, circle the number that indicates the degree to which you agree or disagree.
2. Give your immediate impressions. There are no right or wrong answers.

Statements	Strongly disagree	Disagree	Neutral	Agree	Strongly agree
1. Employees need to be supervised closely, or they are not likely to do their work.	1	2	3	4	5
2. Employees want to be a part of the decision-making process.	1	2	3	4	5
3. In complex situations, leaders should let subordinates work problems out on their own.	1	2	3	4	5
4. It is fair to say that most employees in the general population are lazy.	1	2	3	4	5
5. Providing guidance without pressure is the key to being a good leader.	1	2	3	4	5
6. Leadership requires staying out of the way of subordinates as they do their work.	1	2	3	4	5
7. As a rule, employees must be given rewards or punishments in order to motivate them to achieve organizational objectives.	1	2	3	4	5
8. Most workers prefer supportive communication from their leaders.	1	2	3	4	5
9. As a rule, leaders should allow subordinates to appraise their own work.	1	2	3	4	5
10. Most employees feel insecure about their work and need direction.	1	2	3	4	5
11. Leaders need to help subordinates accept responsibility for completing their work.	1	2	3	4	5
12. Leaders should give subordinates complete freedom to solve problems on their own.	1	2	3	4	5
13. The leader is the chief judge of the achievements of the members of the group.	1	2	3	4	5

Statements	Strongly disagree	Disagree	Neutral	Agree	Strongly agree
14. It is the leader's job to help subordinates find their "passion."	1	2	3	4	5
15. In most situations, workers prefer little input from the leader.	1	2	3	4	5
16. Effective leaders give orders and clarify procedures.	1	2	3	4	5
17. People are basically competent and if given a task will do a good job.	1	2	3	4	5
18. In general, it is best to leave subordinates alone.	1	2	3	4	5

Scoring

1. Sum the responses on items 1, 4, 7, 10, 13, and 16 (authoritarian leadership).

2. Sum the responses on items 2, 5, 8, 11, 14, and 17 (democratic leadership).

3. Sum the responses on items 3, 6, 9, 12, 15, and 18 (laissez-faire leadership).

Total Scores

Authoritarian Leadership _____

Democratic Leadership _____

Laissez-Faire Leadership _____

Scoring Interpretation

This questionnaire is designed to measure three common styles of leadership: authoritarian, democratic, and laissez-faire. By comparing your scores, you can determine which styles are most dominant and least dominant in your own style of leadership.

If your score is 26–30, you are in the very high range.

If your score is 21–25, you are in the high range.

If your score is 16–20, you are in the moderate range.

If your score is 11–15, you are in the low range.

If your score is 6–10, you are in the very low range.

3.2   Observational Exercise

 Visit www.sagepub.com/northouseintro2e for downloadable versions of these questionnaires

Leadership Styles

Purpose

1. To become aware of authoritarian, democratic, and laissez-faire styles of leadership

2. To compare and contrast these three styles

Directions

1. From all of the coaches, teachers, music directors, or managers you have had in the past 10 years, select one who was authoritarian, one who was democratic, and one who was laissez-faire.

    Authoritarian leader (name) _____

    Democratic leader (name) _____

    Laissez-faire leader (name) _____

2. On another sheet of paper, briefly describe the unique characteristics of each of these leaders.

Questions

1. What differences did you observe in how each leader tried to influence you?

2. How did the leaders differ in their use of rewards and punishment?

3. What did you observe about how others reacted to each leader?

4. Under which leader were you most productive? Why?

3.3   Reflection and Action Worksheet

 Visit www.sagepub.com/northouseintro2e for downloadable versions of these questionnaires

Leadership Styles

Reflection

1. As you reflect on the assumptions of Theory X and Theory Y, how would you describe your own philosophy of leadership?

2. Of the three styles of leadership (authoritarian, democratic, and laissez-faire), what style comes easiest for you? Describe how people respond to you when you use this style.

3. One of the aspects of democratic leadership is to help subordinates take responsibility for themselves. How do you assess your own ability to help others help themselves?

Action

1. If you were to try to strengthen your philosophy of leadership, what kinds of changes would you have to make in your assumptions about human nature and work?

2. As you look at your results on the Leadership Styles Questionnaire, what scores would you like to change? What would you have to do to make those changes?

3. List three specific activities you could use to improve your leadership style.

4. If you make these changes, what impact will this have on others?

4

Before you begin reading . . .

Complete the *Task and Relationship Questionnaire*, which you will find on pp. 79–80. As you read the chapter, consider your results on the questionnaire.

Attending to Tasks and Relationships

4

Most people would agree that good doctors are expert at treating disease *and*, at the same time, care about their patients. Similarly, good teachers are informed about the subject matter *and*, at the same time, are sensitive to the personal lives of their students. In leadership, the same is true. Good leaders understand the work that needs to be done *and*, at the same time, can relate to the people who help them do the job.

When we look at what leaders do—that is, at their behaviors—we see that they do two major things: (1) They attend to *tasks,* and (2) they attend to their *relationships* with people. The degree to which leaders are successful is determined by how these two behaviors are exhibited. Situations may differ, but every leadership situation needs a degree of both task and relationship behaviors.

Audio Link 4.1
Listen to indicators of task and relationship orientation.

Through the years, many articles and books have been written on how leaders behave (Blake & McCanse, 1991; Kahn, 1956; Misumi, 1985; Stogdill, 1974). A review of these writings underscores the topic of this chapter: The essence of leadership behavior has two dimensions— task behaviors and relationship behaviors. Certain circumstances may call for strong task behavior, and other situations may demand strong relationship behavior, but some degree of each is required in every situation. Because these dimensions are inextricably tied together, it is the leader's challenge to integrate and optimize the task and relationship dimensions in his or her leadership role.

▶ WHAT IS YOUR PERSONAL STYLE?

One way to explore our own task and relationship perspectives on leadership is to explore our **personal styles** in these two areas. All of us have developed unique habits regarding work and play, which have been ingrained over many years, probably beginning as far back as elementary school. Rooted in the past, these habits regarding work and play form a very real part of who we are as people and of how we function. Many of these early habits stay with us over the years and influence our current styles.

In considering your personal style, it is helpful to describe in more detail your task-oriented and relationship-oriented behaviors. What is your inclination toward tasks and relationships? Are you more work oriented or people oriented in your personal life? Do you find more rewards in the process of "getting things done" or in the process of relating to people? We all have personal styles that incorporate some combination of work and play. The Task and Relationship Questionnaire you completed before reading this chapter can help identify your personal style. Although these descriptions imply that individuals are either one style or the other, it is important to remember that each of us exhibits *both* behaviors to some degree.

Video Link 4.1
Watch more about personal styles.

Journal Link 4.1
Read more on task versus relationship.

TASK-ORIENTED STYLE

Task-oriented people are goal oriented. They want to achieve. Their work is meaningful, and they like things such as "to do" lists, calendars, and daily planners. Accomplishing things and doing things is the raison d'être for this type of person. That is, these individuals' *reason for being* comes from *doing*. Their "in-box" is never empty. On vacations, they try to see and do as much as they possibly can. In all avenues of their lives, they find meaning in doing.

In his book titled *Work and Love: The Crucial Balance* (1980), psychiatrist Jay Rohrlich showed how work can help people organize, routinize, and structure their lives. Doing tasks gives people a sense of control and self-mastery. Achievement sharpens our self-image and helps us define ourselves. Reaching a goal, like running a race or completing a project, makes people feel good because it is a positive expression of who they are.

Some clear examples of task-oriented people include those who use color codes in their daily planners, who have sticky-back notes in every room of their house, or who, by 10:00 on Saturday morning, have washed the car, done the laundry, and cleaned the apartment. Task-oriented people also are likely to make a list for everything, from grocery shopping to the series of repetitions in their weight-lifting workouts. Common to all of these people is their interest in achieving the goal and accomplishing the work.

RELATIONSHIP-ORIENTED STYLE

Relationship-oriented people differ from task-oriented people because they are not as goal directed. The relationship-oriented person finds meaning in *being* rather than in *doing*. Instead of seeking out tasks, relationship-oriented people want to connect with people. They like to celebrate relationships and the pleasures relationships bring.

Furthermore, relationship-oriented people often have a strong orientation in the present. They find meaning in the moment rather than in some future objective to be accomplished. In a group situation, sensing and feeling the company of others is appealing to these people. They have been described by some as "relationship junkies." They are the people who are the last to turn off their cell phones as the airplane takes off and the first to turn the phones back on when the airplane lands. Basically, they are into connectedness.

In a work setting, the relationship-oriented person wants to connect or attach with others. For example, the relationship-oriented person would not be afraid to interrupt someone who was working hard on a task to talk about the weather, sports, or just about anything. When working out a problem, relationship-oriented people like to talk to and be associated with others in addressing the problem. They receive satisfaction from being connected to other people. A task-oriented friend described a relationship-oriented person perfectly when he said, "He is the kind of person who stands and talks to you, coffee mug in hand, when you're trying to do something like mow the lawn or cover the boat." The meaning in "doing" is just not paramount in the relationship-oriented person's style.

Journal Link 4.2
Read about style and trust.

WHAT KIND OF LEADER ARE YOU? ◄

In the previous section, you were asked to consider your *personal* style regarding tasks and relationships. In this section, we are going to consider the task and relationship dimensions of your *leadership* style.

Video Link 4.2

Watch more
about using leadership
styles.

Figure 4.1 illustrates dimensions of leadership along a task-relationship continuum. **Task-oriented leadership**, which appears on the left end of the continuum, represents leadership that is focused predominantly on procedures, activities, and goal accomplishments. **Relationship-oriented leadership**, which appears on the right end of the continuum, represents leadership that is focused primarily on the well-being of subordinates, how they relate to each other, and the atmosphere in which they work. Most leadership falls midway between the two extremes of task- and relationship-oriented leadership. This style of leadership is represented by the *midrange* area, a blend of the two types of leadership.

Figure 4.1   Task-Relationship Leadership Continuum

As was discussed at the beginning of this chapter, good leaders understand the work that needs to be done, as well as the need to understand the people who will do it. The process of "doing" leadership requires that leaders attend to both tasks and relationships. The specific challenge for the leader is to decide how much task and how much relationship is required in a given context or situation.

TASK LEADERSHIP

Task leadership behaviors facilitate goal accomplishment—they are behaviors that help group members to achieve their objectives. Researchers have found that task leadership includes many behaviors. These behaviors are frequently labeled in different ways, but are always about task accomplishment. For example, some have labeled task leadership as **initiating structure**, which means the leader organizes work, defines role responsibilities, and schedules work activities (Stogdill, 1974). Others have labeled task leadership as **production orientation**, which means the leader stresses the production and technical aspects of the job (Bowers & Seashore, 1966). From this perspective, the leader pays attention to new product development, workload matters, and sales volume, to name a few aspects. A third label for task leadership is **concern for production** (Blake & Mouton, 1964). It includes policy decisions, new product development, workload, sales volume, or whatever the organization is seeking to accomplish.

In short, task leadership occurs any time the leader is *doing something* that assists the group in reaching its goals. This can be something as simple as handing out an agenda for an upcoming meeting or as complex as describing the multiple quality control standards of a product development process. Task leadership includes many behaviors: Common to each is influencing people toward goal achievement.

As you would expect, people vary in their ability to show task-oriented leadership. There are those who are very task oriented and those who are less task oriented. This is where a person's personal style comes into play. Those who are task oriented in their personal lives are naturally more task oriented in their leadership. Conversely, those who are seldom task oriented in their personal lives will find it difficult to be task oriented as a leader.

Whether a person is very task oriented or less task oriented, the important point to remember is that, as a leader, he or she will always be required to exhibit some degree of task behavior. For certain individuals this will be easy and for others it will present a challenge, but some task-oriented behavior is essential to each person's effective leadership performance.

RELATIONSHIP LEADERSHIP

Relationship leadership behaviors help subordinates feel comfortable with themselves, with each other, and with the situation in which they find themselves. For example, in the classroom, when a teacher requires each student to know every other student's name, the teacher is demonstrating relationship leadership. The teacher is helping the students to feel comfortable with themselves, with other students, and with their environment.

Researchers have described relationship leadership in several ways that help to clarify its meaning. It has been labeled by some researchers as **consideration behavior** (Stogdill, 1974), which includes building camaraderie, respect, trust, and regard between leaders and followers. Other researchers describe relationship leadership as having an **employee orientation** (Bowers & Seashore, 1966), which involves taking an interest in workers as human beings, valuing their uniqueness, and giving special attention to their personal needs. Another line of research has simply defined relationship leadership as being

Handbook Link 4.1
Read more about leadership in organizations.

concern for people (Blake & Mouton, 1964). Within an organization, concern for people includes building trust, providing good working conditions, maintaining a fair salary structure, and promoting good social relations.

Essentially, relationship leadership behavior is about three things: (1) treating followers with dignity and respect, (2) building relationships and helping people get along, and (3) making the work setting a pleasant place to be. Relationship leadership behavior is an integral part of effective leadership performance.

In our fast-paced and very diverse society, the challenge for a leader is finding the time and energy to listen to all followers and do what is required to build effective relationships with each of them. For those who are highly relationship oriented in their personal lives, being relationship oriented in leadership will come easily; for those who are highly task oriented, being relationship oriented in leadership will present a greater challenge. Regardless of your personal styles, every leadership situation demands a degree of relationship leadership behavior.

Box 4.1   Student Perspectives on Task and Relationship Styles

The following examples are personal observations written by college students. These papers illuminate the distinct differences task and relationship orientations can have in real-life experiences.

Taken to Task

I am definitely a task-oriented person. My mother has given me her love of lists, and my father has instilled in me the value of finishing things once you start them. As a result, I am highly organized in all aspects of my life. I have a color-coded planner with all of the activities I need to do, and I enjoy crossing things off my lists. Some of my friends call me a workaholic, but I don't think that is accurate. There are just a lot of things I have to do.

My roommate Steph, however, is completely different from me. She will make verbal lists for her day, but usually will not accomplish any of them [the items listed]. This drives me crazy when it involves my life. For example, there were boxes all over the place until about a month after we moved into our house. Steph would say every day that she was going to focus and get her

room organized that day, but she'd fail miserably most of the time. She is easily distracted and would pass up the opportunity to get unpacked to go out with friends, get on Facebook, or look at YouTube videos.

No matter how much Steph's life stresses me out, I have learned from it. I'm all about having a good time in the right setting, but I am coming to realize that I don't need to be so planned and scheduled. No matter how carefully you do plan, something will always go awry. I don't know that Steph is the one who has taught me that or if I'm just getting older, but I'm glad I'm learning that regardless.

—*Jessica Lembke*

Being Rather Than Doing

I am an extremely relationship-oriented person. While I know that accomplishing tasks is important, I believe the quality of work people produce is directly related to how they feel about themselves and their leader.

I had the privilege of working with fifth graders in an after-school program last year. There was a range of issues we dealt with including academic, behavioral, and emotional problems, as well as kids who did not have safe homes (i.e., no running water or electricity, physical and emotional abuse, and drug addictions within the home). The "goal" of our program was to help these kids become "proficient" students in the classroom.

The task-oriented leaders in administration emphasized improving students' grades through repetition of school work, flash cards, and quizzes. It was important for our students to improve their grades because it was the only way statistically to gauge if our program was successful. Given some of the personal trials these young people were dealing with, the last thing in my "relationship-oriented" mind was working on their academics. These young people had so much potential and wisdom that was stifled when they were asked to blindly follow academic assignments. In addition, they did not know how to self-motivate, self-encourage, or get the work done with so many of life's obstacles in their way.

Instead of doing school work, which the majority of my students struggled with and hated, I focused on building relationships with and between the students. We used discussion, role play, dance parties, and leadership projects to build their self-confidence and emotional intelligence. The students put together service projects to improve their school and community including initiating a trash pickup and recycling initiative at the school and making cards for a nearby nursing home. By the end of the year almost every one of my students had improved his or her grades significantly. More important, at our daily "cheer-for-each-other" meetings, the students would beam with pride for their own and others' successes.

I guess my point in telling this story is that relationship-oriented leadership is more important to me than task. I much prefer "being" than "doing." I am not an organized, goal-oriented person. I rarely make it out of my house without going back two or three times to grab something I forgot, and my attention span is shorter than that of a fruit fly. However, I feel that my passion for relationships and human connection is what motivates me.

—*Elizabeth Mathews*

A Blend of Both

The Style Approach categorizes leaders as being either task oriented or relationship oriented. While I agree that there are these styles of leadership, I disagree that everyone can be placed concretely into one or the other. The Ohio State study says it well by stating that there are "two different continua." When it comes to determining where I stand on each continuum, I'd have to say I'm about even. Not surprisingly, my results of the Task and Relationship Questionnaire reflect these thoughts: I scored a solid 41 in both task- and relationship-oriented styles; I'm equally task and relationship oriented, with each of these styles becoming more prevalent in certain situations.

While I truly enjoy being around other people, making sure everyone is happy and that we all enjoy our time, I'm very focused and goal oriented. If I'm at the movies with my friends I'm not worrying about a to-do list; alternatively, if I'm working on a group project for school, I'm not as concerned about making friends with the group members.

Completing tasks is very important to me. I have an agenda that I keep with me at all times, partly because without it I would never remember anything, and partly because it provides satisfaction and peace of mind. I make to-do lists for myself: groceries, household chores, homework, and goals. I thrive when I'm busy, but not if I'm disorganized. For example, this semester I'm taking 20 credits, applying to graduate schools, taking the GRE, and working at the bookstore. For me it is comforting to have so many responsibilities. If I have downtime I usually waste it, and I hate that feeling.

I also feel, however, that I'm very relationship oriented. My task oriented nature doesn't really affect how I interact with people. I like to make sure people are comfortable and confident in all situations. While I pressure myself to get things done and adhere to a schedule, I'd never think of pushing those pressures onto someone else. If I were the leader of a group that wasn't getting things done, I'd set an example, rather than tell someone what he or she should be doing.

For me, the idea of "two continua" really makes sense. Whether I am task or relationship focused depends on the situation. While I certainly want to have fun with people, I'm a proponent of the "time and place" attitude, in which people remember when it is appropriate to socialize and when it is appropriate to get a job done.

—*Sally Johnson*

WHAT KIND OF LEADER DO YOUR FOLLOWERS NEED?

As discussed earlier in this chapter, task and relationship leadership behaviors are inextricably tied together, and a leader's challenge is to integrate the two in an optimal way while effectively adapting to followers' needs. For example, task leadership is critically important in a company or an organization with a large number of newly hired employees or at a junior high school with a cadre of new faculty members. In situations like these, the followers feel uncertain about their roles and responsibilities, and they want a leader who clarifies their tasks and tells them what is expected of them. In fact, in nearly every group or situation there are some individuals who want and need task direction from their leader, and in these circumstances it is paramount that the leader exhibit strong task-oriented leadership.

Audio Link 4.2
Listen to a leader speak about follower needs.

On the other hand, it is also true that many groups or situations will also have individuals who want to be affiliated with or connected to others more than they want direction. For example, in a sorority, in a classroom, or even at a workplace like McDonald's, there are individuals who want the leader to befriend them and relate to them on a human level. The followers are willing to work, but they are primarily interested in being recognized and feeling related to others. Clearly, in these situations, the leader needs to connect with these followers by utilizing relationship-oriented behaviors.

In society, the most effective leaders recognize and adapt to followers' needs. Whether they are team leaders, teachers, or managers, they appropriately demonstrate the right degrees of task and relationship leadership. This is no small challenge because different followers and situations demand different amounts of task and relationship leadership. When followers are unclear, confused, or lost, the leader needs to show direction and exhibit task-oriented leadership. At the same time, a leader needs to be able to see the need for affiliation and attachment in followers and be able to meet those needs, without sacrificing task accomplishment.

In the end, the best leader is the leader who helps followers achieve the goal by attending to the task and by attending to each follower as a person. We all know leaders who do this: They are the coaches who force us to do drills until we are blue in the face to improve our physical performance, but who then caringly listen to our personal problems. They are the managers who never let us slack off for even a second but who make work a fun place to be. The list goes on, but the bottom line is that the best leaders get the job done and care about others in the process.

CASE STUDY

The following case study describes a leadership dilemma faced by Mark Schmidt who runs a small cleaning business. As you read the case, try to apply ideas from the chapter about task-oriented and relationship-oriented leadership to the situation. At the end of the case, questions are provided to help you analyze the leadership challenges presented in this situation.

From Two to One

Mark Schmidt runs Co-Ed Cleaners, a business that employs teams of college students to clean offices and schools during the night hours. Due to the economic downturn over the past two years, Co-Ed Cleaners has lost customers, and although Mark has trimmed everywhere he can think of he has come to the conclusion that he has to cut back further. This will require letting go of one of his two team managers and consolidating responsibilities under the other manager's leadership.

Dan Cali manages the Schools Team, which cleans school buildings. Because his team cleans two different schools each night, Dan is often on the go, visiting teams at each school while they are working. His employees describe him as an efficient taskmaster who has checklists they are all required to follow and sign off on as they complete each job. Dan initiates most ideas for changing processes based on his own judgment of what should be done. When something goes wrong on a job, Dan insists he be alerted and brought in to solve it. "Dan is a traditional, top-down, the-buck-stops-here kind of boss," says one of his team members. "There is no one that works harder than he does or knows more about our jobs. But if he doesn't think you are doing your job, you won't have one for very long."

Asher Roland is the manager of the Office Team, overseeing several two-person teams that clean offices and businesses. Because Asher has up to 10 teams working a night, he relies on his team members to do their jobs and keep him apprised of problems. He takes turns working alongside his teams to understand the challenges they may face, but most of the time the teams are on their own. He brings them in once a month for a "Great Job Breakfast" where they bond and share stories. One of his team managers describes him this way: "Asher is very hands-off. He will always advocate for his teams and listens when we have ideas or problems, but allows us to manage our own jobs the way we think best. He trusts us to do the right things, and we trust him to be fair and honest with us."

Mark likes both Dan and Asher, and in their own way they are both good managers. Mark worries, however, about how each manager's individual style will affect his ability to take on the responsibilities for the other team. He must let one go, but he doesn't know which one.

Questions

1. Using ideas from the chapter, describe Dan's and Asher's styles of leadership.
2. How will Asher's employees, who are used to being able to manage themselves in their own way, respond to Dan's task-oriented style?
3. How will Dan's employees, who are used to being given clear direction and procedures, respond to Asher's more relationship-oriented style?
4. If you were an employee at Co-Ed Cleaners, whom would you want Mark to let go? Explain your choice.

Summary

Good leaders are both task oriented and relationship oriented. Understanding your personal styles of work and play can provide a better recognition of your leadership. Task-oriented people find meaning in doing, while relationship-oriented people find meaning in being connected to others. Effective leadership requires that leaders be both task oriented and relationship oriented.

 Go to **http://www.sagepub.com/northouseintro2e/** *for additional exercises and study resources. Select Chapter 4, Attending to Tasks and Relationships, for chapter-specific activities.*

Glossary Terms

concern for people   74

concern for production   72

consideration behavior   73

employee orientation   73

initiating structure   72

personal styles   70

production orientation   72

relationship-oriented leadership   72

task-oriented leadership   72

References

Blake, R. R., & McCanse, A. A. (1991). *Leadership dilemmas: Grid solutions.* Houston, TX: Gulf Publishing.

Blake, R. R., & Mouton, J. S. (1964). *The managerial grid.* Houston, TX: Gulf Publishing.

Bowers, D. G., & Seashore, S. E. (1966). Predicting organizational effectiveness with a four-factor theory of leadership. *Administrative Science Quarterly, 11,* 238–263.

Kahn, R. L. (1956). The prediction of productivity. *Journal of Social Issues, 12,* 41–49.

Misumi, J. (1985). *The behavioral science of leadership: An interdisciplinary Japanese research program.* Ann Arbor: University of Michigan Press.

Rohrlich, J. B. (1980). *Work and love: The crucial balance.* New York: Summit Books.

Stogdill, R. M. (1974). *Handbook of leadership: A survey of theory and research.* New York: Free Press.

4.1   Task and Relationship Questionnaire

 Visit www.sagepub.com/northouseintro2e for downloadable versions of these questionnaires

Purpose

1. To identify how much you emphasize task and relationship behaviors in your life
2. To explore how your task behavior is related to your relationship behavior

Directions

For each item below, indicate on the scale the extent to which you engage in the described behavior. Move through the items quickly. Do not try to categorize yourself in one area or another.

Statements	Never	Rarely	Sometimes	Often	Always
1. Make a "to do" list of the things that need to be done.	1	2	3	4	5
2. Try to make the work fun for others.	1	2	3	4	5
3. Urge others to concentrate on the work at hand.	1	2	3	4	5
4. Show concern for the personal well-being of others.	1	2	3	4	5
5. Set timelines for when the job needs to be done.	1	2	3	4	5
6. Help group members get along.	1	2	3	4	5
7. Keep a checklist of what has been accomplished.	1	2	3	4	5
8. Listen to the special needs of each group member.	1	2	3	4	5
9. Stress to others the rules and requirements for the project.	1	2	3	4	5
10. Spend time exploring other people's ideas for the project.	1	2	3	4	5

Scoring

1. Sum scores for the odd-numbered statements (task score).
2. Sum scores for the even-numbered statements (relationship score).

Total Scores

Task score: _____

Relationship score: _____

Scoring Interpretation

This questionnaire is designed to measure your task-oriented and relationship-oriented leadership behavior. By comparing your scores, you can determine which style is more dominant in your own style of leadership. If your task score is higher than your relationship score, you tend to give more attention to goal accomplishment and somewhat less attention to people-related matters. If your relationship score is higher than your task score, your primary concern tends to be dealing with people, and your secondary concern is directed more toward tasks. If your scores are very similar to each other, it suggests that your leadership is balanced and includes an equal amount of both behaviors.

If your score is 20–25, you are in the high range.

If your score is 15–19, you are in the high moderate range.

If your score is 10–14, you are in the low moderate range.

If your score is 5–9, you are in the low range.

4.2   Observational Exercise

 Visit www.sagepub.com/northouseintro2e for downloadable versions of these questionnaires

Task and Relationship

Purpose

1. To understand how leadership includes both task and relationship behaviors

2. To contrast different leaders' task and relationship behaviors

Directions

1. Over the next couple of days, observe the leadership styles of two different leaders (e.g., teacher, athletic coach, choir director, restaurant manager, work supervisor).

2. Record your observations of the styles of each person.

Leader #1 (name) _____

Task behaviors   Relationship behaviors

- _____   - _____
- _____   - _____
- _____   - _____
- _____   - _____

Leader #2 (name) _____

Task behaviors   Relationship behaviors

- _____   - _____
- _____   - _____
- _____   - _____
- _____   - _____

Questions

1. What differences did you observe between the two leaders?

2. What did you observe about the leader who was most task oriented?

3. What did you observe about the leader who was most relationship oriented?

4. How effective do you think you would be in each of these leadership positions?

4.3   Reflection and Action Worksheet

 Visit **www.sagepub.com/northouseintro2e** for downloadable versions of these questionnaires

Task and Relationship

Reflection

1. As you reflect on what has been discussed in this chapter and on your own leadership style, how would you describe your own style in relation to task and relationship orientations? What are your strengths and weaknesses?

2. What biases do you maintain regarding task style and relationship style? How do your biases affect your leadership?

3. One of the most difficult challenges leaders face is to integrate their task and relationship behaviors. Do you see this as a challenge in your own leadership? How do you integrate task and relationship behaviors?

Action

1. If you were to change in an effort to improve your leadership, what aspect of your style would you change? Would you try to be more task oriented or more relationship oriented?

2. Identify three specific task or relationship changes you could carry out.

3. What barriers will you face as you try to make these changes?

4. Given that you believe this change will improve your overall leadership, what can you do (i.e., what strategies can you use) to overcome the barriers you cite in Action Item #3 above?

Before you begin reading . . .

Complete the *Leadership Skills Questionnaire*, which you will find on pp. 103–104. As you read the chapter, consider your results on the questionnaire.

Developing Leadership Skills

5

Whether it is playing the guitar, a video game, or the stock market, most of life's activities require us to have skills if we are to be successful. The same is true of leadership—skills are required. As was discussed in the first chapter, leadership skills refer to learned competencies that leaders are able to demonstrate in performance (Katz, 1955). Leadership skills give people the capacity to influence others. They are a critical component in successful leadership.

Even though skills play an essential role in the leadership process, they have received little attention by researchers (Lord & Hall, 2005; Mumford, Campion, & Morgeson, 2007). Leadership traits rather than leadership skills have been the focus of research for more than 100 years. However, in the past 10 years a shift has occurred, and leadership skills are now receiving far more attention by researchers and practitioners alike (Mumford, Zaccaro, Connelly, & Marks, 2000; Yammarino, 2000).

WHAT ARE YOUR CORE LEADERSHIP SKILLS? ◄

Although there are many different leadership skills, they are often considered as groups of skills. In this chapter, leadership skills are grouped into three categories: *administrative skills, interpersonal skills,*

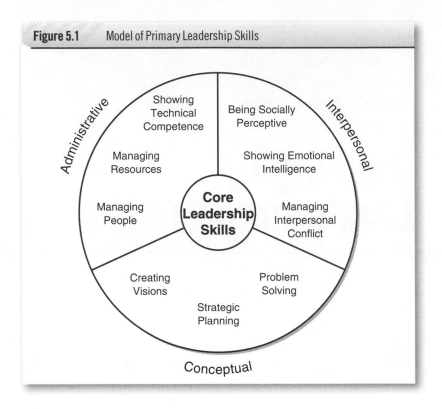

Figure 5.1   Model of Primary Leadership Skills

and *conceptual skills* (see Figure 5.1). The next section describes each group of skills and explores the unique ways they affect the leadership process.

ADMINISTRATIVE SKILLS

While often devalued because they are not glamorous or exciting, **administrative skills** play a primary role in effective leadership. Administrative skills help a leader to accomplish the mundane but critically important aspects of showing leadership. Some would even argue that administrative skills are the most fundamental of all the skills required of a leader.

What are administrative skills? Administrative skills refer to those competencies a leader needs to run an organization in order to carry out the organization's purposes and goals. These involve planning, organizing work, assigning the right tasks to the right people, and coordinating work activities (Mann, 1965). For purposes of our discussion, administrative skills are divided into three specific sets of skills: (1) managing people, (2) managing resources, and (3) showing technical competence.

Managing People

Any leader of a for-profit or nonprofit organization, if asked what occupies the most time, will reply, "Managing people." Few leaders can do without the skill of being able to manage people. The phrase *management by walking around* captures the essence of managing people. An effective leader connects with people and understands the tasks to be done, those skills required to perform them, and the environment in which people work. The best way to know this is to be involved rather than to be a spectator. For a leader to deal effectively with people requires a host of abilities such as helping employees to work as a team, motivating them to do their best, promoting satisfying relationships among employees, and responding to their requests. The leader also needs to find time to deal with urgent staff matters. Staff issues are a daily fact of life for any leader. Staff members come to the leader for advice on what to do about a problem, and the leader needs to respond appropriately.

Journal Link 5.1
Read more about administrative skills.

A leader must also pay attention to recruiting and retaining employees. In addition, leaders need to communicate effectively with their own board of directors, as well as with any external constituencies such as the public, stockholders, or other outside groups that have a stake in the organization.

Consider the leadership of Nate Parker, the director of an after-school recreation program serving 600 kids in a large metropolitan community. Nate's program is funded by an $800,000 government grant. It provides academic, fitness, and enrichment activities for underserved children and their families. Nate has managers who assist him in running the after-school program in five different public schools. Nate's own responsibilities include setting up and running staff meetings, recruiting new staff, updating contracts, writing press releases, working with staff, and establishing relationships with external constituencies. Nate takes great pride in having created a new and strong relationship between the city government and the school district in which he works. Until he came on board, the relationship between the schools and city government was tense. By communicating effectively across groups,

Nate was able to bring the entire community together to serve the children. He is now researching the possibility of a citywide system to support after-school programming.

Managing Resources

Although it is not obvious to others, a leader is often required to spend a significant amount of time addressing resource issues. Resources, the lifeblood of an organization, can include people, money, supplies, equipment, space, or anything else needed to operate an organization. Managing resources requires a leader to be competent in both obtaining and allocating resources. Obtaining resources can include a wide range of activities such as ordering equipment, finding work space, or locating funds for special projects. For example, a middle school cross-country coach wanted to replace her team's outdated uniforms, but had no funds to do so. In order to buy new uniforms, the coach negotiated with the athletic director for additional funds. The coach also encouraged several parents in the booster club to sponsor a few successful fund-raisers.

In addition to obtaining resources, a leader may be required to allocate resources for new staff or new incentive programs, or to replace old equipment. While a leader may often engage staff members to assist in managing resources, the ultimate responsibility of resource management rests on the leader. As the sign on President Harry S. Truman's desk read, "The buck stops here."

Showing Technical Competence

Technical competence involves having specialized knowledge about the work we do or ask others to do. In the case of an organization, it includes understanding the intricacies of how an organization functions. A leader with technical competence has organizational know-how—he or she understands the complex aspects of how the organization works. For example, a university president should be knowledgeable about teaching, research, student recruitment, and student retention; a basketball coach should be knowledgeable about the basics of dribbling, passing, shooting, and rebounding; and a sales manager should have a thorough understanding of the product the salespeople are selling. In short, a leader is more effective when he or she has the knowledge and technical competence about the activities subordinates are asked to perform.

Technical competence is sometimes referred to as "functional competence" because it means a person is competent in a particular function or area. No one is required to be competent in all avenues of life. So, too, a leader is not required to have technical competence in every situation. Having technical skills means being competent in a particular area of work, the area in which one is leading.

The importance of having technical competence can be seen in the example of an orchestra conductor. The conductor's job is to direct rehearsals and performances of the orchestra. To do this, the conductor needs technical competence pertaining to rhythm, music composition, and all the many instruments and how they are played. Technical competence gives the conductor the understanding required to direct the many different musicians to perform together successfully.

INTERPERSONAL SKILLS

In addition to administrative skills, effective leadership requires interpersonal skills (see Figure 5.1). **Interpersonal skills** are people skills—those abilities that help a leader to work effectively with subordinates, peers, and superiors to accomplish the organization's goals. While some people downplay the importance of interpersonal skills or disparage them as "touchy-feely" and inconsequential, leadership research has consistently pointed out the importance of interpersonal skills to effective leadership (Bass, 1990; Blake & McCanse, 1991; Katz, 1955). In our discussion, interpersonal skills are divided into three parts: (1) being socially perceptive, (2) showing emotional intelligence, and (3) managing interpersonal conflicts.

Encyclopedia Link 5.1
Read about
developing skills.

Being Socially Perceptive

To successfully lead an organization toward change, a leader needs to be sensitive to how her or his own ideas fit in with others' ideas. **Social perceptiveness** includes having insight into and awareness of what is important to others, how they are motivated, the problems they face, and how they react to change. It involves understanding the unique needs, goals, and demands of different organizational constituencies (Zaccaro, Gilbert, Thor, & Mumford, 1991). A leader with social perceptiveness has a keen sense of how employees will respond to any proposed change in the organization. In a sense, you could say a socially perceptive leader has a finger on the pulse of employees on any issue at any time.

Leadership is about change, and people in organizations often resist change because they like things to stay the same. Novel ideas, different rules, or new ways of doing things are often seen as threatening because they do not fit in with how people are used to things being done. A leader who is socially perceptive can create change more effectively if he or she understands how the proposed change may affect all the people involved.

One example that demonstrates the importance of social perceptiveness is illustrated in the events surrounding the graduation ceremonies at the University of Michigan in the spring of 2008. The university anticipated 5,000 students would graduate, with an expected audience of 30,000. In prior years, the university traditionally held spring graduation ceremonies in the football stadium, which, because of its size, is commonly known as "the Big House." However, because the stadium was undergoing major renovations, the university was forced to change the venue for graduation and decided to hold the graduation at the outdoor stadium of nearby Eastern Michigan University. When the university announced the change of location, the students, their families, and the university's alumni responded immediately and negatively. There was upheaval as they made their strong opinions known.

Clearly, the leadership at the university had not perceived the significance to seniors and their families of where graduation ceremonies were to be held. It was tradition to graduate in the Big House, so changing the venue was offensive to many. Phone calls came into the president's office, and editorials appeared in the press. Students did not want to graduate on the campus of another university. They thought that they deserved to graduate on their own campus. Some students, parents, and alumni even threatened to withhold future alumni support.

To correct the situation, the university again changed the venue. Instead of holding the graduation at Eastern Michigan University, the university spent $1.8 million to set up a temporary outdoor stage in the center of campus, surrounded by the University of Michigan's classroom buildings and libraries. The graduating students and their families were pleased that the ceremonies took place where their memories and traditions were so strong. The university ultimately was successful because it adapted to the deeply held beliefs of its students and their families. Clearly, if the university had been more socially perceptive at the outset, the initial dissatisfaction and upheaval that arose could have been avoided.

Showing Emotional Intelligence

Another important skill for a leader is being able to show emotional intelligence. Although emotional intelligence emerged as a concept less than 20 years ago, it has captivated the interests of many scholars and practitioners of leadership (Caruso & Wolfe, 2004; Goleman, 1995; Mayer & Salovey, 1995). **Emotional intelligence** is concerned with a person's ability to understand his or her own and others' emotions, and then to apply this understanding to life's tasks. Specifically, emotional intelligence can be defined as the ability to perceive and express emotions, to use emotions to facilitate thinking, to understand and reason with emotions, and to manage emotions effectively within oneself and in relationships with others (Mayer, Salovey, & Caruso, 2000).

Audio Link 5.1
Listen to the importance of skill development.

The underlying premise of research on emotional intelligence is that people who are sensitive to their own emotions and the impact their emotions have on others will be more effective leaders. Since showing emotional intelligence is positively related to effective leadership, what should a leader do to enhance his or her emotional skills?

First, leaders need to work on *becoming aware* of their own emotions, taking their emotional pulse, and identifying their feelings as they happen. Whether it is mad, glad, sad, or scared, a leader needs to assess constantly how he or she is feeling and what is causing those feelings.

Second, a leader should train to become aware of the emotions of others. A leader who knows how to read others' emotions is better equipped to respond appropriately to these people's wants and needs. Stated another way, a leader needs to have empathy for others. He or she should understand the feelings of others as if those feelings were his or her own. Salovey and Mayer (1990) suggested that empathy is the critical component of emotional intelligence. Empathy and how to demonstrate it is discussed further in Chapter 8, "Listening to Out-Group Members."

Third, a leader needs to learn how to regulate his or her emotions and put them to good use. Whenever a leader makes a substantial decision, the leader's emotions are involved. Therefore, emotions need to be embraced and managed for the good of the group or organization. When a leader is sensitive to others and manages his or her own emotions appropriately, that leader increases the chances that the group's decisions will be effective. For example, a high school principal sensed that she was becoming extremely angry with some students who pulled a prank during an assembly. Instead of expressing her anger—"losing it"—she

Video Link 5.1

Watch more on
social intelligence.

maintained her composure and helped to turn the prank into a learning experience. The key point here is that people with emotional intelligence understand emotions and incorporate these in what they do as leaders. To summarize, a leader with emotional intelligence listens to his or her own feelings and the feelings of others, and is adept at regulating these emotions in service of the common good.

Handling Conflict

A leader also needs to have skill in handling conflict. Conflict is inevitable. Conflict creates the need *for* change and occurs as the result *of* change. Conflict can be defined as a struggle between two or more individuals over perceived differences regarding substantive issues (e.g., the correct procedure to follow) or over perceived differences regarding relational issues (e.g., the amount of control each individual has within a relationship). When confronted with conflict, leaders and followers often feel uncomfortable because of the strain, controversy, and stress that accompany conflict. Although conflict is uncomfortable, it is not unhealthy, nor is it necessarily bad. If conflict is managed in effective and productive ways, the result is a reduction of stress, an increase in creative problem solving, and a strengthening of leader-follower and team-member relationships.

Because conflicts are usually very complex, and addressing them is never simple, Chapter 9, "Handling Conflict," provides a more thorough examination of the components of conflict and offers several practical communication approaches that a leader can take to constructively resolve differences.

CONCEPTUAL SKILLS

Whereas administrative skills are about organizing work, and interpersonal skills are about dealing effectively with people, **conceptual skills** are about working with concepts and ideas. Conceptual skills involve the thinking or cognitive aspects of leadership. Conceptual skills for leaders can be divided into three parts: (1) problem solving, (2) strategic planning, and (3) creating vision.

Problem Solving

We all know people who are especially good at problem solving. When something goes wrong or needs to be fixed, they are the first ones to jump in and address the problem. Problem solvers do not sit idly by when there are problems. They are quick to ask, "What went wrong?" and they are ready to explore possible answers to "How can it be fixed?" Problem-solving skills are essential for effective leadership.

What are problem-solving skills? **Problem-solving skills** refer to a leader's cognitive ability to take corrective action in a problem situation in order to meet desired objectives. The skills include identifying the problem, generating alternative solutions, selecting the best solution from among the alternatives, and implementing that solution. These skills do not function in a vacuum, but are carried out in a particular setting or context.

Step 1: Identify the problem. The first step in the problem-solving process is to identify or recognize the problem. The importance of this step cannot be understated. Seeing a problem and addressing it is at the core of successful problem solving. All of us are confronted with many problems every day, but some of us fail to see those problems or even to admit that they exist. Others may recognize that something is wrong but then do nothing about it. People with problem-solving skills see problems and address them.

Some problems are simple and easy to define, while others are complex and demand a great deal of scrutiny. Problems arise when there is a difference between what is expected and what actually happens. Identifying the problem requires awareness of these differences. The questions we ask in this phase of problem solving are "What is the problem?" "Are there multiple aspects to it?" and "What caused it?" Identifying the exact nature of the problem precedes everything else in the problem-solving process.

Step 2: Generate alternative solutions. After identifying the problem and its cause or causes, the next step in problem solving is to generate alternative solutions where there is more than one possible resolution to the problem. Because problems are often complex, there are usually many different ways of trying to correct them. During this phase of problem solving, it is important to consider as many solutions as possible and not dismiss any as unworthy. For example, consider a person with a major health concern (e.g., cancer or multiple sclerosis). There are often many ways to treat the illness, but before choosing a course of treatment it is important to consult a health professional and explore all the treatment options. Every treatment has different side effects and different probabilities for curing the illness. Before choosing an option, people often want to be sure that they have fully considered all of the possible treatment options. The same is true in problem solving. Before going forward, it is important to consider all the available options for dealing with a problem.

Step 3: Selecting the best solution. The next step in problem solving is to select the best solution to the problem. Solutions usually differ in how well they address a particular problem, so the relative strengths and weaknesses of each solution need to be addressed. Some solutions are straightforward and easy to enact, while others are complex or difficult to manage. Similarly, some solutions are inexpensive while others are costly. Many criteria can be used to judge the value of a particular solution as it applies to a given problem. Selecting the best solution is the key to solving a problem effectively.

The importance of selecting the best solution can be illustrated in a hypothetical example of a couple with marital difficulties. Having struggled in their marriage for more than 2 years, the couple decides that they must do something to resolve the conflict in their relationship. Included in the list of what they could do are attend marital counseling, receive individual psychiatric therapy, separate, date other people even though they are married, or file for divorce. Each of these solutions would have a different impact on what happens to the couple and their marital relationship. While not exhaustive, the list highlights the importance in problem solving of selecting the best solution to a given problem. The solutions we choose have a major impact on how we feel about the outcome of our problem solving.

Step 4: Implementing the solution. The final step in problem solving is implementing the solution. Having defined the problem and selected a solution, it is time to put the solution into action. Implementing the solution involves shifting from thinking about the problem to doing something about the problem. It is a challenging step: It is not uncommon to meet with resistance from others when trying to do something new and different to solve a problem. Implementing change requires communicating with others about the change, and adapting the change to the wants and needs of those being affected by the change. Of course, there is always the possibility that the chosen solution will fail to address the problem; it might even make the problem worse. Nevertheless, there is no turning back at this phase. There is always a risk in implementing change, but it is a risk that must be taken to complete the problem-solving process.

To clarify what is meant by problem-solving skills, consider the following example of John and Kristen Smith and their troublesome dishwasher. The Smiths' dishwasher was 5 years old, and the dishes were no longer coming out clean and sparkling. Analyzing the situation, the Smiths determined that the problem could be related to several possible causes: their use of liquid instead of powdered dish detergent, a bad seal on the door of the dishwasher, ineffective water softener, misloading of the dishwasher, or a defective water heater. Not knowing what the problem was, John thought they should implement all five possible solutions at once. Kristen disagreed, and suggested they address one possible solution at a time to determine the cause. The first solution they tried was to change the dish detergent, but this did not fix the problem. Next, they changed the seal on the door of the dishwasher—and this solved the problem. By addressing the problem carefully and systematically, the Smiths were able to find the cause of the dishwasher malfunction and to save themselves a great deal of money. Their problem-solving strategy was effective.

Strategic Planning

A second major kind of conceptual skill is **strategic planning**. Like problem solving, strategic planning is mainly a cognitive activity. A leader needs to be able to think and consider ideas to develop effective strategies for a group or an organization. Being strategic requires developing careful plans of action based on the available resources and personnel to achieve a goal. It is similar to what generals do in wartime: They make elaborate plans of how to defeat the enemy given their resources, personnel, and the mission they need to accomplish. Similarly, athletic coaches take their knowledge of their players and their abilities to create game plans for how to best compete with the opposing team. In short, strategic planning is about designing a plan of action to achieve a desired goal.

Video Link 5.2
Watch more on strategic planning.

In their analysis of research on strategic leadership, Boal and Hooijberg (2000) suggested that strategic leaders need to have the ability to learn, the capacity to adapt, and managerial wisdom. The *ability to learn* includes the capability to absorb new information and apply it toward new goals. It is a willingness to experiment with new ideas and even to accept failures. The *capacity to adapt* is about being able to respond quickly to changes in the environment. A leader needs to be open to and accepting of change. When competitive conditions change, an effective leader will have the capacity to change. Having *managerial wisdom* refers to possessing a deep understanding of the people and the environment in which a leader works. It is about having the good sense to make the right decisions at the right time, and to do so with the best interests of everyone involved.

To illustrate the complexity of strategic planning, consider the following example of how NewDevices, a startup medical supply company, used strategic thinking to promote itself. NewDevices developed a surgical scanner to help surgical teams reduce errors during surgery. Although there were no such scanners on the market at that time, two companies were developing a similar product. The potential market for the product was enormous, and included all the hospitals in the United States (almost 8,000 hospitals). Because it was clear that all hospitals would eventually need this scanner, NewDevices knew it was going to be in a race to capture the market ahead of the other companies.

NewDevices was a small company with limited resources, so management was well aware of the importance of strategic planning. Any single mistake could threaten the survival of the company. Because everyone at NewDevices, including the sales staff, owned stock in the company, everyone was strongly motivated to work to make the company succeed. Sales staff members were willing to share effective sales approaches with each other because, rather than being in competition, they had a common goal.

Every Monday morning the management team met for 3 hours to discuss the goals and directions for the company. Much time was spent on framing the argument for why hospitals needed the NewDevices scanner more than its competitors' scanners. To make this even more challenging, the NewDevices scanner was more expensive than the competition, although it was also safer. NewDevices chose to sell the product by stressing that it could save money in the long run for hospitals because it was safer and would reduce the incidence of malpractice cases.

Managers also developed strategies about how to persuade hospitals to sign on to their product. They contacted hospitals to inquire as to whom they should direct their pitch for the new product. Was it the director of surgical nursing or some other hospital administrator? In addition, they analyzed how they should allocate the company's limited resources. Should they spend more money on enhancing their website? Did they need a director of advertising? Should they hire more sales representatives? All of these questions were the subject of much analysis and debate. NewDevices knew the stakes were very high; if management slipped even once, the company would fail.

This example illustrates that strategic planning is a multifaceted process. By planning strategically, however, leaders and their employees can increase the likelihood of reaching their goals and achieving the aims of the organization.

Creating Vision

Similar to strategic planning, creating vision takes a special kind of cognitive and conceptual ability. It requires the capacity to challenge people with compelling visions of the future. To create vision, a leader needs to be able to set forth a picture of a future that is better than the present, and then move others toward a new set of ideals and values that will lead to the future. A leader must be able to articulate the vision and engage others in its pursuit. Furthermore, the leader needs to be able to implement the vision and model the principles set forth in the vision. A leader with a vision has to "walk the walk," and not just "talk the talk." Building vision is an important leadership skill and one that receives extensive discussion in Chapter 6, "Creating a Vision."

CASE STUDY

The following case study describes a CEO who steps down. The questions at the end of the case will help you analyze the case using ideas from the different conceptual perspectives provided in the chapter.

Why Twitter's C.E.O. Demoted Himself

October 30, 2010
By Claire Cain Miller, *The New York Times*

At an annual gathering of techies in Austin, Tex., conference organizers had chosen a hangar-size room to accommodate their star speaker: Evan Williams, the co-founder of Twitter, the messaging and social networking site that had become a digital phenomenon.

In a private moment before the doors opened, Mr. Williams, who is famously deliberate and cautious, snapped a photograph of the endless rows of chairs facing the stage and posted it on Twitter.

"Gulp," he wrote.

It is no small irony, of course, that a man so ill at ease on the big stage is a pivotal force in a communications revolution, one that has made it easier for people to chat, disseminate information and mobilize locally and globally with almost anyone who has a cellphone or an Internet connection.

(Continued)

(Continued)

And Twitter has become one of the rare but fabled Web companies with a growth rate that resembles the shape of a hockey stick. It has 175 million registered users, up from 503,000 three years ago and 58 million just last year. It is adding about 370,000 new users a day.

It has helped transform the way that news is gathered and distributed, reshaped how public figures from celebrities to political leaders communicate, and played a role in popular protests in Iran, China and Moldova. Because of that, Twitter is on the cusp of becoming the next big, independent Internet company—or the next start-up to be swallowed whole by a giant like Google or, possibly, the next start-up to run out of steam.

Now the company is trying to instill some of the rigor and sense of purpose it needs to ensure that it is, indeed, the next big thing.

But in September 2010, Mr. Williams unexpectedly announced that he had decided to step down as chief executive and give the job to Dick Costolo, who had been Twitter's chief operating officer. Mr. Williams, who remains on the company's board, now focuses on product strategy. People who have worked with him say he excels at understanding what Internet users want and contemplating Twitter's future, but isn't a detail-oriented task manager.

For his part, Mr. Williams may embody a classic Silicon Valley type—the inspired, talented start-up guy with good ideas, but not the one to execute a sophisticated business strategy once things get rolling, says Steve Blank, an entrepreneurship teacher at Stanford.

And Mr. Williams may have also earned the self-awareness and confidence to recognize exactly who he is.

"The thing I've learned that's much different than any other time in my life is I have a team that is really, really great," says Mr. Williams, 38. "I've been studying this stuff for a really long time, and I've screwed up in many, many, many ways in terms of managing people and product decisions and business."

Twitter was born in 2006 as a side project. While sitting on a children's slide at a park eating Mexican food one day, a work colleague of Williams's, Jack Dorsey, suggested to colleagues a simple way to send status updates by using text messages.

Mr. Dorsey and Twitter's third co-founder, Biz Stone, built a prototype in two weeks. Twitter was a unique entrant on the social media scene. People could follow others without being followed back, and all posts were public by default—and limited to 140 characters so they could fit inside cellphone text messages. Mr. Dorsey served as Twitter's first chief executive, Mr. Stone as creative director and Mr. Williams as chairman.

By the end of 2008, Twitter's growth was exploding—and things inside the company were beginning to break down. Mr. Williams suggested to Twitter's board that it push Mr. Dorsey out. Mr. Williams had run three companies, directors reasoned, so they figured that he would do a better job.

Even with Mr. Williams as C.E.O., Twitter was growing faster than he or anyone else at the company could handle. In 2009, Twitter ballooned to 71.3 million registered users from 5 million. The Web site crashed often, and the "fail whale"—an image of a whale that appears on the site whenever Twitter falters—became the butt of jokes. "The mistake I made was definitely underhiring, both in quantity and in experience, in several areas, for a long time," Mr. Williams says now. He attributes that mistake to the daily distractions of running Twitter and not anticipating how big it would become.

Video Link 5.3
Watch Evan Williams.

Yet even though Twitter's executives say their heads are finally above water, Mr. Williams still describes the company as "a 6-foot-tall sixth grader—there's a lack of maturity, despite size and the perception of outsiders."

He says Twitter now has a team that can realize the company's ambitions—a revelation coming from someone who arrived in Silicon Valley with something to prove and volumes to learn about working with others.

Williams grew up on a farm in Nebraska, "90 miles and an eternity" from Lincoln, he says. And he didn't fit in. He dropped out of the University of Nebraska and started a business in Lincoln, financed by his father, designing Web sites for local businesses and making CD-ROMs about Nebraska football and the Internet. The business ended up being Mr. Williams's first failure.

California loomed in his imagination as a place where he could truly carve out his own niche as an entrepreneur. He made his first move west in 1997, with a marketing job at O'Reilly Media, the technology publisher in Sebastopol, Calif. He left O'Reilly after seven months—"I was bad at working for people," he says. And in January 1999, at the height of the dot com bubble, he started his second company, Pyra Labs, which made a Web-based project management tool. He soon saw a different opportunity: a tool that allowed users to easily post articles and photographs to personal blogs. That became Blogger, one of the first Web services that automated blog publishing.

Soon after, the tech bubble burst, and Blogger was running out of money. Mr. Williams told his five employees he could no longer pay them and that he would run the company alone. But six months later Blogger started making money by charging for added features, and Mr. Williams had a budget that allowed him to hire new workers. In 2003, Google acquired Blogger.

"I don't think he took care of the people who got him to where he was," says Ms. Hourihan, a former Blogger partner who earned millions of dollars from the sale. "It was bitter, horrible and tough. He's not C.E.O. material. It doesn't play to his strengths. He's a better inventor; he's better at coming up with ideas."

Mr. Williams doesn't fit the Silicon Valley stereotype. He is neither a back-slapping former frat boy nor a socially awkward programmer most content behind a computer screen. He is at ease with himself, and convivial and dryly funny in small settings, but tends to be quiet in large groups and is ambivalent about his newfound celebrity. He rarely posts personal messages to the 1.3 million people who follow him.

"Often there will be a room with five people having a conversation and he says the least, but when he does talk, everyone listens intently, and it's a gem," says Mr. Kaplan, his friend.

In business, that trait can be beneficial. In 2008, Facebook tried to buy Twitter, and financiers asked Mr. Williams if he wanted to sell. He said he wanted to sleep on it, and the next day sent them a long e-mail about why he wanted Twitter to stay independent.

"He's got this ability to be patient in this very productive way," says Bijan Sabet, who is on Twitter's board and is a partner at Spark Capital, which invested in the company. "It was not just this flip e-mail but very thoughtful— what we could accomplish by when, why there's still so much we have left to do. It was pretty inspiring."

But others say Mr. Williams's methodical approach can get in the way. "Ev is very difficult to work with because he has a tough time making a final decision on products," says the C.E.O. of a Silicon Valley social networking company who requested anonymity because the company works with Twitter.

That's why from Mr. Williams's point of view, his division of labor with Mr. Costolo is a sign of success. After failing early on to work with others, Mr. Williams says he has figured out how to be part of a team.

"Dick is hard-charging and very focused on urgency and executing now, and I tend to be very contemplative," he says. "My weakness is probably taking too long to make a decision, and his is being too hasty."

The company, meanwhile, is trying to avoid the bureaucracy that plagues larger businesses. The topic is important to Mr. Williams, who says he started companies because he didn't believe in aligning himself with institutions.

Speaking to a group of new hires at an orientation session last spring, Mr. Williams said Twitter had three goals: to change the world, to build a business and to have fun.

"You can succeed by only building a business, and many companies do," he said. "We won't consider it success unless it's all three."

1. In terms of administrative skills, how would you describe Evan Williams's abilities?

2. How did Williams use his conceptual abilities to motivate others?

3. Williams admittedly rates his own interpersonal skills as not his strength. Would you agree or disagree? Why?

4. What kind of skills should Twitter's new leader utilize to continue to be successful?

Source: "Why Twitter's C.E.O. Demoted Himself" by Claire Cain Miller, *The New York Times.* Used with permission.

Summary

In recent years, the study of leadership skills has captured the attention of researchers and practitioners alike. Skills are essential to being an effective leader. Unlike traits that are innate, leadership skills are *learned* competencies. Everyone can learn to acquire leadership skills. In this chapter, we considered three types of leadership skills: administrative skills, interpersonal skills, and conceptual skills.

Often thought of as unexciting, *administrative skills* play a primary role in effective leadership. These are the skills a leader needs to run the organization and carry out its purposes. These are the skills needed to plan and organize work. Specifically, administrative skills include managing people, managing resources, and showing technical competence.

A second type of skills is *interpersonal skills,* or people skills. These are the competencies that a leader needs to work effectively with subordinates, peers, and superiors to accomplish the organization's goals. Research has shown unequivocally that interpersonal skills are of fundamental importance to effective leadership. Interpersonal skills can be divided into being socially perceptive, showing emotional intelligence, and managing interpersonal conflict.

A leader also needs *conceptual skills*. Conceptual skills have to do with working with concepts and ideas. These are cognitive skills that emphasize the thinking ability of a leader. Although these cover a wide array of competencies, conceptual skills in this chapter are divided into problem solving, strategic planning, and creating vision.

In summary, administrative, interpersonal, and conceptual skills play a major role in effective leadership. Through practice and hard work, we can all become better leaders by improving our skills in each of these areas.

Journal Link 5.2
Read more about skills.

Go to **http://www.sagepub.com/northouseintro2e/** *for additional exercises and study resources. Select Chapter 5, Developing Leadership Skills, for chapter-specific activities.*

Glossary Terms

administrative skills   86

conceptual skills   92

emotional intelligence   91

interpersonal skills   89

problem-solving skills   93

social perceptiveness   89

strategic planning   95

technical competence   88

References

Bass, B. M. (1990). *Bass & Stogdill's handbook of leadership: Theory, research, and managerial applications* (3rd ed.). New York: Free Press.

Blake, R. R., & McCanse, A. A. (1991). *Leadership dilemmas: Grid solutions.* Houston, TX: Gulf.

Boal, K. B., & Hooijberg, R. (2000). Strategic leadership research: Moving on. *Leadership Quarterly, 11,* 515–549.

Caruso, D. R., & Wolfe, C. J. (2004). Emotional intelligence and leadership development. In D. V. Day, S. J. Zaccaro, & S. M. Halpin (Eds.), *Leader development for transforming organizations: Growing leaders for tomorrow* (pp. 237–266). Mahwah, NJ: Erlbaum.

Goleman, D. (1995). *Emotional intelligence.* New York: Bantam Books.

Katz, R. L. (1955). Skills of an effective administrator. *Harvard Business Review, 33*(1), 33–42.

Lord, R. G., & Hall, R. J. (2005). Identity, deep structure and the development of leadership skill. *Leadership Quarterly, 16,* 591–615.

Mann, F. C. (1965). Toward an understanding of the leadership role in formal organization. In R. Dubin, G. C. Homans, F. C. Mann, & D. C. Miller (Eds.), *Leadership and productivity* (pp. 68–103). San Francisco: Chandler.

Mayer, J. D., & Salovey, P. (1995). Emotional intelligence and the construction and regulation of feelings. *Applied and Preventive Psychology, 4,* 197–208.

Mayer, J. D., Salovey, P., & Caruso, D. R. (2000). Models of emotional intelligence. In R. J. Sternberg (Ed.), *Handbook of intelligence* (pp. 396–420). Cambridge, MA: Cambridge University Press.

Miller, C. C. (2010, October 10). Why Twitter's C.E.O. demoted himself. *The New York Times,* p. BU1.

Mumford, M. D., Zaccaro, S. J., Connelly, M. S., & Marks, M. A. (2000). Leadership skills: Conclusions and future directions. *Leadership Quarterly, 11*(1), 155–170.

Mumford, T. V., Campion, M. A., & Morgeson, F. P. (2007). The leadership skills strataplex: Leadership skill requirements across organizational levels. *Leadership Quarterly, 18,* 154–166.

Salovey, P., & Mayer, J. D. (1990). Emotional intelligence. *Imagination, Cognition, and Personality, 9,* 185–221.

Yammarino, F. J. (2000). Leadership skills: Introduction and overview. *Leadership Quarterly, 11*(1), 5–9.

Zaccaro, S. J., Gilbert, J., Thor, K. K., & Mumford, M. D. (1991). Leadership and social intelligence: Linking social perceptiveness and behavioral flexibility to leader effectiveness. *Leadership Quarterly, 2,* 317–331.

5.1   Leadership Skills Questionnaire

 Visit www.sagepub.com/northouseintro2e for downloadable versions of these questionnaires

Purpose

1. To identify your leadership skills
2. To provide a profile of your leadership skills showing your strengths and weaknesses

Directions

1. Place yourself in the role of a leader when responding to this questionnaire.
2. For each of the statements below, circle the number that indicates the degree to which you feel the statement is true.

Statements	Not true	Seldom true	Occasionally true	Somewhat true	Very true
1. I am effective with the detailed aspects of my work.	1	2	3	4	5
2. I usually know ahead of time how people will respond to a new idea or proposal.	1	2	3	4	5
3. I am effective at problem solving.	1	2	3	4	5
4. Filling out forms and working with details comes easily for me.	1	2	3	4	5
5. Understanding the social fabric of the organization is important to me.	1	2	3	4	5
6. When problems arise, I immediately address them.	1	2	3	4	5
7. Managing people and resources is one of my strengths.	1	2	3	4	5
8. I am able to sense the emotional undercurrents in my group.	1	2	3	4	5
9. Seeing the big picture comes easily for me.	1	2	3	4	5
10. In my work, I enjoy responding to people's requests and concerns.	1	2	3	4	5
11. I use my emotional energy to motivate others.	1	2	3	4	5
12. Making strategic plans for my company appeals to me.	1	2	3	4	5
13. Obtaining and allocating resources is a challenging aspect of my job.	1	2	3	4	5

Statements	Not true	Seldom true	Occasionally true	Somewhat true	Very true
14. The key to successful conflict resolution is respecting my opponent.	1	2	3	4	5
15. I enjoy discussing organizational values and philosophy.	1	2	3	4	5
16. I am effective at obtaining resources to support our programs.	1	2	3	4	5
17. I work hard to find consensus in conflict situations.	1	2	3	4	5
18. I am flexible about making changes in our organization.	1	2	3	4	5

Scoring

1. Sum the responses on items 1, 4, 7, 10, 13, and 16 (administrative skill score).

2. Sum the responses on items 2, 5, 8, 11, 14, and 17 (interpersonal skill score).

3. Sum the responses on items 3, 6, 9, 12, 15, and 18 (conceptual skill score).

Total Scores

Administrative skill: _____

Interpersonal skill: _____

Conceptual skill: _____

Scoring Interpretation

The Leadership Skills Questionnaire is designed to measure three broad types of leadership skills: administrative, interpersonal, and conceptual. By comparing your scores, you can determine where you have leadership strengths and where you have leadership weaknesses.

If your score is 26–30, you are in the very high range.

If your score is 21–25, you are in the high range.

If your score is 16–20, you are in the moderate range.

If your score is 11–15, you are in the low range.

If your score is 6–10, you are in the very low range.

5.2   Observational Exercise

 Visit www.sagepub.com/northouseintro2e for downloadable versions of these questionnaires

Leadership Skills

Purpose

1. To develop an understanding of different types of leadership skills

2. To examine how leadership skills affect a leader's performance

Directions

1. Your task in this exercise is to observe a leader and evaluate that person's leadership skills. This leader can be a supervisor, a manager, a coach, a teacher, a fraternity or sorority officer, or anyone who has a position that involves leadership.

2. For each of the groups of skills listed below, write what you observed about this leader.

Name of leader: _____

Administrative skills	1	2	3	4	5
Managing people	Poor	Weak	Average	Good	Very good
Managing resources	Poor	Weak	Average	Good	Very good
Showing technical competence	Poor	Weak	Average	Good	Very good
Comments:					

Interpersonal Skills	1	2	3	4	5
Being socially perceptive	Poor	Weak	Average	Good	Very good
Showing emotional intelligence	Poor	Weak	Average	Good	Very good
Managing conflict	Poor	Weak	Average	Good	Very good
Comments:					

Conceptual skills	1	2	3	4	5
Problem solving	Poor	Weak	Average	Good	Very good
Strategic planning	Poor	Weak	Average	Good	Very good
Creating vision	Poor	Weak	Average	Good	Very good
Comments:					

Questions

1. Based on your observations, what were the leader's strengths and weaknesses?

2. In what setting did this leadership example occur? Did the setting influence the kind of skills that the leader used? Discuss.

3. If you were coaching this leader, what specific things would you tell this leader about how he or she could improve leadership skills? Discuss.

4. In another situation, do you think this leader would exhibit the same strengths and weaknesses? Discuss.

5.3   Reflection and Action Worksheet

 Visit www.sagepub.com/northouseintro2e for downloadable versions of these questionnaires

Leadership Skills

Reflection

1. Based on what you know about yourself and the scores you received on the Leadership Skills Questionnaire in the three areas (administrative, interpersonal, and conceptual), how would you describe your leadership skills? Which specific skills are your strongest, and which are your weakest? What impact do you think your leadership skills could have on your role as a leader? Discuss.

2. This chapter suggests that emotional intelligence is an interpersonal leadership skill. Discuss whether you agree or disagree with this assumption. As you think about your own leadership, how do your emotions help or hinder your role as a leader? Discuss.

3. This chapter divides leadership into three kinds of skills (administrative, interpersonal, and conceptual). Do you think some of these skills are more important than others in some kinds of situations? Do you think lower levels of leadership (e.g., supervisor) require the same skills as upper levels of leadership (e.g., CEO)? Discuss.

Action

1. One unique aspect of leadership skills is that they can be practiced. List and briefly describe three things you could do to improve your administrative skills.

2. Leaders need to be *socially perceptive*. As you assess yourself in this area, identify two specific actions that would help you become more perceptive of other people and their viewpoints. Discuss.

3. What kind of problem solver are you? Are you slow or quick to address problem situations? Overall, what two things could you change about yourself to be a more effective problem solver?

Before you begin reading . . .

Complete the *Leadership Vision Questionnaire*, which you will find on pp. 123–124. As you read the chapter, consider your results on the questionnaire.

Creating a Vision

6

An effective leader creates compelling visions that guide people's behavior. In the context of leadership, a **vision** is a mental model of an ideal future state. It offers a picture of what could be. Visions imply change and can challenge people to reach a higher standard of excellence. At the same time, visions are like a guiding philosophy that provides people with meaning and purpose.

In developing a vision, a leader is able to visualize positive outcomes in the future and communicate these to others. Ideally, the leader and the members of a group or an organization share the vision. Although this picture of a possible future may not always be crystal clear, the vision itself plays a major role in how the leader influences others and how others react to his or her leadership.

For the past 25 years, vision has been a major topic in writings on leadership. Vision plays a prominent role in training and development literature. For example, Covey (1991) suggested that vision is one of seven habits of highly effective people. He argued that effective people "begin with the end in mind" (p. 42)—that they have a deep understanding of their goals, values, and mission in life, and that this understanding is the basis for everything they do. Similarly, Loehr and Schwartz (2001), in their full-engagement training program, stressed that people are a mission-specific species, and their goal in life should be to mobilize their sources of energy to accomplish their intended mission. Kouzes and Posner

(2003), whose Leadership Practices Inventory is a widely used leadership assessment instrument, identified vision as one of the five practices of exemplary leadership. Clearly, vision has been an important aspect of leadership training and development in recent years.

Vision also plays a central role in many of the common theories of leadership (Zaccaro & Banks, 2001). For example, in transformational leadership theory, vision is identified as one of the four major factors that account for extraordinary leadership performance (Bass & Avolio, 1994). In charismatic leadership theories, vision is highlighted as a key to organizational change (Conger & Kanungo, 1998; House, 1977). Charismatic leaders create change by linking their vision and its values to the self-concept of followers. For example, through her charisma Mother Teresa linked her vision of serving the poor and disenfranchised to her followers' beliefs of personal commitment and self-sacrifice. Some theories are actually titled visionary leadership theories (see Nanus, 1992; Sashkin, 1988, 2004) because vision is their defining characteristic of leadership.

Encyclopedia Link 6.1
Read more about
visionary leadership.

To better understand the role of vision in effective leadership, this chapter will address the following questions: "What are the characteristics of a vision?" "How is a vision articulated?" and "How is a vision implemented?" In our discussion of these questions, we will focus on how you can develop a workable vision for whatever context you find yourself in as a leader.

▶ WHAT ARE THE CHARACTERISTICS OF A VISION?

Given that it is essential for a leader to have a vision, how are visions formed? What are the main characteristics of a vision? Research on visionary leadership suggests that visions have five characteristics: a picture, a change, values, a map, and a challenge (Nanus, 1992; Zaccaro & Banks, 2001).

A PICTURE

A vision creates a **picture** of a future that is better than the **status quo**. It is an idea about the future that requires an act of faith by followers. Visions paint an ideal image of where a group or an organization should be going. It may be an image of a situation that is more exciting, more affirming, or more inspiring. As a rule, these mental images are of a time and place where people are working productively to achieve a common goal. Although it is easier for followers to comprehend a detailed vision, a leader's vision is not always fully developed. Sometimes a leader's vision provides only a general direction to followers or gives limited guidance to them. At other times, a leader may have only a bare-bones notion of where he or she is leading others; the final picture may not emerge for a number of years. Nevertheless, when a leader is able to paint a picture of the future that is attractive and inspiring, it can have significant impact on his or her ability to lead others effectively.

Video Link 6.1
Watch a leader talk about the future.

A CHANGE

Another characteristic of a vision is that it represents a **change** in the status quo, and moves an organization or a system toward something more positive in the future. Visions point the way to new ways of doing things that are better than how things were done in the past. They take the best features of a prior system and strengthen them in the pursuit of a new goal.

Audio Link 6.1
Listen to the vision for rebuilding New Orleans.

Changes can occur in many forms: rules, procedures, goals, values, or rituals, to name a few. Because visions imply change, it is not uncommon for a leader to experience resistance to the articulated vision. Some leaders are even accused of "stirring the pot" when promoting visionary changes. Usually, though, visions are compelling and inspire others to set aside old ways of doing things and to become part of the positive changes suggested by a leader's vision.

VALUES

A third characteristic of a vision is that it is about **values**, or the ideas, beliefs, and modes of action that people find worthwhile or desirable. To advocate change within a group or an organization requires an understanding of one's own values, the values of others, and the values of the organization. Visions are about changes in those values. For example, if a leader creates a vision that emphasizes that everyone in the company is important, the dominant value being expressed is human dignity. Similarly, if a leader develops a vision that suggests that everyone in the company is equal, the dominant value being expressed is fairness and justice. Visions are grounded in values. They advocate a positive change and movement toward some new set of ideals. In so doing, they must address values.

The following example illustrates the centrality of values in visionary leadership. Chris Jones was a new football coach at a high school in a small rural community in the Midwest. When Jones started coaching, there were barely enough players to fill the roster. His vision was to have a strong football program that students liked and that instilled pride in the parents and school community. He valued good physical conditioning, self-discipline, skills in all aspects of the game, esprit de corps, and an element of fun throughout the process. In essence, he wanted a top-notch, high-quality football program.

Over a period of 5 years, the number of players coming out for football grew from 15 to 95. Parents wanted their kids to go out for football because Jones was such a good coach. Players said they liked the team because Coach Jones treated them as individuals. He was very fair with everyone. He was tough about discipline but also liked to have fun. Practices were always a challenge but seldom dull or monotonous. Because of his program, parents formed their own booster club to support team dinners and other special team activities.

Although Coach Jones's teams did not always win, his players learned lessons in football that were meaningful and long lasting. Coach Jones was an effective coach whose vision promoted individual growth, competence, camaraderie, and community. He had a vision about developing a program around these strong values, and he was able to bring his vision to fruition.

A MAP

Video Link 6.2
Watch a visionary leader speak.

A vision provides a **map**—a laid-out path to follow—that gives direction so followers know when they are on track and when they have slipped off course. People often feel a sense of certainty and calmness in knowing they are on the right course, and a vision provides this assurance. It is also comforting for people to know they have a map to direct them toward their short- and long-term goals.

At the same time, visions provide a guiding philosophy for people that gives them meaning and purpose. When people know the overarching goals, principles, and values of an organization, it is easier for them to establish an identity and know where they fit within the organization. Furthermore, seeing the larger purpose allows people to appreciate the value of their contributions to the organization and to something larger than their own interests. The value of a vision is that it shows others the meaningfulness of their work.

A CHALLENGE

A final characteristic of a vision is that it **challenges** people to transcend the status quo to do something to benefit others. Visions challenge people to commit themselves to worthwhile causes. In his inaugural address in 1961, President John F. Kennedy challenged the American people by saying, "Ask not what your country can do for you—ask what you can do for your country." This challenge was inspiring because it asked people to move beyond self-interest to work for the greater good of the country. Kennedy's vision for America (see Box 6.1) had a huge impact on the country.

An example of an organization that has a vision with a clear challenge component is the Leukemia and Lymphoma Society's Team In Training program. The primary goal of this program is to raise funds for cancer research, public education, and patient aid programs. As a part of Team In Training, participants who sign up to run or walk a marathon (26.2 miles) are asked to raise money for cancer research in return for the personalized coaching and fitness training they receive from Team In Training staff. Since its inception in the late 1980s, the program has raised more than $600 million for cancer research. A recent participant said of Team In Training, "I was inspired to find something I could do both to push myself a little harder and to accomplish something meaningful in the process." When people are challenged to do something good for others, they often become inspired and committed to the task. Whether it is to improve their own group, organization, or community, people like to be challenged to help others.

Journal Link 6.1
Read more about vision.

To summarize, a vision has five main characteristics. First, it is a mental *picture* or image of a future that is better than the status quo. Second, it represents a *change* and points to new ways of doing things. Third, it is grounded in *values*. Fourth, it is a *map* that gives direction and provides meaning and purpose. Finally, it is a *challenge* to change things for the better.

The next section discusses how a leader articulates a vision to others and describes specific actions that a leader can take to make the vision clear and understandable.

▶ HOW IS A VISION ARTICULATED?

Audio Link 6.2

Listen to leaders articulate their vision.

Although it is very important for a leader *to have* a vision, it is equally important for a leader to be able *to articulate*—explain and describe—the vision to others. Although some are better than others at this, there are certain ways all leaders can improve the way they communicate their visions.

First, a leader must communicate the vision by *adapting the vision* to his or her audience. Psychologists tell us that most people have a drive for consistency and when confronted with the need to change will do so only if the required change is not too different from their present state (Festinger, 1957). A leader needs to articulate the vision to fit within others' latitude of acceptance by adapting the vision to the audience (Conger & Kanungo, 1987). If the vision is too demanding and advocates too big a change, it will be rejected. If it is articulated in light of the status quo and does not demand too great a change, it will be accepted.

A leader also needs to *highlight the values* of the vision by emphasizing how the vision presents ideals worth pursuing. Presenting the values of the vision helps individuals and group members find their own work worthwhile. It also allows group members to identify with something larger than themselves, and to become connected to a larger community (Shamir, House, & Arthur, 1993).

Articulating a vision also requires *choosing the right language*. A leader should use *words and symbols* that are motivating and inspiring (Sashkin, 2004; Zaccaro & Banks, 2001). Words that describe a vision need to be affirming, uplifting, and hopeful, and describe the vision in a way that underscores its worth. The following speech by President John F. Kennedy (see Box 6.1) is an example of how a leader used inspiring language to articulate his vision.

Box 6.1   Inaugural Address by President John Fitzgerald Kennedy

Delivered on the steps of the Capitol, in Washington, DC, on January 20, 1961:

Vice President Johnson, Mr. Speaker, Mr. Chief Justice, President Eisenhower, Vice President Nixon, President Truman, Reverend Clergy, fellow citizens:

We observe today not a victory of party but a celebration of freedom—symbolizing an end as well as a beginning—signifying renewal as well as change. For I have sworn before you and Almighty God the same solemn oath our forebears prescribed nearly a century and three-quarters ago.

The world is very different now. For man holds in his mortal hands the power to abolish all forms of human poverty and all forms of human life. And yet the same revolutionary beliefs for which our forebears fought are still at issue around the globe—the belief that the rights of man come not from the generosity of the state but from the hand of God.

We dare not forget today that we are the heirs of that first revolution. Let the word go forth from this time and place, to friend and foe alike, that the torch has been passed to a new generation of Americans—born in this century, tempered by war, disciplined by a hard and bitter peace, proud of our ancient heritage—and unwilling to witness or

permit the slow undoing of those human rights to which this nation has always been committed, and to which we are committed today at home and around the world.

Let every nation know, whether it wishes us well or ill, that we shall pay any price, bear any burden, meet any hardship, support any friend, oppose any foe to assure the survival and the success of liberty.

This much we pledge—and more.

To those old allies whose cultural and spiritual origins we share, we pledge the loyalty of faithful friends. United there is little we cannot do in a host of cooperative ventures. Divided there is little we can do—for we dare not meet a powerful challenge at odds and split asunder.

To those new states whom we welcome to the ranks of the free, we pledge our word that one form of colonial control shall not have passed away merely to be replaced by a far more iron tyranny. We shall not always expect to find them supporting our view. But we shall always hope to find them strongly supporting their own freedom—and to remember that, in the past, those who foolishly sought power by riding the back of the tiger ended up inside.

To those people in the huts and villages of half the globe struggling to break the bonds of mass misery, we pledge our best efforts to help them help themselves, for whatever period is required—not because the Communists may be doing it, not because we seek their votes, but because it is right. If a free society cannot help the many who are poor, it cannot save the few who are rich.

To our sister republics south of our border, we offer a special pledge—to convert our good words into good deeds—in a new alliance for progress—to assist free men and free governments in casting off the chains of poverty. But this peaceful revolution of hope cannot become the prey of hostile powers. Let all our neighbors know that we shall join with them to oppose aggression or subversion anywhere in the Americas. And let every other power know that this Hemisphere intends to remain the master of its own house.

To that world assembly of sovereign states, the United Nations, our last best hope in an age where the

Video Link 6.3
Watch the Inaugural address.

(Continued)

(Continued)

instruments of war have far outpaced the instruments of peace, we renew our pledge of support—to prevent it from becoming merely a forum for invective—to strengthen its shield of the new and the weak—and to enlarge the area in which its writ may run.

Finally, to those nations who would make themselves our adversary, we offer not a pledge but a request: that both sides begin anew the quest for peace, before the dark powers of destruction unleashed by science engulf all humanity in planned or accidental self-destruction.

We dare not tempt them with weakness. For only when our arms are sufficient beyond doubt can we be certain beyond doubt that they will never be employed.

But neither can two great and powerful groups of nations take comfort from our present course—both sides overburdened by the cost of modern weapons, both rightly alarmed by the steady spread of the deadly atom, yet both racing to alter that uncertain balance of terror that stays the hand of mankind's final war.

So let us begin anew—remembering on both sides that civility is not a sign of weakness, and sincerity is always subject to proof. Let us never negotiate out of fear. But let us never fear to negotiate.

Let both sides explore what problems unite us instead of belaboring those problems which divide us.

Let both sides, for the first time, formulate serious and precise proposals for the inspection and control of arms—and bring the absolute power to destroy other nations under the absolute control of all nations.

Let both sides seek to invoke the wonders of science instead of its terrors. Together let us explore the stars, conquer the deserts, eradicate disease, tap the ocean depths and encourage the arts and commerce.

Let both sides unite to heed in all corners of the earth the command of Isaiah—to "undo the heavy burdens . . . [and] let the oppressed go free."

And if a beachhead of cooperation may push back the jungle of suspicion, let both sides join in creating a new endeavor, not a new balance of power, but a new world of law, where the strong are just and the weak secure and the peace preserved.

All this will not be finished in the first one hundred days. Nor will it be finished in the first one thousand days, nor in the life of this Administration, nor even perhaps in our lifetime on this planet. But let us begin.

In your hands, my fellow citizens, more than mine, will rest the final success or failure of our course. Since this country was founded, each generation of Americans has been summoned to give testimony to its national loyalty. The graves of young Americans who answered the call to service surround the globe.

Now the trumpet summons us again—not as a call to bear arms, though arms we need—not as a call to battle, though embattled we are—but a call to bear the burden of a long twilight struggle, year in and year out, "rejoicing in hope, patient in tribulation"—a struggle against the common enemies of man: tyranny, poverty, disease and war itself.

Can we forge against these enemies a grand and global alliance, North and South, East and West, that can assure a more fruitful life for all mankind? Will you join in that historic effort?

In the long history of the world, only a few generations have been granted the role of defending freedom in its hour of maximum danger. I do not shrink from this responsibility—I welcome it. I do not believe that any of us would exchange places with any other people or any other generation. The energy, the faith, the devotion which we bring to this endeavor will light our country and all who serve it—and the glow from that fire can truly light the world.

And so, my fellow Americans: ask not what your country can do for you—ask what you can do for your country.

My fellow citizens of the world: ask not what America will do for you, but what together we can do for the freedom of man.

Finally, whether you are citizens of America or citizens of the world, ask of us here the same high standards of strength and sacrifice which we ask of you. With a good conscience our only sure reward, with history the final judge of our deeds, let us go forth to lead the land we love, asking His blessing and His help, but knowing that here on earth God's work must truly be our own.

Source: John Fitzgerald Kennedy Library, http://www.jfklibrary.org/.

Symbols are often adopted by leaders in an effort to articulate a vision and bring group cohesion. A good illustration of this is how, in 1997, the University of Michigan football team and coaching staff chose to use Jon Krakauer's book *Into Thin Air* and "conquering Mount Everest" as a metaphor for what they wanted to accomplish. Krakauer provided a firsthand account of a team's challenging journey up Mount Everest that was successful, although five climbers lost their lives in the process. One of the Michigan coaches said, "It's amazing how many similarities there are between playing football and climbing a mountain. . . . The higher you get on a mountain, the tougher it gets. The longer you play during the season, the harder it gets to keep playing the way you want to play." Throughout the season, the coaches frequently emphasized that achieving great feats required tremendous discipline, perseverance, strength, and teamwork. In the locker room, real climbing hooks and pitons were hung above the door to remind everyone who exited that the mission was to "conquer the mountain"—that is, to win the title. The imagery of mountain climbing in this example was a brilliant way to articulate the vision the coaches had for that season. This imagery proved to be well chosen: The team won the 1997 National Collegiate Athletic Association National Championship.

Visions also need to be described to others *using inclusive language* that links people to the vision and makes them part of the process. Words such as *we* and *our* are inclusive words and are better to use than words such as *they* or *them*. The goal of this type of language is to enlist participation of others and build community around a common goal. Inclusive language helps bring this about.

In general, to articulate a vision clearly requires that a leader *adapt the content* to the audience, emphasize the vision's *intrinsic value,* select *words and symbols* that are uplifting, and use language that is *inclusive*. If a leader is able to do these things, he or she will increase the chances that the vision will be embraced and the goal achieved.

HOW IS A VISION IMPLEMENTED? ◄

In addition to creating and articulating a vision, a leader needs to *implement* the vision. Perhaps the real test of a leader's abilities occurs in the implementation phase of a vision. Implementing a vision requires a great deal of effort by a leader over an extended period. Although some leaders can "talk the talk," leaders who implement the vision "walk the walk." Most important, in implementing a vision the leader

Journal Link 6.2
Read more
about visionary
leadership in action.

must model to others the attitudes, values, and behaviors set forth in the vision. The leader is a living example of the ideals articulated in the vision. For example, if the vision is to promote a deeply humanistic organization, the leader needs to demonstrate qualities such as empathy and caring in every action. Similarly, if the vision is to promote community values, the leader needs to show interest in others and in the common good of the broader community. When a leader is seen *acting out the vision,* he or she builds credibility with others. This credibility inspires people to express the same kind of values.

Implementing a vision also requires a leader to set high performance expectations for others. Setting challenging goals motivates people to accomplish a mission. An example of setting high expectations and worthwhile goals is illustrated in the story of the Marathon of Hope (see Box 6.2). Terry Fox was a cancer survivor and amputee who attempted to run across Canada to raise awareness and money for cancer research. Fox had a vision and established an extremely challenging goal for himself and others. He was courageous and determined. Unfortunately, he died before completing his journey, but his vision lives on. Today, the Terry Fox Foundation continues to thrive.

Box 6.2   Marathon of Hope

Terry Fox was born in Winnipeg, Manitoba, and raised in Port Coquitlam, British Columbia, a community near Vancouver on Canada's west coast. An active teenager involved in many sports, Fox was only 18 years old when he was diagnosed with osteogenic sarcoma (bone cancer). In order to stop the spread of the cancer, doctors amputated his right leg 15 centimeters (6 inches) above the knee in 1977.

While in the hospital, Fox was so overcome by the suffering of other cancer patients—many of them young children—that he decided to run across Canada to raise money for cancer research. He called his journey the Marathon of Hope.

After 18 months and running more than 5,000 kilometers (3,107 miles) to prepare, Fox started his run in St. John's, Newfoundland, on April 12, 1980, with little fanfare. Although it was difficult to garner attention in the beginning, enthusiasm soon grew, and the money collected along his route began to mount. He ran 42 kilometers (26 miles) a day through Canada's Atlantic provinces, through Quebec, and through part of Ontario. It was a journey that Canadians never forgot.

On September 1, 1980, after 143 days and 5,373 kilometers (3,339 miles), Fox was forced to stop running outside Thunder Bay, Ontario, because cancer had

appeared in his lungs. An entire nation was saddened when he passed away on June 28, 1981, at the age of 22.

The heroic Canadian was gone, but his legacy was just beginning. To date, more than $400 million has been raised worldwide for cancer research in his name through the annual Terry Fox Run, held in Canada and in countries around the world.

The process of carrying out a vision does not happen rapidly but takes continuous effort. It is a step-by-step process, and not one that occurs all at once. For this reason, it is imperative for a leader's eyes to stay on the goal. By doing so, the leader encourages and supports others in the day-to-day efforts to reach the larger goal. A leader alone cannot implement a vision. The leader must work *with* others and empower them in the implementation process. It is essential that leaders share the work and collaborate with others to accomplish the goal.

CASE STUDY

The following case describes how Nancy Brinker created the *Susan G. Komen for the Cure* foundation. Questions are provided at the end of the case that will help you analyze the case and explore how vision plays a role in effective leadership.

The Promise of the Pink Ribbon

It started with a deathbed promise and a shoebox full of names. In 1980, Nancy Brinker's only sister, Susan Komen, was dying of breast cancer at the age of 36. She asked her younger sister to do something so other women didn't have to suffer her fate. "I really want you to put an end to breast cancer," she said. Nancy replied, "Suzy, I promise. I'll help. Even if it takes me the rest of my life."

Nancy, who was a recently divorced single mother, worked in retail marketing and public relations. She soon met millionaire Norman Brinker, who had lost his first wife to ovarian cancer, and the two bonded over their mutual desire to do something about the devastating disease. They married, and the new financial freedom allowed Nancy to quit her job and begin to make good on her promise.

With only $200, a typewriter, 12 volunteers, and a shoebox full of index cards with names of contacts she had copied from her husband's Rolodex, *Susan G. Komen for the Cure* was born. From the start, the nonprofit foundation's mission was to eradicate the disease by improving research, screening, education, and treatment. But Nancy found that people were hesitant to talk about the disease,

(Continued)

(Continued)

especially the male CEOs she approached for corporate donations. People called it "The Big C," and some thought it was contagious. Nancy quickly determined that raising money wasn't the challenge, but reshaping the public perception about the disease was.

"There was so much fear about this disease, of the treatment, and for good reasons. People died so easily and quickly of it," she says. "There can be no change until there's awareness. It wasn't just a question of changing what was happening in the clinics and changing science. It was changing the culture" (Stahl, 2010).

Nancy believed the best way to do that was through cause-related marketing. Soon, the little pink ribbon adopted by the foundation and the color pink became synonymous with breast cancer. Nancy forged partnerships with major companies, including automobile, food, cosmetics, and appliance manufacturers, to design and promote pink products, donating back a portion of the profits to the foundation. As one supporter said, "Nancy knows how to translate corporate goodwill into programs that have meaningful results" (Stahl, 2010).

In 1984, the foundation developed Race for the Cure, a 5-kilometer running/walking event to raise money and awareness, and in 1986, it began promoting October as the official Breast Cancer Awareness Month. Nancy's efforts to publicize its cause resulted with the Empire State Building in New York City turning all its lights pink, as well as having pink lights shine on the White House. With each new link to a corporate sponsor and each new pink product, Nancy saw opportunity to educate more people about the disease.

The foundation was doing well enough by 1984 to award its first grants for research and education. At the same time, Nancy was diagnosed with the same kind of breast cancer that took her sister. She took an aggressive approach to treating her cancer, including a double mastectomy and several rounds of chemotherapy. She emerged from the battle even more determined to help those with the disease.

By 1989, two researchers who were partly funded by the Susan G. Komen foundation received Nobel Prizes for their discoveries about cancer genes. A few years later other foundation-supported researchers identified the BRCA gene mutation, which is linked to hereditary breast cancer. By 2010, *Susan G. Komen for the Cure* had become the world's largest source of nonprofit funds for breast cancer, having invested $1.5 billion since 1982. The foundation now has a presence in 120 U.S. communities and 50 countries.

In 2009, Nancy Brinker was awarded the U.S. Presidential Medal of Freedom. She admits that when she began, she didn't know it would take so long to get to where the foundation is today. "In the beginning, I don't think many scientists and physicians took us real seriously, but they didn't realize we were going to work this hard for this long," she says. "I'd like to think I survived all these years because I'm supposed to do this work. I realized I may not have enough time to live out this promise, so I've always kind of felt I am in a race personally to get this done" (Farwell, 2009).

Questions

1. Visions create a *picture* of the future that is better than the status quo. What mental image or picture of the future did Nancy have before beginning *Susan G. Komen for the Cure?*

2. What kind of change in values did Nancy's vision about cancer research create? What kind of resistance did she confront to her articulated vision?

3. From a leadership perspective, how big a role did vision play in what Nancy created?

4. After reading the case, how did you feel? If you could talk to Nancy, what would you want to tell her about her accomplishments?

Summary

A competent leader will have a compelling vision that challenges people to work toward a higher standard of excellence. A vision is a mental model of an ideal future state. It provides a *picture* of a future that is better than the present, is grounded in *values,* and advocates *change* toward some new set of ideals. Visions function as a *map* to give people direction. Visions also *challenge* people to commit themselves to a greater common good.

First, an effective leader clearly articulates the vision to others. This requires the leader to adapt the vision to the attitudes and values of the audience. Second, the leader highlights the *intrinsic values* of the vision, emphasizing how the vision presents ideals worth pursuing. Third, a competent leader uses language that is *motivating* and *uplifting* to articulate the vision. Finally, the leader uses *inclusive language* that enlists participation from others and builds community.

A challenge for a leader is to carry out the difficult processes of implementing a vision. To implement a vision, the leader needs to be a living *model* of the ideals and values articulated in the vision. In addition, he or she must *set high performance expectations* for others, and *encourage and empower* others to reach their goals.

 Go to **http://www.sagepub.com/northouseintro2e/** *for additional exercises and study resources. Select Chapter 6, Creating a Vision, for chapter-specific activities.*

Glossary Terms

challenge   113   status quo   110

change   111   vision   109

map   112   value   111

picture   110

References

Bass, B. M., & Avolio, B. J. (1994). *Improving organizational effectiveness through transformational leadership.* Thousand Oaks, CA: Sage.

Conger, J. A., & Kanungo, R. N. (1987). Toward a behavioral theory of charismatic leadership in organizational settings. *Academy of Management Review, 12*(4), 637–647.

Conger, J. A., & Kanungo, R. N. (1998). *Charismatic leadership in organizations*. Thousand Oaks, CA: Sage.

Covey, S. R. (1991). *Principle-centered leadership*. New York: Simon & Schuster.

Farwell, S. (2009, August 9). Dedication to breast cancer fight defines and drives Nancy Brinker. *The Dallas Morning News*. Retrieved December 17, 2010, from http://www.dallasnews.com/sharedcontent/dws/dn/latestnews/stories/080909dnmetbrinker.3fd20b5.html

Festinger, L. (1957). *A theory of cognitive dissonance*. Stanford, CA: Stanford University Press.

House, R. J. (1977). A 1976 theory of charismatic leadership. In J. G. Hunt & L. L. Larson (Eds.), *Leadership: The cutting edge* (pp. 189–207). Carbondale: Southern Illinois University Press.

Kouzes, J. M., & Posner, B. Z. (2003). *The leadership challenge* (3rd ed.). San Francisco: Jossey-Bass.

Loehr, J., & Schwartz, T. (2001). *The power of full engagement: Managing energy, not time, is the key to high performance and personal renewal*. New York: Simon & Schuster.

Nanus, B. (1992). *Visionary leadership: Creating a compelling sense of direction for your organization*. San Francisco: Jossey-Bass.

Sashkin, M. (1988). The visionary leader. In J. A. Conger & R. N. Kanungo (Eds.), *Charismatic leadership: The elusive factor in organizational effectiveness* (pp. 122–160). San Francisco: Jossey-Bass.

Sashkin, M. (2004). Transformational leadership approaches: A review and synthesis. In J. Antonaki, A. T. Cianciolo, & R. J. Sternberg (Eds.), *The nature of leadership* (pp. 171–196). Thousand Oaks, CA: Sage.

Shamir, B., House, R. J., & Arthur, M. B. (1993). The motivational effects of charismatic leadership: A self-concept based theory. *Organization Science, 4*(4), 577–594.

Stahl, L. (2010, September 12). Nancy Brinker's life is a promise in pink and a force against breast cancer. *The Dallas Morning News*. Retrieved December 17, 2010, from http://www.dallasnews.com/sharedcontent/dws/dn/latestnews/stories/091210dnmetbrinker.2780489.html

Zaccaro, S. J., & Banks, D. J. (2001). Leadership, vision, and organizational effectiveness. In S. J. Zaccaro & R. J. Klimoski (Eds.), *The nature of organizational leadership: Understanding the performance imperatives confronting today's leaders* (pp. 181–218). San Francisco: Jossey-Bass.

6.1 Leadership Vision Questionnaire

 Visit www.sagepub.com/northouseintro2e for downloadable versions of these questionnaires

Purpose

1. To assess your ability to create a vision for a group or an organization
2. To help you understand how visions are formed

Directions

1. Think for a moment of a work, school, social, religious, musical, or athletic organization in which you are a member. Now, think what you would do if you were the leader and you had to create a vision for the group or organization. Keep this vision in mind as you complete the exercise.
2. Using the following scale, circle the number that indicates the degree to which you agree or disagree with each statement.

Statements	Strongly disagree	Disagree	Neutral	Agree	Strongly agree
1. I have a mental picture of what would make our group better.	1	2	3	4	5
2. I can imagine several changes that would improve our group.	1	2	3	4	5
3. I have a vision for what would make our organization stronger.	1	2	3	4	5
4. I know how we could change the status quo to make things better.	1	2	3	4	5
5. It is clear to me what steps we need to take to improve our organization.	1	2	3	4	5
6. I have a clear picture of what needs to be done in our organization to achieve a higher standard of excellence.	1	2	3	4	5
7. I have a clear picture in my mind of what this organization should look like in the future.	1	2	3	4	5
8. It is clear to me what core values, if emphasized, would improve our organization.	1	2	3	4	5
9. I can identify challenging goals that should be emphasized in my group.	1	2	3	4	5
10. I can imagine several things that would inspire my group to perform better.	1	2	3	4	5

Scoring

Sum the numbers you circled on the questionnaire (visioning ability skill).

Total Scores

Visioning ability skill: _____

Scoring Interpretation

The Leadership Vision Questionnaire is designed to measure your ability to create a vision as a leader.

If your score is 41–50, you are in the very high range.

If your score is 31–40, you are in the high range.

If your score is 21–30, you are in the moderate range.

If your score is 10–20, you are in the low range.

6.2   Observational Exercise

 Visit www.sagepub.com/northouseintro2e for downloadable versions of these questionnaires

Leadership Vision

Purpose

1. To understand the way visions are constructed by leaders in ongoing groups and organizations
2. To identify strategies that leaders employ to articulate and implement their visions

Directions

1. For this exercise, select two people in leadership positions to interview. They can be leaders in formal or informal positions at work, at school, or in society. The only criterion is that the leader influences others toward a goal.
2. Conduct a 30-minute interview with each leader, by phone or in person. Ask the leaders to describe the visions they have for their organizations. In addition, ask, "How do you *articulate* and *implement* your visions?"

Leader #1 (name) _____

Vision content   Vision articulation   Vision implementation

Leader #2 (name) _____

Vision content   Vision articulation   Vision implementation

Questions

1. What differences and similarities did you observe between the two leaders' visions?

2. Did the leaders advocate specific values? If yes, what values?

3. Did the leaders use any unique symbols to promote their visions? If yes, what symbols?

4. In what ways did the leaders' behaviors model their visions to others?

6.3   Reflection and Action Worksheet

 Visit **www.sagepub.com/northouseintro2e** for downloadable versions of these questionnaires

Leadership Vision

Reflection

1. Stephen Covey (1991) contended that effective leaders "begin with the end in mind." These leaders have a deep understanding of their own goals and mission in life. How would you describe your own values and purpose in life? In what way is your leadership influenced by these values?

2. Creating a vision usually involves trying to change others by persuading them to accept different values and different ways of doing things. Are you comfortable influencing people in this way? Discuss.

3. As we discussed in this chapter, effective visions can be articulated with strong symbols. How do you view yourself as being able to do this? Are you effective at generating language and symbols that can enhance a vision and help make it successful?

Action

1. Based on your score on the Leadership Vision Questionnaire, how do you assess your ability to create a vision for a group? Identify specific ways you could improve your abilities to create and carry out visions with others.

2. Good leaders *act out the vision*. Describe what ideals and values you act out or could act out as a leader.

3. Take a few moments to think about and describe a group or an organization to which you belong presently or belonged to in the past. Write a brief statement describing the vision you would utilize if you were the leader of this group or organization.

Complete the *Setting the Tone Questionnaire*, which you will find on pp. 145–146. As you read the chapter, consider your results on the questionnaire.

Setting the Tone

7

As we discussed earlier, a leader needs to attend to tasks and to people. A leader also has to have a vision that he or she can express and implement. Equally important, a leader must be able to *set the tone* for the people in a group or an organization.

Setting the tone demands that a leader provide structure, clarify norms, build cohesiveness, and promote standards of excellence. By setting the tone for the group, a leader ensures that members work more effectively together.

When a leader sets the tone in productive ways, he or she helps group members perform at their highest levels of excellence (Larson & LaFasto, 1989). This chapter will discuss the importance of each of the four factors in setting the tone, and will illustrate how these contribute to effective group performance.

PROVIDE STRUCTURE ◄

Because working in groups can be chaotic and challenging, it is helpful when a leader provides a sense of **structure** for group members. Providing structure is much like giving group members an architectural blueprint for their work. The drawing gives form and meaning to the purposes of the group's activities. Instilling structure into the organization provides people with a sense of security, direction, and stability. It helps them to understand where they fit in and what goals they need to accomplish. Working in a group *without* structure is more difficult for everyone involved.

How does a leader give structure to a group? First, a leader needs to communicate to the group the group's goals. When a leader gives a clear picture of assignments and responsibilities, group members gain a better sense of direction. For example, soldiers in the military are given orders to carry out a specific **mission**. The mission is the goal toward which they are working, and it provides organization to the rest of their activities. Another example is a group meeting where the leader provides an agenda.

Audio Link 7.1
Hear the importance of group structure.

In most college classrooms on the first day of class, professors hand out and discuss syllabi. Going over the syllabus is important to students because it provides information about the structure of the class. The syllabus also gives details about the professor, the course objectives, reading and writing assignments, tests, attendance requirements, and exam schedules. Some professors even include a calendar of lecture topics for each week to help students prepare more effectively. The syllabus sets the tone for the class by giving a structure for what will be accomplished. Students usually leave the first class feeling confident about what the class is going to be like and what will be required of them.

Journal Link 7.1
Read about the effects of synergy.

A leader also provides structure by identifying the unique ways that each individual member can contribute to the group. Effective groups use the talents of each individual and, as a result, accomplish a great deal. This is known as **synergy**, when the group outcome is greater than the sum of the individual contributions. The challenge for a leader is to find how each individual group member can contribute to the group's mission, and to encourage the group to recognize these contributions. For example, some people are good at generating ideas, while others are skilled at building consensus. Additionally, some people are good at setting agendas, and others are adept at making sure the proper supplies are available at meetings. Each person has a distinctive talent and can make a unique contribution. Effective leaders know how to discover these talents to benefit the entire group.

▶ CLARIFY NORMS

In addition to structuring the group, a leader also needs to clarify group norms. **Norms** are the rules of behavior that are established and shared by group members. Social psychologists have argued for years that norms play a major role in the performance and effectiveness of groups (Cartwright & Zander, 1968; Harris & Sherblom, 2007; Napier & Gershenfeld, 2004). Norms are like a road map for navigating how we are supposed to behave in a group. They tell us what is appropriate or inappropriate, what is right or wrong, and what is allowed or not allowed (Schein, 1969). Norms do not emerge on their own—they are the outcome of people interacting with each other and with the leader.

Encyclopedia Link 7.1
Read more about norms.

A leader can have a significant impact on establishing group norms. When a leader brings about constructive norms, it can have a positive effect on the entire group. The following example illustrates how a leader positively influences group norms. Home from college for the summer, Matt Smith was asked to take over as coach of his little brother's baseball team because the previous coach was leaving. Before taking over coaching the team, Matt observed several practices and became aware of the norms operating on the team. Among other things, he observed that team members frequently arrived 15 to 30 minutes late for practice, they often came without their baseball shoes or gloves, and they goofed off a lot during drills. Overall, Matt observed that the kids did not seem to care about the team or have much pride in what they were doing. Matt knew that coaching this team was going to be a real challenge.

After Matt had coached for a few weeks, the team's norms gradually changed. Matt continually stressed the need to start practice on time, encouraged players to "bring their stuff" to practice, and complimented players when they worked hard during drills. By the end of the summer, they were a different team. Players grew to enjoy the practice sessions, they worked hard, and they performed well. Most important, they thought their baseball team was "the greatest."

In this situation, the norms the players were operating under with the old coach interfered with the team and its goals. Under Matt's leadership, the players developed new norms that enabled them to function better.

Audio Link 7.2
Hear more about norms.

Norms are an important component of group functioning. They develop early in a group and are sometimes difficult to change. A leader should pay close attention to norm development and try to shape norms that will maximize group effectiveness.

► BUILD COHESIVENESS

The third way a leader sets the tone is to build cohesiveness. Cohesiveness is often considered an elusive but essential component of highly functioning groups. **Cohesiveness** is described as a sense of "we-ness," the cement that holds a group together, or the esprit de corps that exists within a group. Cohesiveness allows group members to express their personal viewpoints, give and receive feedback, accept opinions different from their own, and feel comfortable doing meaningful work (Corey & Corey, 2006). When a group is cohesive, the members feel a special connection with each other and with the group as a whole. Members appreciate the group, and in turn are appreciated by the group.

Cohesiveness has been associated with a number of positive outcomes for groups (see Table 7.1) (Cartwright, 1968; Shaw, 1976). First, high cohesiveness is frequently associated with *increased participation* and *better interaction* among members. People tend to talk more readily and listen more carefully in cohesive groups. Second, in highly cohesive groups, group membership tends to be more *consistent*. Members *develop positive feelings toward one another* and *are more willing to attend* group meetings. Third, highly cohesive groups are able to exert a *strong influence* on group members. Members *conform more closely to group norms* and *engage in more goal-directed behavior* for the group. Fourth, *member satisfaction is high* in cohesive groups; members tend to feel more secure and find enjoyment participating in the group. Finally, members of a cohesive group usually are *more productive* than members of a group that is less cohesive. Members of groups with greater cohesion can direct their energies toward group goals without spending a lot of time working out interpersonal issues and conflicts.

Given the positive outcomes of cohesiveness, how can a leader help groups become cohesive? Group cohesiveness does not develop instantaneously, but is created gradually over time. A leader can assist

Table 7.1	Positive Outcomes of Cohesive Groups

- There is increased participation from members.
- There is better interaction among members.
- Group membership is more consistent.
- Members develop positive feelings toward one another.
- Members are more willing to attend group meetings.
- Members influence each other.
- Members conform more closely to group norms.
- Group behavior is more goal directed.
- Member satisfaction is high.
- Members are more productive.

Sources: Cartwright, 1968; Shaw, 1976.

a group in building cohesiveness by incorporating the following actions in his or her leadership:

- Help groups to create a climate of trust
- Invite group members to become active participants
- Encourage passive or withdrawn members to become involved
- Be willing to listen and accept group members for who they are
- Help group members to achieve their individual goals
- Promote the free expression of divergent viewpoints in a safe environment
- Allow group members to share the leadership responsibilities
- Foster and promote member-to-member interaction instead of only leader-to-follower interaction (Corey & Corey, 2006)

When a leader is able to do some of the things described on this list, it increases the chance that the group will build a sense of cohesiveness.

Consider the following example of a service-learning group of five students that had a goal of raising money for Special Olympics by sponsoring a rock concert. The group included *John,* a student who was hard of hearing, and who felt alienated and excluded from college life; *Emily,* an energetic student with high hopes of earning an A in the class; *Bill,* an older student with very definite opinions; *Abby,* a free spirit with a strong interest in rock bands; and *Dane,* a talented student who resented having to work with others on a group project.

During its initial meetings, the group was very disjointed and had low group cohesion. The two people in the group with musical talent (Emily and Abby) thought they would have to do all of the work to put on the concert to raise $200. John never spoke, and Bill and Dane had attitudes that put them on the sidelines. During these early meetings, the group members were unenthusiastic and had negative feelings about each other. However, after the professor for the class encouraged Emily to reach out to John and try to include him in the group, a gradual change started to take place, and the group began moving in a more positive direction. Emily found it difficult to communicate with John because he could only hear if people spoke directly into a special handheld microphone. Emily spent an hour or so with John outside the group and soon established a meaningful association with him. At the same time, Bill, who initially was certain that John could not contribute to the group, started to change his mind when he saw how well Emily and John were getting along. Since Emily was talking to John through the microphone, Bill thought he should try it, too.

Because Abby knew people in three local bands, she put her energies into finding a good band to play for their concert. When John, who was an engineering student, came up with the idea of making posters and handing out flyers to advertise the concert, the energies in the group became focused. Within two weeks of John's offer, the group had completed a massive promotion throughout the community. The rekindled energies of John, Bill, and Dane were put to good use, and the group far exceeded its previous expectations.

By the end of the project, the group had raised $450 for Special Olympics, and walked away as friends. John claimed that this group project was one of the most meaningful experiences in his college education. Dane wanted to take credit for knowing the most people who came to the concert. Bill was ecstatic that the group had far exceeded his expectations. Abby was pleased to have hired the band and that the concert was a great hit, and Emily was proud of her leadership and the success of the group.

The service-learning group in the above example was a group with low cohesion when it started, but was highly cohesive by the end of the project. Cohesiveness was created because group members developed trust, and withdrawn and passive members were encouraged to participate and become involved. Group members learned to listen and respect one another's opinions, and to accept each other as unique people. From this example, the lesson for leaders is to help their group to build cohesiveness. When they do, the results can far exceed expectations.

▶ PROMOTE STANDARDS OF EXCELLENCE

Video Link 7.1

Watch how a group uses standards of excellence.

Finally, a leader sets the tone by promoting **standards of excellence**. In a classic study, Larson and LaFasto (1989) analyzed the characteristics of 75 highly successful teams. Included in their study were famous teams such as the DeBakey-Cooley cardiac surgery team, the *Challenger* disaster investigation team, the 1966 Notre Dame championship football team, and even the McDonald's Chicken McNugget team. In their analysis, researchers found that standards of excellence were a crucial factor associated with team success.

What are standards of excellence? These standards are the expressed and implied expectations for performance that exist within a group or an organization. Standards of excellence include six factors that are essential for members to function effectively:

1. What group members need to know and what skills they need to acquire

2. How much initiative and effort they need to demonstrate

3. How group members are expected to treat one another

4. The extent to which deadlines are significant

5. What goals they need to achieve

6. What the consequences are if they achieve or fail to achieve these goals (Larson & LaFasto, 1989, p. 95)

Journal Link 7.2
Read examples of standards.

In essence, standards of excellence refer to the established benchmarks of desired performance for a group. A good example of standards of excellence can be seen in the slogan (see Figure 7.1) of The Upjohn Company, a pharmaceutical manufacturing firm in Kalamazoo, Michigan. Founded in 1885, Upjohn was known for revolutionizing the drug industry through its invention of the "friable pill," which can crumble under the pressure of a person's thumb. In addition to this innovation, over the years Upjohn made many other drug discoveries, and grew to become one of the largest pharmaceutical companies in the world. For many years, the internal slogan promoted throughout the company was "Keep the quality up."

Figure 7.1   Standard of Excellence Slogan

KEEP THE QUALITY UP

W. E. UPJOHN

Sources: Courtesy of the WMU Archives and Regional History Collections.

"Keep the quality up" captures the essence of what standards of excellence are all about. This slogan is clear, direct, and forceful. It puts responsibility on employees to work toward maintaining quality—a standard of excellence. The slogan strongly suggests that employees should work consistently toward these standards over time. In addition, "Keep the quality up" stresses a positive expectation that has value for both employees and the company; quality is the valued benchmark of the company's desired performance for its employees.

Based on studies of more than 600 team leaders and 6,000 team members, LaFasto and Larson (2001) identified several specific ways that a leader can influence performance and promote standards of excellence. To influence performance, the authors contend that a leader must stress the "three Rs": (1) *Require* results, (2) *Review* results, and (3) *Reward* results.

1. *Require results*. A leader needs to articulate clear, concrete expectations for team members. Working together, a leader and team members should establish mutual goals and identify specific objectives for achieving the results associated with those goals. Without clear expectations, team members flounder and are uncertain about what is required of them. They are unsure what results they are expected to achieve. Requiring results is the critical first step in managing performance (LaFasto & Larson, 2001).

For example, students in a research course were expected to form a group with four or five of their classmates and work together to complete a "utilization project" by the end of the course. Although the professor had a clear idea of what she wanted students to accomplish, students had no idea what a utilization project was or how to go about developing it. After a number of students expressed frustration at the lack of clear guidelines, the professor explained that a utilization project involved taking findings from a research study and applying them to a real-world situation. She developed evaluation criteria for the project that outlined what students were supposed to do, the level of depth required for the project, and the key elements of the project that needed to be reported in the evaluation paper. With these explicit instructions, students' anxiety about the utilization project decreased, and they were able to work more effectively in their groups.

In this example, the professor initially required results that were unclear. When she clarified her expectations, the students were able to produce the results. Giving clear objectives and instructions is the first step to high-quality performance.

2. *Review results*. In addition to requiring results, a leader also needs to review results. According to LaFasto and Larson (2001), a leader does this by giving constructive feedback and resolving performance issues.

Giving constructive feedback is a must for a leader if he or she is going to help group members maintain standards of excellence (see

Table 7.2). Constructive feedback is honest and direct communication about a group member's performance. It is not mean-spirited or paternalistic, nor is it overly nice or patronizing. Constructive feedback helps group members know if they are doing the right things, in the right way, and at the right speed. Although it is not easy to do, giving constructive feedback is a skill that everyone can learn. When done correctly, constructive feedback allows group members to look at themselves honestly and know what they need to maintain or improve (LaFasto & Larson, 2001).

Handbook Link 7.1
Read more about performance assessment.

Table 7.2	Tips for Giving Constructive Feedback

People benefit greatly from feedback that is delivered in a noncontrontational, constructive manner. Unfortunately, not many of us have the innate skill for delivering feedback this way. There are, however, some simple communication methods that can improve your ability to provide constructive feedback.

1. Address behaviors.

Use facts to describe the behavior that is problematic, rather than focusing on personal traits. For example, a leader might say, "Jane, I have noticed that you have been late for the past three mornings. Can you explain why?" rather than "Why aren't you able to arrive on time?"

2. Describe specifically what you have observed.

Observations are what you have seen occur; an interpretation is your analysis or opinion of what has occurred. By telling the person what you have seen and not what you think of what you have seen, you provide observations that are more factual and less judgmental. For example, a leader might say, "Dan, I noticed and highlighted several factual and grammatical errors in the report you submitted," rather than "Dan, all these mistakes make me wonder if you were doing this report at the last minute."

3. Use "I" language.

Employing "I" statements rather than "you" statements will help reduce the defensiveness of the person you are addressing. For example, if you say, "Joe, because our cubicles are so close together I have a hard time concentrating when you play music on your computer," rather than "It is really inconsiderate of you to play music when other people are trying to work," you are more likely to elicit the change you would like.

4. Give the feedback in calm, unemotional language.

Avoid "need to" phrases (e.g., "You need to improve this . . .") or using a tone that implies anger, frustration, or disappointment. Rather than saying, "If you'd just learn the software, you'd do a better job," a leader should say, "I am sure you will be much faster now that you understand how to use this software."

5. Check to ensure clear communication has occurred.

Solicit feedback from the other person to ensure he or she understands what you have been trying to communicate to him or her. For example, a leader might say, "Ann, do you know the procedure for ordering the supplies? Can you go over it to be sure I covered everything?" rather than "Ann, you got all that, didn't you?"

Consider the following example of two restaurant managers (Managers A and B) and their waitstaff. Manager A was known for being very blunt and sometimes even mean. Although he wanted the best for the restaurant, his performance reviews were always disasters. Manager A was brutally honest; he did not know how to be diplomatic. If a server was slow or inefficient, he let the person know it in no uncertain terms. In fact, staff members often thought Manager A was attacking them. Although Manager A wanted people to perform well, he did not know how to make that behavior happen. As he frequently told his employees, "Around this place, I don't sugarcoat anything. If your performance is poor, you're going to hear about it!"

In contrast, Manager B was very careful in how she treated the waitstaff. Manager B cared about staff, and it showed in how she did performance reviews. If waitstaff did something wrong, Manager B would always comment on it, but never in a mean way. When giving praise or criticism, the feedback was always objective and never extreme; the feedback never attacked the person. Manager B consistently evaluated her staff, but always in a way that made them feel better about themselves and that made them want to try harder.

Manager A and Manager B were very different in how they gave feedback to their staff. Manager A's feedback was destructive and debilitating, while Manager B's feedback was constructive and helped to improve performance. As a result, the waitstaff liked working for Manager B and disliked working for Manager A. Staff performed better when Manager B was in charge and worse when Manager A was in charge.

Video Link 7.2
Watch a
performance review.

Resolving performance issues is the second part of reviewing results. LaFasto and Larson (2001) found that, more than anything else, the distinguishing characteristic of effective leaders was their willingness to confront and resolve inadequate performance by team members. Clearly, individuals in groups want their leaders to keep other group members "on track." If some group members are slacking off, or not doing their part, the leader needs to address the situation.

Working in groups is a collective effort—everyone must be involved. Group members are interdependent, and all members share the responsibility of trying to achieve group goals. When some members do not pull their own weight, it affects everyone in the group. This is why a leader must address the inadequate performance of any group members. If the leader fails to do so, contributing group members will feel angry and slighted, as if their work does not really matter.

Confronting inadequate performance by group members is a challenging and emotionally charged process that requires much of leaders (LaFasto & Larson, 2001). It is not easy, but it is a necessary part of leadership. An effective leader is proactive and confronts problems when they occur. In problem situations, a leader has to communicate with low-performing group members and explain how their behaviors hinder the group from meeting its goals. The leader also has to explain what needs to be done differently. After the changes have been clearly identified, the leader needs to monitor the behaviors of the low-performing group members. If the group members make satisfactory changes, they can remain in the group. If a group member refuses to change, the leader needs to counsel him or her about leaving the group. When a leader addresses behavioral problems in a timely fashion, it is beneficial both to the person with the performance problem and to the entire group.

An example of a performance review can be seen in the story of Sam Wilson, a principal at a private, suburban high school. Sam is a highly effective leader who is respected by students, teachers, and parents of his school. As principal, he is responsible for hiring all the teachers at the school. During one fall semester, Sam noticed that Michelle Long, a teacher he had hired to teach geometry, appeared to be slacking off in her work. Michelle was coming to work late, was skipping faculty meetings, and did not seem very excited about teaching. Seeing that she was underperforming, Sam called Michelle into his office to discuss his concerns. During the meeting, Sam described thoroughly his concerns about Michelle's work and asked Michelle to give her point of view on these concerns. After a long discussion, Sam identified several changes Michelle needed to make if she wanted to continue to teach at the high school.

Following the meeting, Michelle temporarily changed her behavior. She came to school on time, attended some of the faculty meetings, and improved her teaching plans. This positive behavior lasted for about a month, and then she fell back into her old habits. In March, when Sam gave Michelle her annual performance review, he told her that her teaching contract would not be renewed for the following year. Although Michelle was not pleased, she understood why she was being let go.

In the ensuing months, Michelle finished the school year and then found a job at another school. While letting Michelle go was not easy, Sam was comfortable with what he had done. Although some teachers at the school were surprised that Michelle had been let go, they also expressed some relief because they realized that her work was not up to the standards of the school.

3. *Reward results*. Finally, an effective leader rewards group members for achieving results (LaFasto & Larson, 2001). Many of the behaviors required to be an effective leader are abstract (such as establishing norms) and challenging (such as building group cohesion). However, that is not the case when it comes to rewarding results. Rewarding results is a very practical, straightforward process. It is something that every leader can do.

In their well-known consulting work on leadership effectiveness, Kouzes and Posner (2002) claimed that rewarding results is one of the five major practices of exemplary leaders. They argued that a leader needs to recognize the contributions of group members and express appreciation for individual excellence. This includes paying attention to group members, offering them encouragement, and giving them personalized appreciation. These expressions can be dramatic, such as a dinner celebration, or simple, such as a short e-mail of praise. When a leader recognizes group members and gives encouragement, members feel valued, and there is a greater sense of group identity and community spirit.

A good example of how to effectively reward performance can be seen in how the leader of a nonprofit organization rewarded one of its members, Christopher Wolf. Christopher was an active member of the board who willingly shared his insights and expertise for 15 consecutive years. To show appreciation for his work, the board president had T-shirts made that characterized Christopher's contributions. On the front of the shirt was a caricature of a wolf in sheep's clothing symbolizing Christopher's many positive contributions to the board. On the back of the shirt were the words "The Wolf Pack" and a list of the names of each of the other board members. Both Christopher and each member of the board were given a shirt, which was a big hit with everyone. Although the shirts were simple and inexpensive, they were a unique way of positively recognizing Christopher and all his fellow board members.

CASE STUDY

The following case study describes the leadership of two different university professors. The questions at the end of the case will help you analyze the case using ideas from the different conceptual perspectives provided in the chapter.

A Tale of Two Classes

Ebony Ellis has two communication classes back-to-back in the same room, but they couldn't be more different.

The first, a class on interpersonal communication, is taught by Steve Gardner, an older professor who has taught at the university for 30 years. The first day of class he verbally set down the rules for class conduct, which were also distributed in a printed handout. Cell phones must be off, no texting is allowed, and, unless a student needs to use one for note taking, laptops are to be closed. He won't tolerate students who come in late or leave early.

Her second class, an organizational communication course taught by Jacinta Morgan, a younger professor in her 40s, has different rules. There aren't any. This professor doesn't care if the students use their laptops during class. Texting and talking are unrestrained. Professor Morgan announced on the first day that all students are responsible for their own learning in the class, and she trusts them to know how they learn best. When students walk in late or leave early, she always says hello or goodbye to them.

Ebony likes her interpersonal communication class a lot. Professor Gardner's manner has succeeded in getting the class of 75 to engage with him and listen to one another. Self-disclosure by students and the professor alike is frequent, and there is often much humor and laughter. In his course, students write a paper every other week, and they have a midterm and final exams.

The atmosphere in the organizational communication class also appeals to Ebony. It is spontaneous and free. Some of the best discussions on the content come from the freestyle, unstructured dialogue between students and teacher. Professor Morgan also assigns papers, but they are short, personal observation papers that aren't given grades but are marked as turned in or not. Students' final grades for the class are dependent on a presentation each student must give on an interpersonal communication topic of his or her choice.

Ebony thinks the two differing styles of the professors would make a great topic for her organizational communication class presentation. To get more information, she interviewed both instructors to learn why their classroom management styles are so different.

Professor Gardner describes his teaching philosophy this way: "I want students to think that this class is unique and the subject is important and has value. It's important that they be on board with the direction the train is going from the start. I try to build a community by getting the students to listen to one another. The fun and spirit of the class comes from the camaraderie they establish.

(Continued)

(Continued)

In order to listen to one another, however, they have to be fully present. To be fully present, they have to be paying full attention. Texting and open laptops suggest to me that the students are disassociated and disconnected from the group. The attention is on self, rather than the community."

Professor Morgan also says her goal is to build community in her classroom, but through a more naturally occurring cohesiveness. "I give the students just enough freedom in class that they will either sink or swim. This freedom allows me to present them with ideas, and they discuss it naturally, like a group of friends gathered together. I think today's students are so multifaceted that they can still pay attention to class while texting or using their laptops. Many times a student will bring up something valuable that he or she has found while surfing the Internet during class that really adds to our discussions. I like to think I know how to control their electronic activities while making sure the material they need to know is presented. They are each responsible for how much of it they absorb."

Ebony also interviewed two students, like herself, who are enrolled in both classes. Ian said he is more comfortable in Professor Gardner's class because he knows what is expected of him and what the norms for class behavior are. Professor Gardner's grading structure is similar to that of most other classes he's had, and Ian likes that there are several graded assignments that allow him to gauge how he's doing through the course of the semester. As for Professor Morgan's class, he enjoys it but finds some of the electronic activity to be distracting and is stressed about his grade being dependent on one big assignment.

Professor Morgan's class, however, is BreeAnn's favorite. She says that while the class feels "a little wild," the discussions are well controlled by the professor so that the class stays on topic and learns the material. And while she doesn't assign students' papers a grade, Professor Morgan writes thoughtful comments on each of their papers to help guide their learning. BreeAnn found the final presentation assignment to be an interesting challenge that tapped into her creativity as well as what she had learned.

Ian and BreeAnn told Ebony that they believe both professors have the respect of their students and are effective teachers. "They are both good," Ian says, "just very, very different."

1. In setting the tone for his or her class, what kind of structure has each professor put in place?

2. How would you describe the group norms for each class?

3. What actions has each professor taken to establish cohesiveness in his or her class?

4. What standards of excellence has each professor established for his or her course?

5. Which class atmosphere would you do best in? Why?

Summary

Setting the tone is a subtle but essential aspect of effective leadership that plays a major role in whether groups or organizations function effectively. Setting the tone is similar to creating a positive climate for workers in a company. It requires that a leader *provide structure, clarify norms, build cohesiveness,* and *promote standards of excellence.*

A leader *provides structure* by establishing concrete goals, giving explicit assignments, and making responsibilities clear. Helping each group member feel included and know that he or she contributes to the overall goals of the group also provides structure.

A leader plays a significant role in helping to develop positive *group norms.* Effective groups establish positive norms that allow them to work productively. When norms for a group are negative or unproductive, the leader needs to help group members to change and develop new norms. By assisting groups in establishing positive norms, a leader facilitates the group in maximizing its performance.

Building cohesiveness is the third facet of setting the tone. Cohesiveness is a special quality of high-functioning groups that feel a strong sense of connectedness and esprit de corps. Associated with many positive outcomes, cohesiveness is established by a leader who assists group members in trusting each other, listening to and respecting one another's opinions, and accepting each other as unique people.

Finally, to set the tone a leader *promotes standards of excellence.* Highly effective teams have strong standards of excellence—they have established benchmarks for desired performance. Standards of excellence are best achieved when the leader *requires results, reviews results,* and *rewards results.*

To summarize, setting the tone is a complex process that involves a great deal of work by a leader. A leader who sets a positive tone will find payoffs in remarkable group performance.

 Go to **http://www.sagepub.com/northouseintro2e/** *for additional exercises and study resources. Select Chapter 7, Setting the Tone, for chapter-specific activities.*

Glossary Terms

cohesiveness 132	standards of excellence 134
mission 130	structure 129
norms 130	synergy 130

References

Cartwright, D. (1968). The nature of group cohesiveness. In D. Cartwright & A. Zander (Eds.), *Group dynamics: Research and theory* (3rd ed., pp. 91–109). New York: Harper & Row.

Cartwright, D., & Zander, A. (Eds.). (1968). *Group dynamics: Research and theory* (3rd ed.). New York: Harper & Row.

Corey, M. S., & Corey, G. (2006). *Groups: Process and practice* (7th ed.). Pacific Grove, CA: Brooks/Cole.

Harris, T. E., & Sherblom, J. C. (2007). *Small group and team communication* (4th ed.). Boston: Pearson.

Kouzes, J. M., & Posner, B. Z. (2002). *The leadership challenge* (3rd ed.). San Francisco: Jossey-Bass.

LaFasto, F. M. J., & Larson, C. E. (2001). *When teams work best: 6,000 team members and leaders tell what it takes to succeed.* Thousand Oaks, CA: Sage.

Larson, C. E., & LaFasto, F. M. J. (1989). *Teamwork: What must go right/what can go wrong.* Newbury Park, CA: Sage.

Napier, R. W., & Gershenfeld, M. K. (2004). *Groups: Theory and experience* (7th ed.). Boston: Houghton Mifflin.

Schein, E. H. (1969). *Process consultation: Its role in management development.* Reading, MA: Addison-Wesley.

Shaw, M. E. (1976). *Group dynamics: The psychology of small group behavior* (2nd ed.). New York: McGraw-Hill.

7.1 Setting the Tone Questionnaire

 Visit www.sagepub.com/northouseintro2e for downloadable versions of these questionnaires

Purpose

1. To develop an understanding of how your leadership affects others
2. To help you understand your strengths and weaknesses in establishing the tone for a group or an organization

Directions

1. For each of the statements below, indicate the frequency with which you engage in the behavior listed.
2. Give your immediate impressions. There are no right or wrong answers.

When I am the leader . . .	Never	Seldom	Sometimes	Often	Always
1. I give clear assignments to group members.	1	2	3	4	5
2. I emphasize starting and ending group meetings on time.	1	2	3	4	5
3. I encourage group members to appreciate the value of the overall group.	1	2	3	4	5
4. I encourage group members to work to the best of their abilities.	1	2	3	4	5
5. I make the goals of the group clear to everyone.	1	2	3	4	5
6. I model group norms for group members.	1	2	3	4	5
7. I encourage group members to listen and to respect each other.	1	2	3	4	5
8. I make a point of recognizing people when they do a good job.	1	2	3	4	5
9. I emphasize the overall purpose of the group assignment to group members.	1	2	3	4	5
10. I demonstrate effective communication to group members.	1	2	3	4	5
11. I encourage group members to respect each other's differences.	1	2	3	4	5
12. I promote standards of excellence.	1	2	3	4	5
13. I help group members understand their purpose for being in the group.	1	2	3	4	5
14. I encourage group members to agree on the rules for the group.	1	2	3	4	5
15. I encourage group members to accept each other as unique individuals.	1	2	3	4	5

When I am the leader . . .	Never	Seldom	Sometimes	Often	Always
16. I give group members honest feedback about their work.	1	2	3	4	5
17. I help group members understand their roles in the group.	1	2	3	4	5
18. I expect group members to listen when another group member is talking.	1	2	3	4	5
19. I help group members build camaraderie with each other.	1	2	3	4	5
20. I show group members who are not performing well how to improve the quality of their work.	1	2	3	4	5

Scoring

1. Sum the responses on items 1, 5, 9, 13, and 17 (providing structure).

2. Sum the responses on items 2, 6, 10, 14, and 18 (clarifying norms).

3. Sum the responses on items 3, 7, 11, 15, and 19 (building cohesiveness).

4. Sum the responses on items 4, 8, 12, 16, and 20 (promoting standards of excellence).

Total Scores

Providing structure: _____

Clarifying norms: _____

Building cohesiveness: _____

Promoting standards of excellence: _____

Scoring Interpretation

This questionnaire is designed to measure four factors related to setting the tone: providing structure, clarifying norms, building cohesiveness, and promoting standards of excellence. By comparing your scores, you can determine your strengths and weaknesses in setting the tone as a leader.

If your score is 20–25, you are in the high range.

If your score is 15–19, you are in the high moderate range.

If your score is 10–14, you are in the low moderate range.

If your score is 5–9, you are in the low range.

7.2   **Observational Exercise**

 Visit www.sagepub.com/northouseintro2e for downloadable versions of these questionnaires

Setting the Tone

Purpose

1. To develop an understanding of how leaders set the tone for a group or an organization

2. To identify how specific factors contribute to effective group performance

Directions

1. For this exercise, you will observe a leader running a meeting, a practice, a class, or some other group-related activity.

2. Attend a full session of the group and record your observations below.

   Name of leader: _____

   Name of the group: _____

   Observations about the structure (organization) of the group.

   Observations about the group's norms:

   Observations about the cohesiveness of the group:

   Observations about the group's standards of excellence:

Questions

1. In what ways did the leader make the goals of the group clear to group members?

2. How did the leader utilize the unique talents of different group members?

3. What were some of the positive and negative norms of this group? How did the leader reinforce these norms?

4. How would you evaluate, on a scale from 1 (*low*) to 5 (*high*), the cohesiveness of this group? In what ways did the leader promote or fail to promote the esprit de corps in the group?

5. A key factor in promoting standards of excellence is rewarding results. How did the leader reward group members for achieving results?

7.3   Reflection and Action Worksheet

 Visit www.sagepub.com/northouseintro2e for downloadable versions of these questionnaires

Setting the Tone

Reflection

1. Based on the scores you received on the Setting the Tone Questionnaire, what are your strengths and weaknesses regarding setting the tone for a group or an organization? Discuss.

   Strengths:

   Weaknesses:

2. How did you react to the example in this chapter (pp. 133–134) of the service-learning group that developed cohesiveness? In what way do you think cohesiveness plays an important role in groups? Have you ever experienced cohesiveness in a group yourself? Discuss.

3. In this chapter, group rules and norms are stressed as being very important to effective teams. Do you agree with this? Explain your answer. Briefly comment on your own desire and ability to adapt to the rules of a group.

4. An important aspect of setting the tone is giving recognition to others. Is rewarding or praising others something that would come easily for you as a leader? Discuss.

Action

1. Imagine that you have been chosen to lead a group project for your class and are preparing for the first meeting. Based on what you have read in this chapter, identify five important actions you could take to help set a positive tone for the group.

2. This chapter argues that setting the tone demands that the leader be a role model for how group members should act. What three values are important to you in a group? How would you demonstrate these values to group members?

3. High-performing teams have strong standards of excellence. Discuss your level of comfort with encouraging others to "keep the quality up." What leadership behaviors could you strengthen to encourage others to work to the best of their ability?

Before you begin reading . . .

Complete the *Responding to Members of the Out-Group Questionnaire*, which you will find on pp. 167–168. As you read the chapter, consider your results on the questionnaire.

Listening to Out-Group Members

8

Listening and responding to out-group members, those individuals in a group or an organization who do not identify with the larger group, is one of the most difficult challenges facing a leader. When a leader fails to meet this challenge, the results can be problematic. Good leaders know the importance of listening to *all* members of a group, especially the out-group members.

It is common to find out-groups in any context where a group of individuals is trying to reach a goal. Out-groups are a natural occurrence in everyday life. They exist in all types of situations at the local, community, and national levels. In nearly all of these situations, when one or more individuals are *not* "on board," the performance of the group is adversely affected. Since out-group members are so common, it is important for anyone who aspires to be a leader to know how to work with them.

Journal Link 8.1
Read more about out-groups.

Out-group members can be identified in many everyday encounters. At school, out-group members are often those kids who do not believe that they are a part of the student body. For instance, they may want to participate in sports, music, clubs, and so on, but for a host of reasons do not do so. At work, there are out-groups comprising people who are at odds with management's vision, or who are excluded from important decision-making committees. On project teams, some out-group members are those who simply refuse to contribute to the activities of the larger group.

This chapter will examine why it is important for a leader to listen to out-group members. The questions it will address are "Who is in the out-group?" "Why do out-groups form?" "What is the impact of out-groups?" and "How should a leader respond to out-groups?" This discussion of out-groups will emphasize specific strategies that leaders can employ to build a sense of belonging and community, and advance the goals of the larger group.

▶ WHO IS IN THE OUT-GROUP?

There are many different ways to define out-groups. For our purposes, the term **out-group** refers to those individuals in a group or an organization who do not identify themselves as part of the larger group. They are individuals who are disconnected and not fully engaged in working toward the goals of the group. They may be in opposition to the will of a larger group or simply disinterested in the group's goals. They may feel unaccepted, alienated, and even discriminated against. In addition, they may think they are powerless because their potential resources have not been fully accepted by the larger group.

Out-groups come in many forms: They can be minorities who think their voice is not being heard, or people who think their ideas are unappreciated. They can be those who simply do not identify with the leader or other members of the primary group. Sometimes out-group members are social loafers—group members who are inclined to goof off or work below their capacity when they are in a group. In short, out-group members sense themselves to be at odds with the larger group.

▶ WHY DO OUT-GROUPS FORM?

There are many different reasons that out-groups form. First, some out-groups form because people disagree with the social, political, or ethical position of the majority—they sense that they are in *opposition* to the larger group. When decisions need to be made in organizational settings, consensus is often difficult to achieve. Without consensus, individuals align themselves either with the majority viewpoint or with the minority. This minority is often seen as an out-group. Even when decisions are made by voting, the results often produce winners and losers, and the losers frequently perceive themselves as members of the out-group.

A second reason that out-groups form is explained by **social identity theory**. This theory suggests that out-groups come about because some individuals *cannot identify* with the beliefs, norms, or values of the dominant group members. Research on groups (Hogg & Abrams, 1988; Tajfel & Turner, 1979, 1986) indicates that individuals in groups often share a social identity and act toward each other in terms of that identity (Abrams, Frings, & Randsley de Moura, 2005). In group settings, members embrace the social identity of other group members and make the group's concerns their own. For example, in a support group for people with cancer, group members are likely to embrace a common identity—as cancer survivors who are coping with the disease. People find meaning in belonging to the group and sharing their experiences with others. They see one another as having a shared experience. However, if one of the members is struggling with a more serious form of cancer and does not feel like a survivor, then that person may become an out-group member. Out-groups are created when individuals in a group cannot identify with the group and, as a result, do not embrace the dominant group's reality.

Journal Link 8.2
Read about intergroup relations.

Closely related to the identity issue, a third reason out-groups form is because people sense that they are *excluded* by the larger group. They do not know where they fit in or whether they are needed by others in the group. Group members may think they are too old, too young, too conservative, too liberal, or just plain different from the larger group. For example, on a high school varsity soccer team, freshmen players might wonder how they fit in with the upperclassmen. Similarly, in a college nursing class made up mostly of women, a male student might feel different from the other nursing students and wonder how he fits in the program. In situations such as these, people often sense that they are alienated from the larger group. In addition, they may also think of themselves as powerless and weak.

A fourth reason for out-group development is that some people *lack communication skills* or *social skills* that are needed to relate to a larger group. In any group of people, there are often one or two people who set themselves apart from the group through their actions. For example, in an undergraduate group project team there may be a student who talks excessively or dominates group discussions and consequently alienates himself from the rest of the group. Or there could be a student who acts very dogmatic, or another who consistently makes off-the-wall remarks. These types of individuals distinguish themselves as different from the rest of the group by how they talk or act. It is as if they are unable to adapt to the norms of the group. As much as they try, these people often find themselves on the outside looking in. Even though they may want to join the larger group, they have difficulty doing so because they do not know how to fit in. In these situations, their lack of communication and social skills often leads them to becoming out-group members.

In reality, there are many possible reasons for out-groups. Any one reason is as legitimate as another. Developing an understanding of these reasons is the first step in trying to resolve out-group issues.

▶ WHAT IS THE IMPACT OF OUT-GROUPS?

Out-groups can have many adverse effects on others. Some of the downsides of out-groups are relatively insignificant, such as causing minor inefficiencies in organizational productivity. Other downsides are more important, such as creating conflict or causing a strike to be called.

Handbook Link 8.1
Read about
intergroup conflict.

So why should a leader be concerned about the negative impact of out-groups? First, *out-groups run counter to building community.* The essence of community is encouraging everyone to be on the same page and moving them in the same direction. Community brings people together and provides a place where they can express similar ideas, values, and opinions, and where they can be heard by members of their team. Community allows people to accomplish great things. It enables people to work hand in hand in pursuit of a shared vision that supports the common good. Through community, people can promote the greater good of everyone in the group.

However, by their very nature out-group members are either in conflict with or avoiding community. Because the community may seem threatening, unfamiliar, or uninteresting to them, some people have a need to pull away from community. Their action detracts from the community being able to use all of its resources to reach a common goal.

The following example occurred in a college social work class; it illustrates how out-groups can have a negative impact on community. Introduction to Social Work is a popular class with a good reputation on campus. Every semester the major assignment in the class is a group service project in which everyone is required to participate.

One semester a few months after Hurricane Katrina had wreaked havoc in the South, several members of the class proposed a service project doing relief work in New Orleans over spring break. Clearly, there was a need for the project, and the project would utilize everyone's talents and skills. To pull it off, the class would need to do a lot of planning and fundraising. Committees were to be formed and T-shirts designed. There seemed to be agreement that a good theme would be "Together—We Can Make Things Better."

Problems arose for the class when some of the students did not want to participate. One student pointed out that he thought it was the government's job to provide relief, not the private sector's. Another student argued that there were already many volunteers in New Orleans, and maybe the class could better serve others by doing cleanup work on the south side of their own city. Two others in the class did not like the idea of working for the poor over spring break because they wanted to go to Cancún, Mexico.

These students could not find common ground. The trip to New Orleans was cancelled, there were no T-shirts printed, and the students ended up doing 40 hours each of tutoring at the local grade school as their service project. The class could not come to an agreement with the out-group members, whose wants and needs prevented the rest of the class from pursuing the project in New Orleans. The interests of the out-group prevented the class from experiencing community and all its benefits.

A second reason that leadership should be concerned with out-groups is that *out-groups have a negative impact on group synergy.* Group synergy is the positive energy created by group members who are working toward a common goal. It is an additive kind of energy that builds on itself. Group synergy is one of the most miraculous features of effective groups and of highly functioning teams. Groups with synergy accomplish far more than groups without it. Group synergy is not just the sum of each person's contribution; it is the sum of each person's contribution *and then some.* It is the "plus more" that allows high-functioning groups to achieve far beyond what would be expected.

Unfortunately, out-groups prevent groups from becoming synergistic. Out-groups take energy *away from* the group rather than *adding energy to* the group. If out-group members are upset and demanding, they take even more energy from the group. This energy is not directed toward the goals of the group and so has a negative impact on productivity. Rather than working together to accomplish a common goal, out-group members stand alone and seek to do their own thing. This is harmful for the group because the unique contributions of out-group members are not expressed, discussed, or utilized for the common good. Every person in a group brings singular talents and abilities that can benefit the group. When out-groups form, the individual contributions of some group members are not utilized, and group synergy is compromised.

A brief example about a fund-raising committee for a nonprofit may help to illustrate this issue. The newly established committee was charged with planning and implementing a new fund-raising event for the organization. A number of the volunteers had some experience in planning special events, while others did not but wanted to be involved. Unfortunately, there were strained relationships between different groups on the committee from the outset. One volunteer wanted a wine tasting event held at a posh country club, while another thought a large rummage sale was a great idea. Two of the committee members were happy to provide input but did not want to have to do any of the actual work. Three of the volunteers were very eager to help but experienced pressure to side with either the wine tasting or the rummage sale supporter. The committee's chair believed that the group members should work things out among themselves. After three meetings, it was clear that agreement could not be reached about what kind of event should be held. As a result, the volunteers who just wanted to provide input stopped coming, and two of the other volunteers lost interest in participating on the committee. Finally, when it appeared that her idea was not going to be accepted, the volunteer in favor of the rummage sale accused the others of being snobs and quit.

In the above example, the committee chair failed to pull the divergent out-group members together into a single group. She needed to recognize the unique contributions of each of the out-group members (e.g., previous event planning experience, connections to those with money, enthusiasm) and use those contributions for the benefit of the entire group. Because the chair was not successful in responding to the out-group members, group synergy was diminished, and the event that was ultimately held was hastily thrown together and not well attended.

A third reason out-groups are of concern to a leader is that *out-group members do not receive the respect they deserve from others*. A central tenet of ethical leadership is the duty to treat each member with respect. As Beauchamp and Bowie (1988) pointed out, people need to be treated as autonomous individuals with their own goals, and not as the means to another person's goals. Being ethical means treating other people's decisions and values with respect: Failing to do so would signify that they are being treated as means to another's ends.

A leader has an ethical responsibility to respond to out-group members. These individuals are not in the out-group without reason. They may have valid grounds for feeling alienated, unaccepted, or discriminated against, or are choosing simply to be uninvolved. No matter what the reasons are, out-group members are people who deserve to be heard by the leader and the other group members.

Encyclopedia Link 8.1
Read more about prejudice.

In summary, the impact of out-groups is substantial. When out-groups exist, they have a negative impact on community, group synergy, and the out-group members themselves. The challenge for every leader is to respond to out-group members in a way that enhances the group and its goals.

HOW SHOULD A LEADER RESPOND TO OUT-GROUPS? ◄

While many ideas about effective leadership are abstract, these strategies for how a leader should respond to out-group members are tangible. They are concrete steps that a leader can take to handle out-group members more effectively. In reading these strategies, ask yourself how you could adopt them to improve your own leadership.

STRATEGY 1: LISTEN TO OUT-GROUP MEMBERS

More than anything else, out-group members want to be heard. Whether they perceive themselves to be powerless, alienated, or discriminated against, out-group members have a need for others to listen to them. Clearly, the fact that some people sense that they are not being heard is at the very center of why out-groups exist. Out-group members have ideas, attitudes, and feelings that they want to express; when they believe they have not been able to or will not be able to express them, they pull away and disassociate from the group.

Listening is one of the most important ways that a leader can respond to out-group members. While it requires paying attention to what people say, it also requires being attentive to what people mean. Listening is both a simple and a complex process that demands concentration, open-mindedness, and tolerance. Listening requires that a leader set aside his or her own biases in order to allow out-group members to express their viewpoints freely. When out-group members think that the leader has heard them, they feel confirmed and more connected to the larger group. Clearly, listening should be a top priority of a leader.

STRATEGY 2: SHOW EMPATHY TO OUT-GROUP MEMBERS

Audio Link 8.1

Listen to more about empathy.

Similar to listening, a leader also needs to show empathy to out-group members. **Empathy** is a special kind of listening that is more demanding than just listening. It requires a leader to try standing in the shoes of out-group members, and to see the world as the out-group member does. Empathy is a process in which the leader suspends his or her own feelings in an effort to understand the feelings of the out-group member.

While showing empathy comes more naturally to some than to others, it is a skill anyone can learn to improve. Techniques for showing empathy include restatement, paraphrasing, reflection, and giving support (see Table 8.1). Through the use of these techniques, a leader can assist out-group members to be understood.

Table 8.1   How to Demonstrate Empathy

A leader can demonstrate empathy through four communication techniques:

1. Restatement
By restating what another person has verbalized without adding any of your own personal thoughts and beliefs, you directly acknowledge and validate another person's point of view. For example, say, "I hear you saying . . . " or "It sounds as if you feel . . ."

2. Paraphrasing
This communication technique involves summarizing in your own words what another person has verbalized. It helps to communicate to the other person that you understand what he or she is saying. For example, say, "In other words, you're saying that . . . " or "Stated another way, you're suggesting that . . ."

3. Reflection
By serving as a mirror or sounding board for another person's expressed or unexpressed emotions and attitudes, you focus on *how* something has been expressed, or the emotional dimension behind the words. This technique helps others gain an understanding of their emotions and assists them in identifying and describing those emotions. For example, say, "So you are pretty confused and angry by it all . . . " or "Am I correct in saying that you are frightened and intimidated by the process?"

4. Support
This communication technique expresses understanding, reassurance, and positive regard to let the other person know that he or she is not "in the boat alone." For example, say, "With your attitude, I know you'll do well . . . " or "I'm impressed with the progress you are making."

STRATEGY 3: RECOGNIZE THE UNIQUE CONTRIBUTIONS OF OUT-GROUP MEMBERS

Expectancy theory (Vroom, 1964) tells us that the first step in motivating others is to let workers know they are competent to do their jobs. Motivation builds when people know they are able to do the work. This is particularly true for out-group members. Out-group members become more motivated when a leader acknowledges their contributions to the larger group. All of us want to know that our contributions are legitimate and that others take us seriously. Out-group members want to believe that their ideas matter and that they are important to the group.

In many situations, it is common for out group members to believe others do not recognize their strengths. To address these concerns, it is important for a leader to identify out-group members' unique abilities and assets, and to integrate these into the group process. For example, if an out-group member suggests a radical but ultimately successful approach to accomplish a difficult task, the leader should express appreciation to the out-group member and let her or him know that the idea was creative and worthwhile. A leader needs to let out-group members know that what they do matters—that it is significant to the larger group.

Another example of a college class in which students had to do a service-learning project helps illustrate the importance of recognizing the unique contributions of out-group members. For their project, one team in this small group communication class chose to build a wheelchair ramp for an elderly woman in the community. In the initial stages of the project, morale in the group was down because one group member (Alissa) chose not to participate. Alissa said she was quite uncomfortable using hand tools, and she chose not to do manual labor. The other team members, who had done a lot of planning on the project, wanted to proceed without her help. As a result, Alissa felt rejected and soon became isolated from the group. Feeling disappointed with her group, Alissa began to criticize the purpose of the project and the personalities of the other team members.

At that point, one of the leaders of the group decided to start being more attentive to Alissa and what she was saying. After carefully listening to many of her concerns, the leader figured out that although Alissa could not work with her hands, she had two amazing talents: She was good with music, and she made wonderful lunches.

Once the leader found this out, things started to change in the group. Alissa started to participate. Her input into the construction of the ramp consisted of playing each group member's and the elderly woman's favorite music for 30 minutes while the other group members worked on the ramp. In addition, Alissa provided wonderful sandwiches and drinks that accommodated each of the group members' unique dietary interests. By the last day, Alissa felt so included by the group, and was so often praised for providing great food, that she decided to help with the manual labor: She began raking up trash around the ramp site with a smile on her face.

Although Alissa's talents had nothing to do directly with constructing a ramp, she made a real contribution to building a successful team. Everybody was included and useful in a community-building project that could have turned sour if one out-group member's talents had not been identified and utilized.

STRATEGY 4: HELP OUT-GROUP MEMBERS FEEL INCLUDED

William Schutz (1966) pointed out that, in small group situations, one of our strongest interpersonal needs is to know whether we belong to the group. Are we "in" or "out"? The very nature of out-groups implies that their members are on the sidelines and peripheral to the action. Out-group members do not feel as if they belong, are included, or are "in." Schutz suggested that people have a need to be connected to others. They want to be in a group, but not so much a part of the group that they lose their own identity. They want to belong, but do not want to belong so much that they lose their sense of self.

Although it is not always easy, a leader can help out-group members be more included. A leader can watch the communication cues given by out-group members and try to respond in appropriate ways. For example, if a person sits at the edge of the group, the leader can put the chairs in a circle and invite the person to sit in the circle. If a person does not follow the group norms (e.g., does not go outdoors with everyone else during breaks), the leader can personally invite the out-group member to join the others outside. Similarly, if a group member is very quiet and has not contributed, a leader can ask for that group member's opinion. Although there are many different ways to help out-group members to be included, the bottom line is that a leader needs to be sensitive to out-group members' needs and try to respond to them in ways that help the out-group members know that they are part of the larger group.

STRATEGY 5: CREATE A SPECIAL RELATIONSHIP WITH OUT-GROUP MEMBERS

The most well-known study on out-groups was conducted by a group of researchers who developed a theory called **Leader-Member Exchange Theory** (Dansereau, Graen, & Haga, 1975; Graen & Uhl-Bien, 1995). The major premise of this theory is that a leader should create a special relationship with each follower. An effective leader has a high-quality relationship with all group members; this results in out-group members becoming a part of the larger group.

Special relationships are built on good communication, respect, and trust. They are often initiated when a leader recognizes out-group members who are willing to step out of scripted roles and take on different responsibilities. In addition, special relationships can develop when a leader challenges out-group members to be engaged and to try new things. If an out-group member accepts these challenges and responsibilities, it is the first step in forging an improved relationship between the leader and the out-group member. The result is that the out-group member feels validated and more connected to everyone else in the group.

An example of how special relationships benefit out-group members can be seen in the following example. Margo Miller was the school nurse at Central High School. She was also the unofficial school counselor, social worker, conflict mediator, and all-around friend to students. Margo noticed that there were a number of very overweight students who were not in any of the groups at school. To address this situation, she began to invite some of these students and others to exercise with her at the track after school. For some of them, it was the first time they had ever taken part in an extracurricular school program. The students and Margo called themselves the Breakfast Club because, like the characters in the movie by the same name, they were a motley crew. At the end of the semester, the group sponsored a school-wide 5K run/walk that was well attended. One overweight girl who finished the 5K said that Margo and the Breakfast Club were the best thing that had ever happened to her. Clearly, it was the special relationships that Margo created with her students that allowed out-group students to become involved and feel good about their involvement in the high school community.

STRATEGY 6: GIVE OUT-GROUP MEMBERS A VOICE AND EMPOWER THEM TO ACT

Giving out-group members a voice lets them be on equal footing with other members of the group. It means the leader and the other group members give credence to the out-group members' ideas and actions. When out-group members have a voice, they know their interests are being recognized and that they can have an impact on the leader and the group. It is quite a remarkable process when a leader is confident enough in his or her own leadership to let out-group members express themselves and have a voice in the affairs of the group.

Empowering others to act means a leader allows out-group members to be more involved, independent, and responsible for their actions. It includes letting them participate in the workings of the group (e.g., planning, decision making). True empowerment requires that a leader relinquish some control, giving out-group members more control. This is why empowerment is such a challenging process for a leader. Finally, empowering others is one of the larger challenges of leadership, but it is also one of the challenges that offers the most benefits for members of the out-group.

CASE STUDY

Audio Link 8.2

Listen to a story about NUMMI.

The following case describes the efforts of a group of General Motors managers chosen to try to transform the organization. Although they were innovators and considered company insiders, they ended up as an out-group. Questions are provided at the end of the case that will help you analyze the case and explore the impacts, positive and negative, that out-groups can have for leaders.

NUMMI Commandos

They called them the NUMMI Commandos.

In 1982, General Motors picked 16 of its rising stars to help start NUMMI, New United Motor Manufacturing Inc., a joint venture between GM and Toyota. The two had much to learn from each other—Toyota wanted to learn to make cars in the United States, and GM, which was beginning to lose market share, needed to learn to make small, fuel-efficient cars. So, together, they created NUMMI in Fremont, California, at a shut-down GM auto plant.

Before NUMMI, the Fremont plant was one of the "worst plants in the industry" (Raine, 1986) with a militant union, high absenteeism, and alleged drug and alcohol abuse on the assembly line floor.

The cars produced by the facility were rife with mistakes. Despite these issues, in opening the new auto plant, NUMMI managers brought back 85% of the former Fremont plant workforce. But it wasn't business as usual (Coloma, 2008).

The new management team decided to fly the plant workers, in groups of 30, to Japan for two weeks of training in the Toyota Production System (TPS). The Japanese system was a radical change: It emphasized the team concept, with groups of four or five employees working together, switching jobs every few hours to lessen the monotony and helping one another out. But the most profound change of all was the andon cord: a dangling rope that was pulled to stop the line if there was a problem. When the andon cord was pulled, team leaders would respond first to solve the problem. If they couldn't, the line was shut down until the problem was resolved. "The line could never stop at GM," says one GM worker. "If you saw a problem and stopped the line, you were fired."

NUMMI was quickly successful. Within three months of its start, the plant was producing cars with quality rates rivaling those of cars made in Japan. Now it was up to the Commandos to spread that success and the lessons they learned within the rest of the GM plants around the country. "We were ready; we were fired up; we were going to change the world," says Steve Berra, a committed Commando.

Video Link 8.1
Watch a NUMMI employee.

But it didn't quite work out that way. GM plant managers from everywhere were brought in to visit NUMMI. Instead of seeing opportunities for improvement, many of these managers saw the changes as a threat, adopting attitudes of "It won't work in my plant." Implementing TPS within GM would mean more cars being produced by fewer workers, and while that greatly appealed to top executives, it rankled the rank and file.

The Commandos had their first opportunity to revamp a plant in neighboring Van Nuys, California. They shut down the plant for two weeks to train management and workers, but encountered strong resistance. The NUMMI methods were challenged and not accepted. The team concept went against union members' deeply ingrained "workers versus management" mentality. In addition, because all team members shared jobs, the seniority that union members had come to covet would become nonexistent.

The resistance wasn't just from union members: Managers, upon learning that they would have to share their cafeteria and parking lot with nonmanagement workers, threatened to quit en masse.

The NUMMI Commandos found those same entrenched, defensive bureaucracies everywhere they turned. They were trying to change the biggest corporation in the world, which really was a collection of "mini empires"—individual car companies like Oldsmobile, Chevrolet, and Buick, each with its own leadership and way of doing things.

Some Commandos have said that the biggest obstacle they faced was the lack of support from above. Although they were considered by many to be the company's future, those at the top didn't seem to know what to do with them or with the lessons from NUMMI. Commandos were told after NUMMI was up and running that they would be deployed elsewhere within the organization to implement the new methods, but were left at NUMMI waiting for reassignments that never came.

In 1991, a recession hit, car sales slumped, and GM lost $20 million. The company's board purged managers, and Jack Smith, who had negotiated with Toyota to start up NUMMI, took over as CEO.

(Continued)

(Continued)

The Commandos finally felt they had a champion in the corner office. But even with clear marching orders from above to change, the rest of GM didn't know how to start. Plant managers still had the power to run the plants as they wanted. One factory manager told a Commando to leave his facility because he wasn't "needed." Another wanted to make his plant "look like NUMMI" by having someone take pictures of the NUMMI plant and then copying everything he saw (Langfitt, 2010).

"You can't copy employee motivation and good relations between workers and management. You can't take a picture of that," one Commando said. "We spent more time trying to convince the plant leadership than on implementation of the system."

Commandos found that to succeed, they had to leave the United States, heading to GM plants in Brazil and Germany. NUMMI was implemented in Brazil in 24 months and soon became the most profitable GM plant.

It took 15 years, but GM slowly started to evolve and implement the lessons from NUMMI across the organization. By 2005, GM developed the Global Manufacturing System in all its plants. Quality improved considerably. But the change didn't come soon enough. In 2009, GM became the largest industrial bankruptcy in history, with $172.81 billion in debt and requiring a government bailout.

One of the Commandos, Mark Hogan, believes that if GM had adopted NUMMI company-wide earlier, the outcome would have been different. "If they had implemented it across the board, it would have saved GM, because the quality and productivity changes would have been so profound," he says. "If they had embraced and adopted the team concept in an honest way, it would have changed everything."

1. Whom would you consider the out-group in this case study? Why did this out-group form?

2. Did this out-group have a negative effect on others? How did others treat the members of the out-group?

3. What *strategies* for responding to out-groups did GM's leaders use with the NUMMI Commandos?

4. How would GM be different today if the company had listened to the NUMMI Commandos?

Summary

In today's society, out-groups are a common occurrence whenever people come together to solve a problem or accomplish a task. In general, the term *out-group* refers to those people in a group who do not sense that they are a part of the larger group. Out-group members are usually people who feel disconnected, unaccepted, discriminated against, or powerless.

Out-groups form for many reasons. Some form because people are in opposition to the larger group. Others form because individuals in a group cannot identify with the larger group or cannot embrace the larger group's reality. Sometimes they form because people feel excluded or because out-group members lack communication and social skills.

Regardless of why they form, the negative impact of out-groups can be substantial. We need to be concerned about out-groups because they run counter to building community and have a negative impact on group synergy. Furthermore, out-group members do not receive the respect they deserve from those in the "in-group."

There are several specific strategies that a leader can use to respond effectively to out-group members. A leader needs to listen to out-group members, show empathy, recognize their unique contributions, help out-group members become included, create a special relationship with out-group members, give out-group members a voice, and empower them to act. A leader who uses these strategies will be more successful in his or her encounters with out-groups, and will be a more effective group leader.

 Go to **http://www.sagepub.com/northouscintro2c/** *for additional exercises and study resources. Select Chapter 8, Listening to Out-Group Members, for chapter specific activities.*

Glossary Terms

empathy   158

listening   157

social identity theory   153

out-group   152

Leader-Member Exchange Theory   161

References

Abrams, D., Frings, D., & Randsley de Moura, G. (2005). Group identity and self-definition. In S. A. Wheelan (Ed.), *Handbook of group research and practice* (pp. 329–350). London: Sage.

Beauchamp, T. L., & Bowie, N. E. (1988). *Ethical theory and business* (3rd ed.). Englewood Cliffs, NJ: Prentice Hall.

Coloma, S. (2008, November 28). Doing right in Detroit. *Business World,* p. S1.

Dansereau, F., Graen, G. G., & Haga, W. (1975). A vertical dyad linkage approach to leadership in formal organizations. *Organizational Behavior and Human Performance, 13,* 46–78.

Graen, G. B., & Uhl-Bien, M. (1995). Relationship-based approach to leadership: Development of leader–member exchange (LMX) theory of leadership more than 25 years: Applying a multi-level, multi-domain perspective. *Leadership Quarterly, 6*(2), 219–247.

Hogg, M. A., & Abrams, D. (1988). *Social identifications: A social psychology of intergroup relations and group processes.* London: Routledge.

Langfitt, F. (Writer). (2010, March 26). NUMMI [Episode 403]. In I. Glass (Executive Producer), *This American Life.* Chicago: Chicago Public Media.

Raine, G. (1986, March 31). Building cars Japan's way. *Newsweek,* p. 43.

Schutz, W. (1966). *The interpersonal underworld.* Palo Alto, CA: Science & Behavior Books.

Tajfel, H., & Turner, J. C. (1979). An integrative theory of intergroup conflict. In S. Worchel & W. G. Austin (Eds.), *The social psychology of intergroup relations* (pp. 33–47). Monterey, CA: Brooks-Cole.

Tajfel, H., & Turner, J. C. (1986). The social identity theory of intergroup behavior. In S. Worchel and L. W. Austin (Eds.), *Psychology of intergroup relations* (pp. 7–24). Chicago: Nelson-Hall.

Vroom, V. H. (1964). *Work and motivation.* New York: Wiley.

8.1   Responding to Members of the Out-Group Questionnaire

 Visit www.sagepub.com/northouseintro2e for downloadable versions of these questionnaires

Purpose

1. To identify your attitudes toward out-group members
2. To explore how you, as a leader, respond to members of the out-group

Directions

1. Place yourself in the role of a leader when responding to this questionnaire.
2. For each of the statements below, circle the number that indicates the degree to which you agree or disagree.

Statements	Strongly disagree	Disagree	Neutral	Agree	Strongly agree
1. If some group members do not fit in with the rest of the group, I usually try to include them.	1	2	3	4	5
2. I become irritated when some group members act stubborn (or obstinate) with the majority of the group.	1	2	3	4	5
3. Building a sense of group unity with people who think differently than I is essential to what I do as a leader.	1	2	3	4	5
4. I am bothered when some individuals in the group bring up unusual ideas that hinder or block the progress of the rest of the group.	1	2	3	4	5
5. If some group members cannot agree with the majority of the group, I usually give them special attention.	1	2	3	4	5
6. Sometimes I ignore individuals who show little interest in group meetings.	1	2	3	4	5
7. When making a group decision, I always try to include the interests of members who have different points of view.	1	2	3	4	5
8. Trying to reach consensus (complete agreement) with out-group members is often a waste of time.	1	2	3	4	5
9. I place a high priority on encouraging everyone in the group to listen to the minority point of view.	1	2	3	4	5
10. When differences exist between group members, I usually call for a vote to keep the group moving forward.	1	2	3	4	5
11. Listening to individuals with extreme (or radical) ideas is valuable to my leadership.	1	2	3	4	5

Statements	Strongly disagree	Disagree	Neutral	Agree	Strongly agree
12. When a group member feels left out, it is usually his or her own fault.	1	2	3	4	5
13. I give special attention to out-group members (i.e., individuals who feel left out of the group).	1	2	3	4	5
14. I find certain group members frustrating when they bring up issues that conflict with what the rest of the group wants to do.	1	2	3	4	5

Scoring

1. Sum the even-numbered items, but reverse the score value of your responses (i.e., change 1 to 5, 2 to 4, 4 to 2, and 5 to 1, with 3 remaining unchanged).

2. Sum the responses of the odd-numbered items and the converted values of the even-numbered items. This total is your leadership out-group score.

Total Score

Out-group score: _____

Scoring Interpretation

This questionnaire is designed to measure your response to out-group members.

- A high score on the questionnaire indicates that you try to help out-group members feel included and become a part of the whole group. You are likely to listen to people with different points of view and to know that hearing a minority position is often valuable in effective group work.

- An average score on the questionnaire indicates that you are moderately interested in including out-group members in the group. Although interested in including them, you do not make out-group members' concerns a priority in your leadership. You may think of out-group members as having brought their out-group behavior on themselves. If they seek you out, you probably will work with them when you can.

- A low score on the questionnaire indicates you most likely have little interest in helping out-group members become a part of the larger group. You may become irritated and bothered when out-group members' behaviors hinder the majority or progress of the larger group. Because you see helping the out-group members as an ineffective use of your time, you are likely to ignore them and make decisions to move the group forward without their input.

    If your score is 57–70, you are in the very high range.

    If your score is 50–56, you are in the high range.

    If your score is 45–49, you are in the average range.

    If your score is 38–44, you are in the low range.

    If your score is 10–37, you are in the very low range.

8.2   Observational Exercise

 Visit www.sagepub.com/northouseintro2e for downloadable versions of these questionnaires

Out-Groups

Purpose

1. To learn to recognize out-groups and how they form
2. To understand the role of out-groups in the leadership process

Directions

1. Your task in this exercise is to identify, observe, and analyze an actual *out-group*. This can be an out-group at your place of employment, in an informal group, in a class group, in a community group, or on a sports team.

2. For each of the questions below, write down what you observed in your experiences with out-groups.

    Name of group: _____

    Identify and *describe* a group in which you observed an out-group.

    Observations of out-group members' actions:

    Observations of the leader's actions:

Questions

1. What is the identity of out-group members? How do they see themselves?

2. How were out-group members treated by the other members in the group?

3. What is the most challenging aspect of trying to deal with this out-group?

4. What does the leader need to do to integrate the out-group members into the larger group?

8.3   Reflection and Action Worksheet

 Visit www.sagepub.com/northouseintro2e for downloadable versions of these questionnaires

Out-Groups

Reflection

1. Based on the score you received on the Responding to Members of the Out-Group Questionnaire, how would you describe your attitude toward out-group members? Discuss.

2. As we discussed in this chapter, out-groups run counter to building community in groups. How important do you think it is for a leader to build community? Discuss.

3. One way to engage out-group members is to *empower* them. How do you see your own competencies in the area of empowerment? What keeps you from empowering others? Discuss.

Action

1. Using items from the Responding to Members of the Out-Group Questionnaire as your criteria, list three specific actions you could take that would show sensitivity to and tolerance of out-group members.

2. In the last section of this chapter, six strategies for responding to out-group members were discussed. Rank these strategies from strongest to weakest with regard to how you use them in your own leadership. Describe specifically what you could do to become more effective in all six strategies.

3. Imagine for a moment that you are doing a class project with six other students. The group has decided by taking a vote to do a fund-raising campaign for the local Big Brothers Big Sisters program. Two people in the group have said they are not enthused about the project and would rather do something for an organization like Habitat for Humanity. While the group is moving forward with the agreed-upon project, the two people who did not like the idea have started missing meetings, and when they do attend, they have been very negative. As a leader, list five specific actions you could take to assist and engage this out-group.

Before you begin reading . . .

Complete the *Conflict Style Questionnaire*, which you will find on pp. 203–205. As you read the chapter, consider your results on the questionnaire.

Handling Conflict

9

C onflict is inevitable in groups and organizations, and it presents both a challenge and a true opportunity for every leader. In the well-known book, *Getting to Yes,* Fisher and Ury (1981) contend that handling conflict is a daily occurrence for all of us. People differ, and because they do, they need to negotiate with others about their differences (pp. xi–xii). *Getting to Yes* asserts that mutual agreement is possible in any conflict situation — if people are willing to negotiate in authentic ways.

When we think of conflict in simple terms, we think of a struggle between people, groups, organizations, cultures, or nations. Conflict involves opposing forces, pulling in different directions. Many people believe that conflict is disruptive, causes stress, and should be avoided.

As we stated before in Chapter 5, while conflict can be uncomfortable, it is not unhealthy, nor is it necessarily bad. Conflict will always be present in leadership situations, and surprisingly, it often produces positive change. The important question we address in this chapter is not "How can we *avoid* conflict and *eliminate* change?" but rather "How can we *manage* conflict and produce *positive* change?" When leaders handle conflict effectively, problem solving increases, interpersonal relationships become stronger, and stress surrounding the conflict decreases.

Communication plays a central role in handling conflict. Conflict is an interactive process between two or more parties that requires effective human interaction. By communicating effectively, leaders and followers can successfully resolve conflicts to bring positive results.

This chapter will emphasize ways to handle conflict. First, we will define conflict and describe the role communication plays in conflict. Next, we will discuss different kinds of conflict, followed by an exploration of Fisher and Ury's (1981) ideas about effective negotiation as well as other communication strategies that help resolve conflict. The final part of the chapter examines styles of approaching conflict and the pros and cons of these styles.

► CONFLICT DEFINED

Conflict has been studied from multiple perspectives, including *intra*personal, *inter*personal, and societal. Intrapersonal conflict refers to the discord that occurs *within* an individual. It is often studied by psychologists and personality theorists who are interested in the dynamics of personality and factors that predispose people to inner conflicts. Interpersonal conflict refers to the disputes that arise *between individuals*. This is the type of conflict we focus on when we discuss conflict in organizations. Societal conflict refers to clashes *between societies and nations*. Studies in this field focus on the causes of international conflicts, war, and peace. The continuing crisis between the Israelis and the Palestinians is a good example of social conflict. This chapter focuses on conflict as an interpersonal process that plays a critical role in effective leadership.

The following definition, based on the work of Wilmot and Hocker (2011, p. 11) best describes conflict. **Conflict** *is a felt struggle between two or more interdependent individuals over perceived incompatible differences in beliefs, values, and goals, or over differences in desires for esteem, control, and connectedness.* This definition emphasizes several unique aspects of conflict (Wilmot & Hocker, 2011).

Journal Link 9.1
Read more about intrapersonal conflict.

First, conflict is a *struggle;* it is the result of opposing forces coming together. For example, there is conflict when a leader and a senior-level employee oppose each other on whether or not all employees must work on weekends. Similarly, conflict occurs when a school principal and a parent disagree on the type of sex education program that should be adopted in a school system. In short, conflict involves a clash between opposing parties.

Second, there needs to be an element of *interdependence* between parties for conflict to take place. If leaders could function entirely independently of each other and their subordinates, there would be no reason for conflict. Everyone could do their own work, and there would be no areas of contention. However, leaders do not work in isolation. Leaders need followers, and followers need leaders. This interdependence sets up an environment in which conflict is more likely.

When two parties are interdependent, they are forced to deal with questions such as "How much influence do I want in this relationship?" and "How much influence am I willing to accept from the other party?" Because of our interdependence, questions such as these cannot be avoided. In fact, Wilmot and Hocker (2011) contend that these questions permeate most conflicts.

Third, conflict always contains an *affective* element, the "felt" part of the definition. Conflict is an emotional process that involves the arousal of feelings in both parties of the conflict (Brown & Keller, 1979). When our beliefs or values on a highly charged issue (e.g., the right to strike) are challenged, we become upset and feel it is important to defend our position. When our feelings clash with others' feelings, we are in conflict.

The primary emotions connected with conflict are not always anger or hostility. Rather, an array of emotions can accompany conflict. Hocker and Wilmot (1995) found that many people report feeling lonely, sad, or disconnected during conflict. For some, interpersonal conflict creates feelings of abandonment—that their human bond to others has been broken. Feelings such as these often produce the discomfort that surrounds conflict.

Video Link 9.1
Watch suggestions for ending conflict.

Fourth, conflict involves *differences* between individuals that are perceived to be incompatible. Conflict can result from differences in individuals' beliefs, values, and goals, or from differences in individuals' desires for control, status, and connectedness. The opportunities for conflict are endless because each of us is unique with particular sets of interests and ideas. These differences are a constant breeding ground for conflict.

In summary, these four elements—struggle, interdependence, feelings, and differences—are critical ingredients of interpersonal conflict. To further understand the intricacies of managing conflict, we'll look at the role of communication in conflict and examine two major kinds of conflict.

► COMMUNICATION AND CONFLICT

When conflict exists in leadership situations, it is recognized and expressed through communication. Communication is the means that people use to express their disagreements or differences. Communication also provides the avenue by which conflicts can be successfully resolved, or worsened, producing negative results.

Journal Link 9.2
Read more about communication and conflict.

To understand conflict, we need to understand communication. When human communication takes place, it occurs on two levels. One level can be characterized as the *content dimension* and the other as the *relationship dimension* (Watzlawick, Beavin, & Jackson, 1967). The **content dimension** of communication involves the objective, observable aspects such as money, weather, and land; the **relationship dimension** refers to the participants' perceptions of their connection to one another. In human communication, these two dimensions are always bound together.

To illustrate the two dimensions, consider the following hypothetical statement made by a supervisor to a subordinate: "Please stop texting at work." The *content* dimension of this message refers to rules and what the supervisor wants the subordinate to do. The *relationship* dimension of this message refers to how the supervisor and the subordinate are affiliated—to the supervisor's authority in relation to the subordinate, the supervisor's attitude toward the subordinate, the subordinate's attitude toward the supervisor, and their feelings about one another. It is the relationship dimension that implicitly suggests how the content dimension should be interpreted, since the content alone can be interpreted in different ways. The exact meaning of the message to the supervisor and subordinate is interpreted as a result of their interaction. If a positive relationship exists between the supervisor and the subordinate, then the content "please stop texting at work" will probably be interpreted by the subordinate as a friendly request by a supervisor who is honestly concerned about the subordinate's job performance. However, if the relationship between the supervisor and the subordinate is superficial or strained, the subordinate may interpret the content of the message as a rigid directive, delivered by a supervisor who enjoys giving orders. This example illustrates how the meanings of messages are not in words alone but in individuals' interpretations of the messages in light of their relationships.

KINDS OF CONFLICT ◄

The content and relationship dimensions provide a lens for looking at conflict. As illustrated in Figure 9.1, there are two major kinds of conflict: conflict over content issues and conflict over relationship issues. Both kinds of conflict are prevalent in groups and organizational settings.

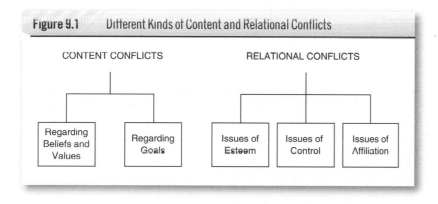

Figure 9.1   Different Kinds of Content and Relational Conflicts

CONFLICT ON THE CONTENT LEVEL

Content conflicts involve struggles between leaders and others who differ on issues such as policies and procedures. Debating with someone about the advantages or disadvantages of a particular rule is a familiar occurrence in most organizations. Sometimes these debates can be very heated (e.g., an argument between two employees about surfing the Internet while working). These disagreements are considered conflicts on the content level when they center on differences in (1) beliefs and values or (2) goals and ways to reach those goals.

Conflict Regarding Beliefs and Values

Each of us has a unique system of beliefs and values that constitutes a basic philosophy of life. We have had different family situations as well as educational and work experiences. When we communicate with others, we become aware that others' viewpoints are often very different from our own. If we perceive what another person is communicating as incompatible with our own viewpoint, a conflict in beliefs or values is likely to occur.

Conflicts arising from differences in beliefs can be illustrated in several ways. For example, members of PETA (People for the Ethical Treatment of Animals) are in conflict with researchers in the pharmaceutical industry who believe strongly in using animals to test new drugs. Another example of a conflict of beliefs can occur when teachers or nurses believe they have the right to strike because of unfair working conditions, while others feel that these kinds of employees should not be allowed to withhold services for any reason. In each of these examples, conflict occurs because one individual feels that his or her *beliefs* are incompatible with the position taken by another individual on the issue.

Conflicts can also occur between people because they have different *values*. When one person's values come into conflict with another's, it can create a difficult and challenging situation. To illustrate, consider the following example of an issue between Emily, a first-generation college student, and her mother. At the beginning of her senior year, Emily asked her mother if she could have a car to get around campus and to get back and forth to work. In order to pay for the car, Emily says she will take fewer credits, work more often at her part-time job, and postpone her graduation date to the following year. Emily is confident that she will graduate and thinks it is "no big deal" to extend her studies for a fifth year. However, Emily's mother does not feel the same. She doesn't want Emily to have a car until after she graduates. She thinks the car will be a major distraction and get in the way of Emily's studies. Emily is the first person in her family to get a college degree, and it is extremely important to her mother that Emily graduates on time. Deep down, her mother is afraid that the longer Emily goes to school, the more student loan debt Emily will have to pay back when she finishes.

The value conflict between Emily and her mother involves Emily's desire to have a car. In this case, both individuals are highly interdependent of one another: To carry out her decision to get a car, Emily needs her mother's agreement; to have her daughter graduate in four years, Emily's mother needs cooperation from Emily. Both individuals perceive the other's values as incompatible with their own, and this makes conflict inevitable. Clearly, the conflict between Emily and her mother requires interpersonal communication about their different values and how these differences affect their relationship.

Conflict Regarding Goals

A second common type of content-related conflict occurs in situations where individuals have different *goals* (see Figure 9.1). Researchers have identified two types of conflict that occur regarding group goals: (1) procedural conflict and (2) substantive conflict (Knutson, Lashbrook, & Heemer, 1976).

Procedural conflict refers to differences between individuals with regard to the approach they wish to take in attempting to reach a goal. In essence, it is conflict over the best means to an agreed-upon goal; it is not about what goal to achieve. Procedural conflicts can be observed in many situations such as determining how to best conduct job interviews, choose a method for identifying new sales territories, or spend advertising dollars. In each instance, conflict can occur when individuals do not agree on how to achieve a goal.

Substantive conflict occurs when individuals differ with regard to the substance of the goal itself, or what the goal should be. For example, two board members of a nonprofit human service agency may have very different views regarding the strategies and scope of a fund-raising campaign. Similarly, two owners of a small business may strongly disagree about whether or not to offer their part-time employees health care benefits. On the international level, in Afghanistan, the Taliban and those not members of the Taliban have different perspectives on whether or not girls should be educated. These illustrations by no means exhaust all the possible examples of substantive conflict; however, they point out that conflict can occur as a result of two or more parties disagreeing on what the goal or goals of a group or an organization should be.

CONFLICT ON THE RELATIONAL LEVEL

Have you ever heard someone say, "I don't seem to get along with her [or him]; we have a personality clash"? The phrase *personality clash* is another way of describing a conflict on the relational level. Sometimes we do not get along with another person, not because of *what* we are talking about (conflict over content issues) but because of *how* we are talking about it. **Relational conflict** refers to the differences we feel between ourselves and others concerning how we relate to each other. For example, at a staff meeting, a manager interrupts employees and talks to them in a critical tone. The employees begin texting on their phones, ignoring the manager. A conflict erupts because both the manager and the employees feel unheard and disrespected. It is typically caused neither by one person nor the other, but arises in their relationship. Relational conflict is usually related to incompatible differences between individuals over issues of (1) esteem, (2) control, and (3) affiliation (see Figure 9.1).

Relational Conflict and Issues of Esteem

The need for esteem and recognition has been identified by Maslow (1970) as one of the major needs in the hierarchy of human needs. Each of us has needs for esteem—we want to feel significant, useful, and worthwhile. We desire to have an effect on our surroundings and to be perceived by others as worthy of their respect. We attempt to satisfy our esteem needs through what we do and how we act, particularly in how we behave in our relationships with our coworkers.

Handbook Link 9.1
Read about
workgroup conflict.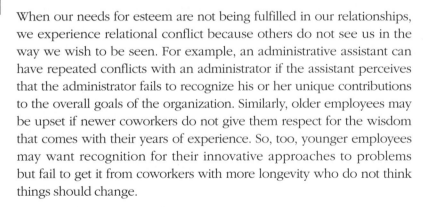

When our needs for esteem are not being fulfilled in our relationships, we experience relational conflict because others do not see us in the way we wish to be seen. For example, an administrative assistant can have repeated conflicts with an administrator if the assistant perceives that the administrator fails to recognize his or her unique contributions to the overall goals of the organization. Similarly, older employees may be upset if newer coworkers do not give them respect for the wisdom that comes with their years of experience. So, too, younger employees may want recognition for their innovative approaches to problems but fail to get it from coworkers with more longevity who do not think things should change.

At the same time that we want our own esteem needs satisfied, others want their esteem needs satisfied as well. If the supply of respect we can give each other seems limited (or scarce), then our needs for esteem will clash. We will see the other person's needs for esteem as competing with our own or taking that limited resource away from us. To illustrate, consider a staff meeting in which two employees are actively contributing insightful ideas and suggestions. If one of the employees is given recognition for her input but the other is not, conflict may result. As this conflict escalates, the effectiveness of their working relationship and the quality of their communication may diminish. When the amount of available esteem (validation from others) seems scarce, a clash develops.

All of us are human and want to be recognized for the contributions we make to our work and our community. When we believe we're not being recognized or receiving our "fair share," we feel slighted and conflicted on the relational level with others.

Relational Conflict and Issues of Control

Struggles over issues of control are very common in interpersonal conflict. Each one of us desires to have an impact on others and the situations that surround us. Having control, in effect, increases our feelings of potency about our actions and minimizes our feelings of helplessness. Control allows us to feel competent about ourselves. However, when we see others as hindering us, or limiting our control, interpersonal conflict often ensues.

Interpersonal conflict occurs when a person's needs for control are incompatible with another's needs for control. In a given situation, each of us seeks different levels of control. Some people like to have a great deal, while others are satisfied (and sometimes even more content) with only a little. In addition, our needs for control may vary from one time to another. For example, there are times when a person's need to control others or events is very high; at other times, this same person may prefer that others take charge. Relational conflict over control issues develops when there is a clash between the needs for control that one person has at a given time (high or low) and the needs for control that others have at that same time (high or low). If, for example, a friend's need to make decisions about weekend plans is compatible with yours, no conflict will take place; however, if both of you want to control the weekend planning and your individual interests are different, then you will soon find yourselves in conflict. As struggles for control ensue, the communication among the participants may become negative and challenging as each person tries to gain control over the other or undermine the other's control.

A graphic example of a conflict over relational control is provided in the struggle between Lauren Smith, a college sophomore, and her parents, regarding what she will do on spring break. Lauren wants to go to Cancún, Mexico, with some friends to relax from the pressures of school. Her parents do not want her to go. Lauren thinks she deserves to go because she is doing well in her classes. Her parents think spring break in Cancún is just a "big party" and nothing good will come of it. As another option, her parents offer to pay Lauren's expenses to go on an alternative spring break to clean up an oil spill in the Gulf of Mexico. Lauren is adamant that she "is going" to Cancún. Her parents, who pay her tuition, threaten that if she goes to Cancún, they will no longer pay for college.

Clearly, in the above example, both parties want to have control over the outcome. Lauren wants to be in charge of her own life and make the decisions about what she does or does not do. At the same time, her parents want to direct her into doing what they think is best for her. Lauren and her parents are interdependent and need each other, but they are conflicted because they each feel that the other is interfering with their needs for control of what Lauren does on spring break.

Conflicts over control are common in leadership situations. Like the parents in the above example, the role of leader brings with it a certain inherent level of control and responsibility. When leaders clash with one another over control or when control issues exist between leaders and subordinates, interpersonal conflicts occur. Later in this chapter, we present some conflict management strategies that are particularly helpful in coping with relational conflicts that arise from issues of control.

Relational Conflict and Issues of Affiliation

In addition to wanting relational control, each of us has a need to feel included in our relationships, to be liked, and to receive affection (Schutz, 1966). If our needs for closeness are not satisfied in our relationships, we feel frustrated and experience feelings of conflict. Of course, some people like to be very involved and very close in their relationships, while others prefer less involvement and more distance. In any case, when others behave in ways that are incompatible with our own desires for warmth and affection, feelings of conflict emerge.

Relational conflict over affiliation issues is illustrated in the following example of a football coach, Terry Jones, and one of his players, Danny Larson. Danny, a starting quarterback, developed a strong relationship with Coach Jones during his junior year in high school. Throughout the year, Danny and Coach Jones had many highly productive conversations inside and outside of school about how to improve the football program. In the summer, the coach employed Danny in his painting business, and they worked side-by-side on a first-name basis. Both Danny and Terry liked working together and grew to know each other quite well. However, when football practice started in the fall, difficulties emerged between the two. During the first weeks of practice, Danny acted like Coach Jones was his best buddy. He called him Terry rather than Coach Jones, and he resisted the player-coach role. As Coach Jones attempted to withdraw from his summer relationship with Danny and take on his legitimate responsibilities as coach, Danny experienced a sense of loss of closeness and warmth. In this situation Danny felt rejection or a loss of affiliation, and this created a relational conflict.

Relational conflicts—whether they are over esteem, control, or affiliation—are seldom overt. Due to the subtle nature of these conflicts, they are often not easy to recognize or address. Even when they are recognized, relational conflicts are often ignored because it is difficult for many individuals to openly communicate that they want more recognition, control, or affiliation.

According to communication theorists, relational issues are inextricably bound to content issues (Watzlawick et al., 1967). This means that relational conflicts will often surface during the discussion of content issues. For example, what may at first appear to be a conflict between two leaders regarding the *content* of a new employee fitness program may really be a struggle over which one of the leaders will ultimately receive credit for developing the program. As we mentioned, relational conflicts are complex and not easily resolved. However, when relational conflicts are expressed and confronted, it can significantly enhance the overall resolution process.

Communication remains central to managing different kinds of conflict in organizations. Leaders who are able to keep channels of communication open with others will have a greater chance of understanding others' beliefs, values, and needs for esteem, control, and affiliation. With increased understanding, many of these common kinds of conflict will seem less difficult to resolve and more open to negotiation.

We now turn to Fisher and Ury's (1981) approach to communicating about conflict. It is one of the most recognized approaches of conflict negotiation in the world.

▶ FISHER AND URY APPROACH TO CONFLICT

Derived from studies conducted by the Harvard Negotiation Project, Fisher and Ury (1981) provide a straightforward, step-by-step method for negotiating conflicts. This method, called **principled negotiation**, emphasizes deciding issues on their merits rather than through competitive haggling or through excessive accommodation. Principled negotiation shows you how to obtain your fair share decently and without having others take advantage of you (Fisher & Ury, 1981).

Video Link 9.2

Watch William Ury speak.

As illustrated in Figure 9.2, the Fisher and Ury negotiation method comprises four principles. Each principle directly focuses on one of the four basic elements of negotiation: people, interests, options, and criteria. Effective leaders frequently understand and utilize these four principles in conflict situations.

Figure 9.2	Fisher and Ury's Method of Principled Negotiation		
Separate the **People** from the Problem	Focus on **Interests,** Not Positions	Invent **Options** for Mutual Gains	Insist on Using Objective **Criteria**

PRINCIPLE 1: SEPARATE THE PEOPLE FROM THE PROBLEM

In the previous section of this chapter, we discussed how conflict has a content dimension and a relationship dimension. Similarly, Fisher and Ury (1981) contend that conflicts comprise a *problem factor* and a *people factor*. To be effective in dealing with conflicts, both of these factors need to be addressed. In particular, Fisher and Ury argue that the people factor needs to be separated out from the problem factor.

Separating people from the problem during conflict is not easy because they are entangled. For example, if a leader and her subordinate are in a heated conversation over the subordinate's negative performance review, it is very difficult for the leader and the subordinate to discuss the review without addressing their relationship and personal roles.

Our personalities, beliefs, and values are intricately interwoven with our conflicts. However, principled negotiation says that people and the problem need to be disentangled.

By separating people from the problem, we enable ourselves to recognize others' uniqueness. Everyone has his or her own distinct thoughts and feelings in different situations. Because we all perceive the world differently, we have diverse emotional responses to conflict. By focusing directly on the *people aspect* of the problem, we become more aware of the personalities and idiosyncratic needs of those with whom we are in conflict.

Perhaps most important, separating people from the problem encourages us to be attentive to our relationships during conflict. Conflicts can strain relationships, so it is important to be cognizant of how one's behavior during conflict affects the other party. Rather than "beat up" on each other, it is useful to work together, alongside each other, and mutually confront the problem. When we separate people from the problem, we are more inclined to work with others to solve problems. Fisher and Ury (1981) suggest that people in conflict need to "see themselves as working side by side, attacking the problem, not each other" (p. 11). Separating the people from the problem allows us to nurture and strengthen our relationships rather than destroy them.

Consider the earlier example of the supervisor and employee conflict over the negative performance review. In order to separate the people from the problem, both the supervisor and the employee need to discuss the negative review by focusing on performance criteria and behavior issues rather than personal attributes. The review indicated that the employee didn't meet performance objectives—the boss could say, "You didn't get your work done," but in separating the people from the problem, the boss would instead explain how the employee was unable to meet the requirements ("The number of contacts you made was below the required number"). The employee, on the other hand, may feel the objectives were unrealistic. Rather than telling her boss it was his fault ("You set unobtainable objectives"), the employee should make her point by providing facts about how these standards are not realistic ("The economic downturn wasn't considered when these objectives were developed"). By focusing on the problem in this way, the employer and the employee are maintaining their relationship but also confronting directly the performance review issues.

PRINCIPLE 2: FOCUS ON INTERESTS, NOT POSITIONS

The second principle, which is perhaps the most well known, emphasizes that parties in a conflict must focus on interests and not just positions. *Positions* represent our stand or perspective in a particular conflict. *Interests* represent what is behind our positions. Stated another way, positions are the opposing points of view in a conflict while interests refer to the relevant needs and values of the people involved. Fisher and Ury (1981) suggest that "your position is something you have decided upon. Your interests are what caused you to so decide" (p. 42).

Focusing on interests expands conflict negotiation by encouraging individuals to explore the unique underpinnings of the conflict. To identify interests behind a position, it is useful to look at the basic concerns that motivate people. Some of our concerns include needs for security, belonging, recognition, control, and economic well-being (Fisher & Ury, 1981). Being attentive to these basic needs and helping people satisfy them is central to conflict negotiation.

Concentrating on interests also helps opposing parties to address the "real" conflict. Addressing both interests *and* positions helps to make conflict negotiation more authentic. In his model of authentic leadership, Robert Terry (1993) advocates that leaders have a moral responsibility to ask the question "*What is really, really going on* in a conflict situation, and what are we going to do about it?" Unless leaders know what truly is going on, their actions will be inappropriate and can have serious consequences. Focusing on interests is a good way to find out what is at the heart of a conflict.

Consider the following conflict between a college professor, Dr. Smith, and his student, Erin Crow, regarding class attendance. Dr. Smith has a mandatory attendance policy, but allows for two absences during the semester. A student's grade is lowered 10% for each additional absence. Erin is a very bright student who has gotten As on all of her papers and tests. However, she has five absences and does not want to be penalized. Based on the attendance policy, Dr. Smith would lower Erin's grade 30%, from an A to a C. Erin's position in this conflict is that she shouldn't be penalized because she has done excellent work despite her absences. Dr. Smith's position is that the attendance policy is legitimate and Erin's grade should be lowered.

In this example, it is worthwhile to explore some of the interests that form the basis for each position. For example, Erin is very reticent and does not like to participate in class. She is carrying 18 credit hours and works two part-time jobs. On the other hand, Dr. Smith is a popular professor who has twice received university-wide outstanding teaching awards. He has 20 years of experience and has a strong publication record in the area of classroom learning methodology. In addition, Dr. Smith has a need to be liked by students, and does not like to be challenged.

Given their interests, it is easy to see that the conflict between Erin and Dr. Smith over class attendance is more complex than meets the eye. If this conflict were to be settled by negotiating positions alone, the resolution would be relatively straightforward, and Erin would most likely be penalized, leaving both parties unsatisfied. However, if the interests of both Erin and Dr. Smith were fully explored, the probability of a mutually agreeable outcome would be far more likely. Dr. Smith is likely to recognize that Erin has numerous obligations that impact her attendance but are important for her economic well-being and security. On the other hand, Erin may come to realize that Dr. Smith is an exemplary teacher who fosters cohesiveness among students by expecting them to show up and participate in class. His needs for control and recognition are challenged by Erin's attendance and lack of class participation.

The challenge for Erin and Dr. Smith is to focus on their interests, communicate them to each other, and remain open to unique approaches to resolving their conflict.

PRINCIPLE 3: INVENT OPTIONS FOR MUTUAL GAINS

The third strategy in effective conflict negotiation presented by Fisher and Ury (1981) is to invent options for mutual gains. This is difficult to do because humans naturally see conflict as an "either-or" proposition. We either win or lose; we get what we want, or the other side gets what it wants. We feel the results will be favorable either to us or to the other side, and we do not see any other possible options.

However, this tendency to see conflict as a fixed choice proposition needs to be overcome by inventing new options to resolve the conflict to the satisfaction of both parties. The method of principled negotiation emphasizes that we need to brainstorm and search hard for creative solutions to conflict. We need to expand our options and not limit ourselves to thinking there is a single best solution.

Focusing on the interests of the parties in conflict can result in this kind of creative thinking. By exploring where our interests overlap and dovetail, we can identify solutions that will benefit both parties. This process of fulfilling interests does not need to be antagonistic. We can help each other in conflict by being sensitive to each other's interests and making it easier, rather than more difficult, for both parties to satisfy their interests. Using the earlier example of Dr. Smith and Erin, Erin could acknowledge Dr. Smith's need for a consistent attendance policy and explain that she understands that it is important to have a policy to penalize less-than-committed students. She should make the case that the quality of her papers indicates she has learned much from Dr. Smith and is as committed to the class as she can be, given her other obligations. Dr. Smith explains that he is not comfortable ignoring her absences and that it is unfair to other students who have also been penalized for missing class. They could agree that Erin's grade will be lowered to a B, rather than a C. While neither party is "victorious," both felt that the best compromise was reached given each person's unique interests.

PRINCIPLE 4: INSIST ON USING OBJECTIVE CRITERIA

Finally, Fisher and Ury (1981) say that effective negotiation requires that objective criteria be used to settle different interests. The goal in negotiation is to reach a solution that is based on principle and not on pressure. Conflict parties need to search for objective criteria that will help them view their conflict with an unbiased lens. Objective criteria can take many forms including

- *precedent,* which looks at how this issue has been resolved previously;
- *professional standards,* which determine if there are rules or standards for behavior based on a profession or trade involved in the conflict;
- *what a court would decide,* which looks at the legal precedent or legal ramifications of the conflict;
- *moral standards,* which consider resolving the conflict based on ethical considerations or "doing what's right";

- *tradition,* which looks at already established practices or customs in considering the conflict; and
- *scientific judgment,* which considers facts and evidence.

For example, if an employee and his boss disagree on the amount of a salary increase the employee is to receive, both the employee and the boss might consider the raises of employees with similar positions and work records. When criteria are used effectively and fairly, the outcomes and final package are usually seen as wise and fair (Fisher & Ury, 1981).

In summary, the method of principled negotiation presents four practical strategies that leaders can employ in handling conflicts: separate the people from the problem; focus on interests, not positions; invent options for mutual gains; and insist on using objective criteria. None of these strategies is a panacea for all problems or conflicts, but used together they can provide a general, well-substantiated approach to settling conflicts in ways that are likely to be advantageous to everyone involved in a conflict situation.

COMMUNICATION STRATEGIES FOR CONFLICT RESOLUTION ◄

Throughout this chapter, we have emphasized the complexity of conflict and the difficulties that arise in addressing it. There is no universal remedy or simple path. In fact, except for a few newsstand-type books that claim to provide quick cures to conflict, only a few sources give practical techniques for resolution. In this section, we describe several practical communication approaches that play a major role in the conflict resolution process: differentiation, fractionation, and face saving. Using these communication strategies can lessen the angst of the conflict, help conflicting parties to reach resolution sooner, and strengthen relationships.

DIFFERENTIATION

Differentiation describes a process that occurs in the early phase of conflict; it helps participants define the nature of the conflict and clarify their positions with regard to each other. It is very important to conflict resolution because it establishes the nature and parameters of the conflict. Differentiation requires that individuals explain and elaborate their own position, frequently focusing on their differences rather than their similarities. It is essential to working through a conflict (Putnam,

Video Link 9.3
Watch more on differentiation.

2010). Differentiation represents a difficult time in the conflict process because it is more likely to involve an escalation of conflict rather than a cooling off. During this time, fears may arise that the conflict will not be successfully resolved. Differentiation is also difficult because it initially personalizes the conflict and brings out feelings and sentiments in people that they themselves are the cause of the conflict (Folger, Poole, & Stutman, 1993).

The value of differentiation is that it defines the conflict. It helps both parties realize how they differ on the issue being considered. Being aware of these differences is useful for conflict resolution because it focuses the conflict, gives credence to both parties' interests in the issue that is in conflict, and, in essence, depersonalizes the conflict. Consistent with Fisher and Ury's (1981) method of negotiation, differentiation is a way to separate the people from the problem.

An example of differentiation involves a group project. Members of the group have complained to the instructor that one member, Jennifer, seldom comes to meetings; when she does come, she does not contribute to the group discussions. The instructor met with Jennifer, who defended herself by stating that the group constantly set meeting times that conflict with her work schedule. She believes they do so on purpose to exclude her. The teacher arranged for the students to sit down together, and then had them explain their differing points of view to one another. The group members said that they believed that Jennifer cared less about academic achievement than they did because she did not seem willing to adjust her work schedule to meet with them. Jennifer, on the other hand, said she believed the others did not respect that she had to work to support herself while going to school, and that she was not in total control of her work schedule.

In the above example, differentiation occurred among group members as they attempted to assess the issues. It was a difficult process because it demanded that each participant talk about his or her feelings about why the group was having conflict. Both sides ultimately understood the other's differing viewpoints. The group and Jennifer set aside a definite time each week when they would meet, and Jennifer made sure her supervisor did not schedule her to work at that time.

FRACTIONATION

Fractionation refers to the technique of breaking down large conflicts into smaller, more manageable pieces (Fisher, 1971; Wilmot & Hocker,

2011). Like differentiation, fractionation usually occurs in the early stages of the conflict resolution process. It is an intentional process in which the participants agree to "downsize" a large conflict into smaller conflicts and then confront just one part of the larger conflict. Fractionating conflict is helpful for several reasons. First, fractionation reduces the conflict by paring it down to a smaller, less complex conflict. It is helpful for individuals to know that the conflict they are confronting is not a huge amorphous mass of difficulties, but rather consists of specific and defined difficulties. Second, it gives focus to the conflict. By narrowing down large conflicts, individuals give clarity and definition to their difficulties instead of trying to solve a whole host of problems at once. Third, downsizing a conflict helps to reduce the emotional intensity of the dispute. Smaller conflicts carry less emotional weight (Wilmot & Hocker, 2011). Last, fractionation facilitates a better working relationship between participants in the conflict. In agreeing to address a reduced version of a conflict, the participants confirm their willingness to work with one another to solve problems.

An example of fractionation at work involves David Stedman, an experienced director of a private school that is on the verge of closing due to low enrollment. School board members are upset with David's leadership and the direction of the school, and David is disappointed with the board. The school had been running on a deficit budget for the previous three years and had used up most of the endowment money it had set aside. The school's board members see the problem one way: The school needs more students. David knows it is not that simple. There are many issues behind the low enrollment: the practices for recruitment of students, retention of students, fund-raising, marketing, and out-of-date technology at the school, as well as bad feelings between the parents and the school. In addition to these concerns, David also has responsibility for day-to-day operations of the school and decisions regarding the education of students. David asked the board members to attend a weekend retreat where, together, they detailed the myriad problems facing the school and narrowed the long list down to three difficulties that they would address together. They agreed to work on an aggressive recruitment plan, fund-raising efforts, and internal marketing toward parents so they would keep their children at the school.

In the end, the retreat was beneficial to both David and the board. The big conflict of "what to do about the school" was narrowed down to three specific areas they could address. In addition, the school board developed an appreciation for the complexity and difficulties of running the school, and David softened his negative feelings about the school board and its members' input. As a result of fractionating their conflict, David Stedman and the school board developed a better working relationship and confirmed their willingness to work on problems in the future.

FACE SAVING

Audio Link 9.1

Listen to more about face saving.

A third skill that can assist a leader in conflict resolution is face saving. **Face saving** refers to communicative attempts to establish or maintain one's self-image in response to threat (Folger et al., 1993; Goffman, 1967; Lulofs, 1994). Face-saving messages help individuals establish how they want to be seen by others. The goal of face-saving messages is to protect one's self-image.

In conflict, which is often threatening and unsettling, participants may become concerned about how others view them in regard to the positions they have taken. This concern for self can be counterproductive to conflict resolution because it shifts the focus of the conflict away from substantive issues and onto personal issues. Instead of confronting the central concerns of the conflict, face-saving concerns force participants to deal with the self-images of the participants as they are related to the conflict.

Interpersonal conflicts can be made less threatening if individuals communicate in a way that preserves the self-image of the other. Conflict issues should be discussed in a manner that minimizes threat to the participants. By using face-saving messages, such as "I think you are making a good point, but I see things differently," the person acknowledges the other's point of view without making that person feel stupid or unintelligent. The threat of conflict is lessened if participants try to support each other's self-image rather than to damage it just to win an argument. It is important to be aware of how people want to be seen by others, how conflict can threaten those desires, and how our communication can minimize those threats (Lulofs, 1994).

In trying to resolve conflicts, face saving should be a concern to participants for two reasons. First, if possible, participants should try to avoid letting the discussions during conflict shift to face-threatening issues. Similar to Fisher and Ury's (1981) principle of separating the people from the problem, this can be done by staying focused on content issues and maintaining interactions that do not challenge the other person's self-image. Second, during the later stages of conflict, face-saving messages can actually be used to assist participants in giving each other validation and support for how they have come across during conflict. Face-saving messages can confirm for others that they have handled themselves appropriately during conflict and that their relationship is still healthy.

The following example illustrates how face saving can affect conflict resolution. At a large university hospital, significant disruptions occurred when 1,000 nurses went on strike after contract negotiations failed. The issues in the conflict were salary, forced overtime, and mandatory coverage of units that were short-staffed. There was much name-calling and personal attacks between nurses and administrators. Early negotiations were inhibited by efforts on both sides to establish an image with the public that what *they* were doing was appropriate, given the circumstances. As a result, these images and issues of right and wrong, rather than the substantive issues of salary and overtime, became the focus of the conflict. If the parties had avoided tearing each other down, perhaps the conflict could have been settled sooner.

Despite these difficulties, face-saving messages did have a positive effect on this conflict. During the middle of the negotiations, the hospital ran a full-page advertisement in the local newspaper describing its proposal and why it thought this proposal was misunderstood. At the end of the ad, the hospital stated, "We respect your right to strike. A strike is a peaceful and powerful means by which you communicate your concern or dissatisfaction." This statement showed that the administration was trying to save face for itself, but also it was attempting to save face for nurses by expressing that their being on strike was not amoral, and that the hospital was willing to accept the nurses' behavior and continue to have a working relationship with them. Similarly, the media messages that both parties released at the end of the strike included affirmation of the other party's self-image. The nurses, who received a substantial salary increase, did not try to claim victory or point out what the hospital lost in the negotiations. In turn, the hospital, which retained control of the use of staff for overtime, did not emphasize what it had won or communicate that it thought the nurses were unprofessional because they had gone out on strike. The point is that these gentle face-saving messages helped both sides to feel good about themselves, reestablish their image as effective health care providers, and salvage their working relationships.

All in all, there are no shortcuts to resolving conflicts. It is a complex process that requires sustained communication. By being aware of differentiation, fractionation, and face saving, leaders can enhance their abilities and skills in the conflict resolution process.

► KILMANN & THOMAS STYLES OF APPROACHING CONFLICT

Video Link 9.4

Watch more about styles of approaching conflict.

There's no doubt that people have different ways of handling conflict and that these different styles affect the outcomes of conflict. A **conflict style** is defined as a patterned response or behavior that people use when approaching conflict. One of the most widely recognized models of conflict styles was developed by Kilmann and Thomas (1975, 1977), based on the work of Blake and Mouton (1964), and is the basis for our Conflict Style Questionnaire on pages 203–205.

The Thomas-Kilmann model identifies five conflict styles: (1) avoidance, (2) competition, (3) accommodation, (4) compromise, and (5) collaboration. This model (see Figure 9.3) describes conflict styles along two dimensions: assertiveness and cooperativeness. *Assertiveness* refers to attempts to satisfy one's own concerns, while *cooperativeness* represents attempts to satisfy the concerns of others. Each conflict style is characterized by how much assertiveness and how much cooperativeness an individual shows when confronting conflict.

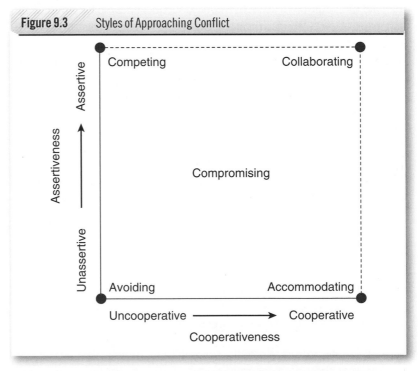

Figure 9.3 Styles of Approaching Conflict

Sources: Reproduced with permission of authors and publisher from Kilmann, R. H., & Thomas, K. W. Interpersonal conflict-handling behavior as reflections of Jungian personality dimensions. *Psychological Reports,* 1975, 37, 971-980. © Psychological Reports, 1975.

In conflict situations, a person's individual style is usually a combination of these five different styles. Nevertheless, because of past experiences or situational factors, some people may rely more heavily on one conflict style than on others. Understanding these styles can help you select the conflict style that is most appropriate to the demands of the situation.

AVOIDANCE

Avoidance is both an unassertive and an uncooperative conflict style. Those who favor the avoidance style tend to be passive and ignore conflict situations rather than confront them directly. They employ strategies such as denying there is a conflict, using jokes as a way to deflect conflict, or trying to change the topic. Avoiders are not assertive about pursuing their own interests, nor are they cooperative in assisting others to pursue theirs.

Advantages and Disadvantages

Avoidance as a style for managing conflict is usually counterproductive, often leading to stress and further conflict. Those who continually avoid conflict bottle up feelings of irritation, frustration, anger, or rage inside themselves, creating more anxiety. Avoidance is essentially a static approach to conflict; it does nothing to solve problems or to make changes that could prevent conflicts.

However, there are some situations in which avoidance may be useful—for example, when an issue is of trivial importance or when the potential damage from conflict would be too great. Avoidance can also provide a cooling-off period to allow participants to determine how to best resolve the conflict at a later time. For example, if Jon is so angry at his girlfriend that he throws his BlackBerry at the wall, he might want to go for a ride in his car and cool down before he tries to talk to his girlfriend about the problem.

COMPETITION

Competition is a conflict style of individuals who are highly assertive about pursuing their own goals but uncooperative in assisting others to reach theirs. These individuals attempt to resolve a struggle by controlling or persuading others in order to achieve their own ends. A competitive style is essentially a win-lose conflict strategy. For example, when Wendy seeks to convince Chris that he is a bad person because he is habitually late for meetings, regardless of his reasons for doing so, it is a win and lose conflict style.

Advantages and Disadvantages

In some situations, competition can produce positive outcomes. It is useful when quick, decisive action is needed. Competition can also generate creativity and enhance performance because it challenges participants to make their best efforts.

Generally, though, competitive approaches to conflict are not the most advantageous because they are more often counterproductive than productive. Resolution options are limited to one party "beating" another, resulting in a winner and a loser. Attempts to solve conflict with dominance and control will often result in creating unstable situations and hostile and destructive communication. Finally, competition is disconfirming; in competition, individuals fail to recognize the concerns and needs of others.

ACCOMMODATION

Accommodation is an unassertive but cooperative conflict style. In accommodation, an individual essentially communicates to another, "You are right, I agree; let's forget about it." An approach that is "other directed," accommodation requires individuals to attend very closely to the needs of others and ignore their own needs. Using this style, individuals confront problems by deferring to others.

Advantages and Disadvantages

Accommodation allows individuals to move away from the uncomfortable feelings that conflict inevitably produces. By yielding to others, individuals can lessen the frustration that conflict creates. This style is productive when the issue is more important to one party than the other or if harmony in the relationship is the most important goal.

The problem with accommodation is that it is, in effect, a lose-win strategy. Although accommodation may resolve conflict faster than some of the other approaches, the drawback is that the accommodator sacrifices his or her own values and possibly a higher-quality decision in order to maintain smooth relationships. It is a submissive style that allows others to take charge. Accommodators also lose because they may fail to express their own opinions and feelings and their contributions are not fully considered.

For example, Jenny's boyfriend is a sports fanatic and always wants to stay home and watch televised sports while Jenny would like to do something like go to a movie or to a club. But to make him happy, Jenny stays home and watches football.

COMPROMISE

As Figure 9.3 indicates, **compromise** occurs halfway between competition and accommodation and involves both a degree of assertiveness and a degree of cooperativeness. Many see compromise as a "give and take" proposition. Compromisers attend to the concerns of others as well as to their own needs. On the diagonal axis of Figure 9.3, compromise occurs midway between the styles of avoidance and collaboration. This means that compromisers do not completely ignore confrontations, but neither do they struggle with problems to the fullest degree. This conflict style is often chosen because it is expedient in finding middle ground while partially satisfying the concerns of both parties.

Advantages and Disadvantages

Compromise is a positive conflict style because it requires attending to one's goals as well as others'. Compromise tends to work best when other conflict styles have failed or aren't suitable to resolving the conflict. Many times, compromise can force an equal power balance between parties.

Among the shortcomings of the compromise style is that it does not go far enough in resolving conflict and can become "an easy way out." In order to reach resolution, conflicting parties often don't fully express their own demands, personal thoughts, and feelings. Innovative solutions are sacrificed in favor of a quick resolution, and the need for harmony supersedes the need to find optimal solutions to conflict. The result is that neither side is completely satisfied. For example, Pat wants to go on a camping vacation, and Mike wants to have a "staycation," hanging around the house. In the end, they agree to spend their vacation taking day trips to the beach and the zoo.

COLLABORATION

Collaboration, the most preferred style of conflict, requires both assertiveness and cooperation. It is when both parties agree to a positive settlement to the conflict and attend fully to the other's concerns while not sacrificing or suppressing their own. The conflict is

Handbook Link 9.2
Read more about collaboration.

not resolved until each side is reasonably satisfied and can support the solution. Collaboration is the ideal conflict style because it recognizes the inevitability of human conflict. It confronts conflict, and then uses conflict to produce constructive outcomes.

Advantages and Disadvantages

The results of collaboration are positive because both sides win, communication is satisfying, relationships are strengthened, and negotiated solutions are frequently more cost-effective in the long run.

Unfortunately, collaboration is the most difficult style to achieve. It demands energy and hard work among participants as well as shared control. Resolving differences through collaboration requires individuals to take time to explore their differences, identify areas of agreement, and select solutions that are mutually satisfying. This often calls for extended conversation in which the participants explore entirely new alternatives to existing problems. For example, residents of a residential neighborhood seek to have an adult entertainment facility in their midst close or leave. The owner refuses. The residents work with city officials to find an alternative location to relocate the facility, and the city gives the facility's owner tax breaks to move.

The five styles of approaching conflict—avoidance, competition, accommodation, compromise, and collaboration—can be observed in various conflict situations. Although there are advantages and disadvantages to each style, the conflict-handling style that meets the needs of the participants while also fitting the demands of the situation will be most effective in resolving conflict.

CASE STUDY

The following case study describes a conflict that occurred between a college student and his father. The questions provided at the end of the case will help you analyze the conflict using ideas from the different conceptual perspectives discussed in the chapter.

Conflict With My Father

John Lawrence

Ever since my 14-year-old sister was very young, her left eye has had visible blood vessels, which are quite large, red, and noticeable. It's a terrible thing for her. She continuously looks like she has pinkeye, hasn't slept, or has used some kind of illegal drug. Curious people ask, "What's wrong with your eye?" compelling her to have to explain the extra blood vessels with which she was born.

Over the past eight years, the blood vessels have grown 50% larger, becoming close to 2 or 3 times the size of normal, healthy blood vessels. My sister and parents went to some specialists who want to conduct an imaging procedure to better identify how the vessels are being blocked in her brain. Then, if they think it necessary—and there is a high likelihood they will find it necessary—they will operate to redirect blood flow into her brain and around the overgrown blood vessels. The surgery will be on the brain's surface and quite dangerous, with a number of possible negative outcomes including brain damage and death.

A few days after we got the bad news, my father came to me and was upset. He said our family needed to be more supportive of my sister through this crisis. He didn't think my mom and I were showing my sister enough love, and we needed to make more of an effort to do so to help her get through the hard times ahead.

My initial reaction was "How dare you!" His words felt like a personal attack of my character. Did he think because I hadn't given her a giant hug in front of him and said, "I love you, I love you" that I didn't "truly" love her? Did I need to "report" to him every last bit of caring I expressed to my sister for him to acknowledge?

I didn't outwardly get upset with my dad because I knew his emotions were running high. I tried to explain to him that I did call my sister after her return from the specialists to hear the news directly from her and I had talked to her several times since. His reaction to these statements, however, implied that my actions aren't "satisfactory love showing," and he repeatedly stated that I needed to do more. This cut me quite deeply.

I didn't continue to defend myself because engaging my dad in an argument would have worsened the whole situation and solved nothing. I don't believe you can measure a person's internal compassion toward another based on stereotypical expressions such as hugs and kisses. Not all people show compassion and care in the same ways. For my dad to use his rating scale of showing compassion to judge me wasn't right. If I had to do it all over again I would try to explain this logic to him. At the time, though, I was so offended by his accusations that I was too mad to try and explain. Instead, I elected to let him say what he wanted, express my opinion in a simple way, and then just take whatever came to me without fighting back.

Source: Adapted from John Lawrence.

Questions

1. How would you describe the conflict between John and his father?

2. In what way are John's and his father's interpersonal concerns the same or different? Is their conflict a relational conflict? If so, what type of relational conflict?

3. From Fisher and Ury's (1981) perspective, what are John's and his father's *positions* and *interests* regarding the conflict?

4. Do you think John handled the conflict in the right way? If you were John, how would you have handled the conflict?

Summary

For leaders and subordinates alike, interpersonal conflict is inevitable. Conflict is defined as a felt struggle between two or more individuals over perceived incompatible differences in beliefs, values, and goals, or over differences in desires for esteem, control, and connectedness. If it is managed in appropriate ways, conflict need not be destructive but can be constructive and used to positive ends.

Communication plays a central role in conflict and in its resolution. Conflict occurs between leaders and others on two levels: content and relational. Conflict on the content level involves differences in beliefs, values, or goal orientation. Conflict on the relational level refers to differences between individuals with regard to their desires for esteem, control, and affiliation in their relationships. Relational conflicts are seldom overt, which makes them difficult for people to recognize and resolve.

One approach to resolving conflicts is the method of principled negotiation by Fisher and Ury (1981). This model focuses on four basic elements of negotiation—people, interests, options, and criteria—and describes four principles related to handling conflicts: Principle 1—Separate the People from the Problem; Principle 2—Focus on Interests, Not Positions; Principle 3—Invent Options for Mutual Gains; and Principle 4—Insist on Using Objective Criteria. Collectively, these principles are extraordinarily useful in negotiating positive conflict outcomes.

Three practical communication approaches to conflict resolution are differentiation, fractionation, and face saving. Differentiation is a process that helps participants to define the nature of the conflict and to clarify their positions with one another. Fractionation refers to the technique of paring down large conflicts into smaller, more manageable conflicts. Face saving consists of messages that individuals express to each other in order to maintain each other's self-image during conflict. Together or singly, these approaches can assist leaders in making the conflict resolution process more productive.

Finally, researchers have found that people approach conflict using five styles: (1) avoidance, (2) competition, (3) accommodation, (4) compromise, and (5) collaboration. Each of these styles characterizes individuals in terms of the degree of assertiveness and cooperativeness they show when confronting conflict. The most constructive approach to conflict is collaboration, which requires that individuals recognize, confront, and resolve conflict by attending fully to others' concerns without sacrificing their own. Managing conflicts effectively leads to stronger relationships among participants and more creative solutions to problems.

 Go to **http://www.sagepub.com/northouseintro2e/** *for additional exercises and study resources. Select Chapter 9, Handling Conflict, for chapter-specific activities.*

Glossary Terms

accommodation   196

avoidance   195

collaboration   197

competition   195

compromise   197

conflict   174

conflict style   194

content conflicts   177

content dimension   176

differentiation   189

face saving   192

fractionation   190

principled negotiation   184

relational conflicts   180

relationship dimension   176

References

Blake, R. R., & Mouton, L. S. (1964). *The managerial grid*. Houston, TX: Gulf.

Brown, C. T., & Keller, P. W. (1979). *Monologue to dialogue: An exploration of interpersonal communication*. Englewood Cliffs, NJ: Prentice-Hall.

Fisher, R. (1971). Fractionating conflict. In C. G. Smith (Ed.), *Conflict resolution: Contributions of the behavioral sciences* (pp. 157–159). South Bend, IN: University of Notre Dame Press.

Fisher, R., & Ury, W. (1981). *Getting to yes: Negotiating agreement without giving in*. New York: Penguin Books.

Folger, J. P., Poole, M. S., & Stutman, R. K. (1993). *Working through conflict: Strategies for relationships, groups, and organizations* (2nd ed.). Glenview, IL: Scott, Foresman.

Goffman, E. (1967). *Interaction ritual: Essays on face-to-face behavior*. New York: Anchor Books.

Hocker, J. L., & Wilmot, W. W. (1995). *Interpersonal conflict* (4th ed.). Dubuque, IA: W. C. Brown.

Kilmann, R. H., & Thomas, K. W. (1975). Interpersonal conflict-handling behavior as reflections of Jungian personality dimensions. *Psychological Reports, 37,* 971–980.

Kilmann, R. H., & Thomas, K. W. (1977). Developing a forced-choice measure of conflict handling behavior: The "mode" instrument. *Educational and Psychology Measurement, 37,* 309–325.

Knutson, T., Lashbrook, V., & Heemer, A. (1976). *The dimensions of small group conflict: A factor analytic study.* Paper presented to the annual meeting of the International Communication Association, Portland, OR.

Lulofs, R. S. (1994). *Conflict: From theory to action.* Scottsdale, AZ: Gorsuch Scarisbrick.

Maslow, A. (1970). *Motivation and personality* (2nd ed.). New York: Harper & Row.

Putnam, L. L. (2010). Communication as changing the negotiation game. *Journal of Applied Communication Research, 38*(4), 325–335.

Schutz, W. C. (1966). *The interpersonal underworld.* Palo Alto, CA: Science and Behavior Books.

Terry, R. W. (1993). *Authentic leadership: Courage in action.* San Francisco: Jossey-Bass.

Watzlawick, P., Beavin, J., & Jackson, D. D. (1967). *Pragmatics of human communication.* New York: Norton.

Wilmot, W. W., & Hocker, J. (2011). *Interpersonal conflict* (8th ed.). New York: McGraw-Hill.

9.1   Conflict Style Questionnaire

 Visit www.sagepub.com/northouseintro2e for downloadable versions of these questionnaires

Purpose

1. To identify your conflict style
2. To examine how your conflict style varies in different contexts or relationships

Directions

1. Think of two different situations (A and B) where you have a conflict, a disagreement, an argument, or a disappointment with someone, such as a roommate or a work associate. Write the name of the person for each situation below.

2. According to the scale below, fill in your scores for Situation A and Situation B. For each question, you will have two scores. For example, on Question 1 the scoring might look like this: 1. 2 | 4

3. Write the name of each person for the two situations here.

Person A _____   Person B _____

1 = never	2 = seldom	3 = sometimes	4 = often	5 = always

Person A	Person B	
1.	|	I avoid being "put on the spot"; I keep conflicts to myself.
2.	|	I use my influence to get my ideas accepted.
3.	|	I usually try to "split the difference" in order to resolve an issue.
4.	|	I generally try to satisfy the other's needs.
5.	|	I try to investigate an issue to find a solution acceptable to both of us.
6.	|	I usually avoid open discussion of my differences with the other.
7.	|	I use my authority to make a decision in my favor.
8.	|	I try to find a middle course to resolve an impasse.
9.	|	I usually accommodate the other's wishes.
10.	|	I try to integrate my ideas with the other's to come up with a decision jointly.
11.	|	I try to stay away from disagreement with the other.
12.	|	I use my expertise to make a decision that favors me.
13.	|	I propose a middle ground for breaking deadlocks.

Person A	Person B	
14.	|	I give in to the other's wishes.
15.	|	I try to work with the other to find solutions that satisfy both our expectations.
16.	|	I try to keep my disagreement to myself in order to avoid hard feelings.
17.	|	I generally pursue my side of an issue.
18.	|	I negotiate with the other to reach a compromise.
19.	|	I often go with the other's suggestions.
20.	|	I exchange accurate information with the other so we can solve a problem together.
21.	|	I try to avoid unpleasant exchanges with the other.
22.	|	I sometimes use my power to win.
23.	|	I use "give and take" so that a compromise can be made.
24.	|	I try to satisfy the other's expectations.
25.	|	I try to bring all our concerns out in the open so that the issues can be resolved.

Source: Adapted from "Confirmatory Factor Analysis of the Styles of Handling Interpersonal Conflict: First-Order Factor Model and Its Invariance Across Groups," by M. A. Rahim and N. R. Magner, 1995, *Journal of Applied Psychology, 80*(1), 122–132. In W. Wilmot and J. Hocker (2011), *Interpersonal Conflict* (pp. 146–148). Published by the American Psychological Association.

Scoring: Add up your scores on the following questions:

A|B	A|B	A|B	A|B	A|B
1. |	2. |	3. |	4. |	5. |
6. |	7. |	8. |	9. |	10. |
11. |	12. |	13. |	14. |	15. |
16. |	17. |	18. |	19. |	20. |
21. |	22. |	23. |	24. |	25. |
| A|B **Avoidance** **Totals**	| A|B **Competition** **Totals**	| A|B **Compromise** **Totals**	| A|B **Accommodation** **Totals**	| A|B **Collaboration** **Totals**

Scoring Interpretation

This questionnaire is designed to *identify* your conflict style and *examine* how it varies in different contexts or relationships. By comparing your total scores for the different styles you can discover which conflict style you rely most heavily upon and which style you use least. Furthermore, by comparing your scores for Person A and Person B, you can determine how your style varies or stays the same in different relationships. Your scores on this questionnaire are indicative of how you responded to a particular conflict at a specific time and therefore might change if you selected a different conflict or a different conflict period. The Conflict Style Questionnaire is not a personality test that labels or categorizes you; rather, it attempts to give you a sense of your more dominant and less dominant conflict styles.

Scores from 21 to 25 are representative of a very strong style.

Scores from 15 to 20 are representative of a strong style.

Scores from 11 to 15 are representative of an average style.

Scores from 6 to 10 are representative of a weak style.

Scores from 0 to 5 are representative of a very weak style.

9.2 Observational Exercise

 Visit www.sagepub.com/northouseintro2e for downloadable versions of these questionnaires

Handling Conflict

Purpose

1. To become aware of the dimensions of interpersonal conflict

2. To explore how to use Fisher and Ury's (1981) method of principled negotiation to address actual conflict

Directions

1. For this exercise, you are being asked to observe an actual conflict. Attend a public meeting at which a conflict is being addressed. For example, you could attend a meeting of the campus planning board, which has on its agenda changes in student parking fees.

2. Take notes on the meeting, highlighting the positions and *interests* of all the people who participated in the meeting.

Questions

1. How did the participants at the meeting frame their arguments? What *positions* did individuals take at the meeting?

2. Identify and describe the interests of each of the participants at the meeting.

3. Discuss whether the participants were able to be objective in their approaches to the problem. Describe how the people involved were able to separate themselves from the problem.

4. In what ways did the participants seek to find mutually beneficial solutions to their conflict?

9.3 Reflection and Action Worksheet

 Visit www.sagepub.com/northouseintro2e for downloadable versions of these questionnaires

Handling Conflict

Reflection

1. How do you react to conflict? Based on the Conflict Style Questionnaire, how would you describe your conflict style? How has your past history influenced your conflict style?

2. Read the story about John Lawrence on page 198. What kind of conflict does it describe? What is John's conflict style? What is his father's conflict style? Do you agree with how John handled the conflict? How would you have reacted if you were John Lawrence?

3. This chapter describes three kinds of relational conflict (i.e., esteem, control, affiliation). Of the three kinds, which is most common in the conflicts you have with others? Discuss.

Action

1. Briefly describe an actual conflict you had with a family member, roommate, or coworker in the recent past. Identify the positions and interests of both you and the other person in the conflict. (Note: Individuals' positions may be easier to identify than their interests. Be creative in detailing your interests and the other person's.)

2. Describe how you could *fractionate* the conflict.

3. Using Fisher and Ury's (1981) methods, describe how you could separate the person from the problem and how you could work together to address the conflict.

4. During your discussions, how could you help the other party in the conflict save face? How could the other party help you save face?

10

Before you begin reading . . .

Complete the *Path-Goal Styles Questionnaire*, which you will find on pp. 224–225.
As you read the chapter, consider your results on the questionnaire.

Overcoming Obstacles

10

" Life is difficult." That is the first sentence in Scott Peck's famous book *The Road Less Traveled* (1978, p. 1). Although hard for some to accept, Peck told us that life is not going to be easy. Obstacles and struggles are an integral part of life. In the work setting, the same is true. Because obstacles always will be present, one of the most important things a leader can do is to help others overcome these obstacles.

Video Link 10.1
Watch Scott Peck read his book.

Whether it is by listening to their complaints, encouraging them, or providing counsel, there are many ways a leader can be helpful to his or her subordinates. The challenge in helping people with obstacles is to first figure out what the problems are; the second challenge is in determining what should be done to solve them. If a leader does this, subordinates will be more motivated, productive, and satisfied with their work.

Research conducted by House (1971, 1996) on **path-goal leadership** directly addresses how a leader can assist others in overcoming obstacles that hinder productivity. Path-goal leadership suggests that a leader should choose a style that best fits the needs of individual group members and the work they are doing. The leader should help these individuals define their goals and the paths they wish to take to reach those goals. When obstacles arise, the leader needs to help individuals confront them. This may mean helping them to navigate around the

Encyclopedia Link 10.1
Read more about path-goal leadership.

Audio Link 10.1

🔊

Listen to people
who have overcome
obstacles.

obstacles, or it may mean helping them remove the obstacle. The leader's job is to help group members reach their goals by directing, guiding, and coaching them along the way.

Based on ideas set forth in path-goal leadership theory, this chapter addresses the **obstacles** that subordinates may face and how a leader can help subordinates overcome them. Although people encounter many obstacles in their lives, this chapter highlights *seven* major obstacles derived from path-goal theory (see Figure 10.1). In the following section, each of the obstacles will be described, and the various ways leaders can respond to these obstacles will be explored.

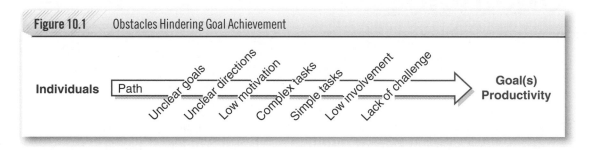

Figure 10.1   Obstacles Hindering Goal Achievement

▶ OBSTACLE 1: UNCLEAR GOALS

We have all known people who selected their career goals early in life. You may remember a grade school friend who said she was going to be a doctor and then subsequently went to college and medical school and became a neurosurgeon. You may remember the high school friend who said he was going to be in the movies who subsequently made it big in Hollywood. These people stand out because they are especially goal oriented—they knew what they wanted to do, *and* they did it. The problem is that these people are the *exception* and not the *rule*. For most people, finding their life goal is a real challenge.

Video Link 10.2

▶

Watch more
about reaching goals.

The same is true in leadership situations. It is not uncommon for individuals to be unclear or confused about their goals. Whether it is the salesperson who is required to meet a new sales quota, a hospital volunteer who is supposed to help patients, or a high school student who must write a term paper, people are often unclear about the goal or how to reach it.

Sometimes the goal is not known, sometimes it is obscure, and sometimes it is hidden among a tangle of competing goals. When goals are not clearly articulated and understood, individuals are less likely to be successful in achieving them. Furthermore, they will be less excited about their work and less gratified about their accomplishments.

It cannot be stressed enough that *the leader needs to make goals clear and understandable.* Just as leaders need to provide a map in articulating their vision (see Chapter 6, "Creating a Vision"), they must help others see the goal, the end toward which everything else is being directed. All members of a group deserve a clear picture of where their efforts are being directed. When the goal is vague, the leader needs to clarify it. Similarly, if the goal is embedded in a complex set of related goals, the leader needs to identify a specific goal for group members and explain how it fits with all the other goals.

The following list provides a few examples of leaders expressing clear goals. The examples may not be glamorous, but they exemplify good leadership.

> *Football coach to team:* "The goal for the defensive team this season is to try to sack the opposing quarterback at least two times in every game."

> *High school physical education teacher to students:* "At the beginning of every class you are required to jog one lap around the track."

> *Orchestra conductor to orchestra:* "Our upcoming rehearsals are going to be difficult because the pieces we are playing are really challenging. If we practice together every week for five hours, this concert could be our best all year."

> *Staff supervisor at a geriatric facility to volunteer staff:* "By helping the staff to fold the laundry of the patients living here, you will help to reduce the spiraling costs of our facility."

> *College speech teacher to students:* "In this speech assignment, you must make sure to do three things: (1) tell the audience what you are going to tell them, (2) tell them, and (3) tell them what you have told them."

In each of these examples, the leaders are helping individuals identify and clarify the goals of their work. The individuals doing the work will be more effective and more satisfied as a result of knowing their goals.

► OBSTACLE 2: UNCLEAR DIRECTIONS

Anyone who has ever bought something that needed to be assembled (e.g., a computer table or futon frame) knows how frustrating it is when the directions are missing from the box, impossible to follow, or written in a foreign language. No matter how much you want to put the product together, you cannot do it. This is what happens in work situations when leaders are not clear with their directions. Bad directions lead to ineffective performance.

A leader needs to *define the path* to the goal by giving clear directions. Directions that are vague, confusing, rambling, imprecise, or incomplete are not helpful to anyone. In fact, unclear directions can have a debilitating effect on individuals. People lose their capacity to move forward when they do not have clear directions on how to proceed. Some individuals are lost without directions. They may have a picture of where they are headed, but they do not know *how* to get there.

Giving good directions takes thought and skill. For example, students in a classroom want clear directions for their assignments. If the assignment is a term paper, the effective teacher describes in detail the required components. The teacher might require a two-paragraph introduction, a thesis sentence, a conceptual framework, a review of the literature, a discussion section, a conclusion, and a bibliography. When clear directions are given, students have a sense of personal control because they know what is required of them. When people know *what* they are supposed to do and *when* they are supposed to do it, they can accomplish their work more easily.

While giving clear directions is important, it is also important to be aware that individuals vary in their need for direction. Some people want very elaborate, specific instructions, while others want general directions that allow them to proceed on their own. It is the leader's job to adapt directions to the needs of each individual.

The metaphor of the global positioning system (GPS), suggested by Betsy Hart (2005), is a good one for leadership (see Box 10.1). Much like drivers who are relieved to have the navigation system tell them what interstate exit to take, subordinates want direction from a calm leader who tells them what they need to do and when they need to do it. When they make a mistake or lose their way, they want the leader to redirect them. Most important, group members want directions that are not evaluative or critical. If they make mistakes, they want to be corrected in a kind

manner. A good leader will give directions that are helpful but not judgmental. People appreciate straightforward directions, and like to hear the
leader say they "have arrived" when they get their work done.

Box 10.1   Car Global Positioning Systems—You Gotta Love 'Em

I finally got one of those global positioning systems for my car. You know, you plug in an address and the device tells you, in words, how to get to where you want to go. Actually, I've had it for a little while, but I just figured out how to work it. Four kids, a new suburb, no choice.

I've found that the key is to tell it what city you want information on. Otherwise, the system will try to find an address on Elm Street in about 17 different locations.

Anyway, I've finally got this thing up and running.

Here's what I love about it. This calm, female voice is constantly ready to give me directions on my terms: "Turn right, ahead." "After two miles, turn left." "Proceed on the current road." (I love that one.) But best of all, "You have arrived at your destination."

Wow. If only somebody would tell me that about my life.

This is why I think these things are so popular. You can never really make a mistake. There are no value judgments. If I were designing one of these things, I'd program it to say, if you made a wrong turn, "You idiot—you have messed up. Pull over and get out of the car. Get out of the car now!"

But no. Inevitably, you miss a turn, and the babe on the GPS doesn't care. No problem. There are no bad road choices. She'll just direct you down a new path and get you back on the right one without once making you feel stupid. Even if she has to say, "Proceed five miles ahead and make a legal U-turn," she doesn't scream, "You idiot. You blew it. You'll never make your party on time. How dumb could you be to miss that turn? Find a way to turn around now!"

I recently loaned a friend my car, and she commented on the calming effect of the guiding voice in a sea of unknown traffic patterns.

If only we could have that in life. What I'm looking for are things like: "Buy this peanut butter instead of that one." "This dress is perfect on you." "Choose this movie." Or maybe, "Children, obey your mother."

Still, I have to face the fact there are times when all of us need to hear things like: "What were you thinking? Are you nuts?" Or, "You dummy—leave the relationship now. Leave it now!" Or, "How could you do that??"

I guess that the idea of a life guided without censure seems really nice. But the fact is, at some point, everybody needs a healthy dose of value judgments. In the end, they are what help to guide us safely to our final destination.

Source: "GPS Systems—You Gotta Love 'Em" by Betsy Hart. Scripps News Service. Copyright © 2005.

OBSTACLE 3: LOW MOTIVATION ◀

What should a leader do when individuals are not motivated? How does
a leader encourage subordinates to work when they do not want to
work? How can a leader make people excited about work? Answers to
questions such as these have been of interest to leaders for a long time.
In fact, hundreds of articles and books have been written in an effort
to explain the underpinnings of human motivation (see Herzberg's
motivation-hygiene theory, 1968; Maslow's hierarchy of needs theory,
1954; and Skinner's work on behaviorism, 1953). All these writings

point to the complexity and challenges leaders face in trying to motivate others.

Video Link 10.3
Watch more on motivation.

Path-goal leadership incorporates **expectancy theory** as a way to motivate others (House, 1996; Vroom, 1964). Expectancy theory suggests that people will be more highly motivated when the effort they put into a task leads to an expected outcome that they value. This occurs for individuals when they feel competent, they get what they expect, and they value what they do. If a leader can help individuals in these three areas, then motivation will be high.

HELP OTHERS FEEL COMPETENT

All of us have a need to feel **competent**. We want to present ourselves in a way that suggests to others (and ourselves) that we know what we are doing. Whether it is learning how to play the guitar, how to swing a golf club, or how to play blackjack, we all want to give a good performance. Letting individuals know that they are competent is the first step in helping them become more highly motivated. For example, after completing a complex assignment, an employee would be gratified to hear the manager say, "You did that assignment exactly the way it needed to be done."

HELP OTHERS GET WHAT THEY EXPECT

People are also more highly motivated when their expectations are met. Knowing that effort will lead to an expected outcome is very important. Achieving an expected result makes the effort worthwhile, but it is disheartening and unmotivating when work does not lead to an expected outcome. In a sense, when individuals do not achieve the results they expect, they distrust the way the system works.

A leader should make sure the outcome that individuals expect from their effort is achievable and will likely occur. A leader must be aware of what outcome individuals expect, and confirm if those outcomes are realistic.

For example, if a salesperson is given a new quota to meet, he or she may expect a pay increase or financial reward for achieving that goal. It is up to the leader to clarify for the salesperson whether or not that reward is possible.

Another example that illustrates this point involves a university instructor who taught a course in public relations. The instructor assigned each group in the class a client for which the student was to develop a campaign, and gave the students a basic outline from which to work. One group struggled with the assignment; the instructor met often with these students outside class to help them develop their plan. At the end of the semester, the group submitted a very basic plan that met the minimum requirements for the assignment and received a grade of a C. Members of the group were very upset with their grade and argued that they deserved a higher score because they had done a lot of work, had completed every task the instructor had given them in their meetings, and had met the requirements for the assignment outlined in the syllabus. The instructor pointed out that higher grades were given to those who went beyond the minimum requirements. It was clear to the teacher that her expectations and those of her students were not the same. As a result, when she taught the class again the teacher specified that the requirements outlined in the syllabus were only a starting point: Higher grades were for those who met and exceeded these requirements in developing their campaign plans. This example illustrates the importance of a leader and the group members having a mutual understanding of what the expected outcomes are.

Not only does a leader need to be sensitive to what others expect from their work and make sure these expectations are realistic, but he or she must also ensure that these expected outcomes are realized. For example, if a student is promised additional points for doing an extra-credit assignment, the teacher must make sure the student receives them. Similarly, if a worker expects a pay raise if he or she meets the new sales quota, the leader needs to make sure the employee receives the pay increase.

HELP OTHERS VALUE WHAT THEY DO

The third aspect of motivating others has to do with outcomes. When people place a high value on what they are doing, they are more motivated. Without a *valued* outcome, people are not motivated to put effort toward a goal.

An example about playing a musical instrument may illustrate this. When Judy, a high school student, takes up a musical instrument (the trumpet), her first concern is about competence. She wonders, "Can I play this thing?" After taking lessons for a period, Judy's thoughts turn to whether or not she can do a solo recital. With long and hard practice, she is successful in the recital. Finally, she asks herself, "What is all of this worth?" This final phase is about the value of the outcome. If Judy really wants to become a good trumpet player, she will continue to be motivated to practice and play. If she does not find real value in playing, her motivation will subside, and she may quit playing altogether.

As a leader, the challenge is to help others see the value in their work performance. Whether this is done through monetary rewards, positive personal feedback, or giving special achievement awards, the key is to help others feel good about those things toward which they are directing their energies.

In summary, the leader's challenge to motivate others is threefold: to help others feel *competent,* to help others get what they *expect,* and to help others see the overall *value* of their work. When all three of these conditions are met, individuals will be more highly motivated about their work.

▶ OBSTACLE 4: COMPLEX TASKS

Sometimes the obstacle facing people is the task itself. When a task is unstructured, ambiguous, or complex, it creates an obstacle for individuals. People are often frustrated and threatened when confronting complex tasks. Some individuals may even be overwhelmed.

When a task is *complex,* the leader needs to be directive—to "take charge" and clarify the path to the goal. **Directive leaders** give others instruction, including what is expected of them, how it is to be done, and a timeline for when it should be completed. Being directive means setting clear standards of performance and making rules and regulations clear for others. When a leader simplifies complex tasks, it helps subordinates to feel more competent about their work.

The following example illustrates how a supervisor effectively used *directive leadership* to help one employee become more productive in her work. Jill Jones was one of four administrative staff working for a team of 45 people in product development at a large corporation. Her job was to do payroll, scheduling, requisitions, and a number of other secretarial tasks as needed. Jill had multiple tasks to coordinate but often seemed overwhelmed about which task to do first. Jill's supervisor recognized that she was having difficulty with her job and decided that Jill needed some guidance in managing her work demands. To reduce Jill's stress, the supervisor reassigned one of Jill's overdue work assignments to another employee. Next, the supervisor met with Jill and asked her to list all of her work responsibilities and the day of the month that each had to be completed. The supervisor had Jill fill out a calendar detailing the days of the week when each specific task needed to be completed (e.g., Monday 9 a.m. to noon—payroll; Tuesday, 3–5 p.m.—requisitions). Jill felt relieved after she worked through this process with her supervisor, and the whole process was win-win. Jill felt better about her work, and her boss was getting more work done. The manager had removed obstacles that were keeping Jill from adequately carrying out her job assignments.

To summarize, Jill was facing a *complex group of tasks,* and her supervisor responded appropriately with *directive leadership.* By reducing the complexity of the task, the supervisor effectively assisted Jill in feeling competent and successful about her work.

OBSTACLE 5: SIMPLE TASKS ◀

Sometimes the obstacle to people's success is not complexity but simplicity. Like complex tasks, simple and repetitive tasks can also have a negative impact on motivation. There is little excitement in doing the same job over and over again. With no variety or nuance, simple tasks become dull and uninteresting.

For work like this, it is important for a leader to use a **supportive** style. The supportive style provides what is missing—the human connection—by encouraging others when they are engaged in tasks that are boring and unchallenging. Supportive leadership offers a sense of human touch for those engaged in mundane mechanical activity.

If you have ever observed people in a weight room at a fitness center, you have seen how support works to counter the unpleasantness of mundane work. People who lift weights are usually engaged in a very simple activity. Doing repetitions is not complex. However, weight rooms are often marked by camaraderie and supportiveness between the people lifting. People spot for each other and often engage in friendly banter and conversation. Their social interaction works to make their repetitive tasks more tolerable and interesting.

To identify situations that involve mundane tasks, you need not look very far. Consider the following situations: working on an assembly line in an automobile plant, swimming laps as part of training for a swim team, washing dishes at a restaurant, or studying vocabulary cards for a foreign-language quiz. Many jobs and many aspects of nearly every job have a simplicity to them that can be negative.

The solution to this problem is for a leader to be supportive and nurturing. A good supervisor senses when jobs are mundane and tries to give people the missing ingredient—social support. Although social support can take a variety of forms (e.g., being friendly, talking about the other's family, or giving compliments), the bottom line is that social support shows care for the well-being and personal needs of the worker. When the task is not challenging, an effective leader will provide stimulation in the form of social support.

▶ OBSTACLE 6: LOW INVOLVEMENT

Journal Link 10.1
Read more on overcoming obstacles.

Having a voice in what happens is very important to people. When people are not involved in a group or an organization, their productivity goes down, and the group or organization suffers. People want to have an identity that is unique from others', but they also want to be included and to fit in with others. By expressing their own thoughts and opinions on different issues, individuals are able to sense that they are contributing to a group. When individuals sense they are not heard, their participation decreases, they contribute less, and often they disengage from the group.

A leader should use a **participative** style to address the issue of low involvement. A participative leader invites others to share in the ways and means of getting things done. They work to establish a climate that is open to new and diverse opinions. This leader consults with others, obtains their ideas and opinions, and integrates their suggestions into the decisions regarding how the group or organization will proceed.

A brief example may help to illustrate the importance of involvement. Oakwood Bistro is a small, upscale restaurant in a college town. It employs about 20 people as bartenders, cooks, and waitstaff. The bistro has two managers, whom we will call Managers A and B. Manager A is very authoritarian and strict. She stresses rules and procedures. She interacts very little with the staff and seldom asks anyone for opinions or feedback. Although Manager A is very competent and runs a tight ship, very few employees like working shifts when she is in charge.

The opposite is true when Manager B is in charge. Manager B is a democratic leader who is friendly with everyone. He is as interested in what the staff and customers are saying as he is in the rules and procedures of the place. He has nicknames for everyone who works at the bistro. In addition, he holds weekly "gripe" sessions during which staff members can express their opinions and make suggestions for how to improve things. Needless to say, individuals like to work for Manager B, and he is effective in his role.

Clearly, Manager B in the above example is a participative leader who allows people to be involved in the workings of the restaurant. The staff appreciates this involvement. In groups or organizations where everyone is involved, there are synergistic effects that create remarkable outcomes. Commitment to the group goes up, and group cohesiveness grows exponentially.

OBSTACLE 7: LACK OF A CHALLENGE ◀

Some people do not work well because they are not *challenged* by what they are doing. Without a challenge, these people find work uninteresting and not worthwhile. As a result, these people work less hard, or they quit and move on to something that they find more engaging.

A leader should adopt an achievement-oriented style of leadership in dealing with individuals who are not challenged. Achievement-oriented leadership is characterized by a leader who challenges individuals to perform at the highest level possible. This leader establishes a high standard of excellence and seeks continuous improvement. In addition to expecting a lot from subordinates, an achievement-oriented leader shows a high degree of confidence that people can reach those challenging goals.

An **achievement-oriented leader** continually challenges others to excel and pushes people to higher levels of success. He or she sets standards of excellence and challenges others to meet those standards. In the classroom, these leaders are the teachers who use an A+ grade as a way of coaxing students to do superior work. On the football field, they are the coaches who promote effort by placing stars on players' helmets for outstanding performance. At work, they are the managers who give end-of-the-year bonuses for individuals who go the extra mile or do more than they are expected to do. An achievement-oriented leader is always looking for ways to challenge people to perform at the highest level possible.

It is important to point out that, while achievement-oriented leadership is good for some people, it is not for everyone. Although some people thrive on competition and like being pushed to do their best, there are those who are internally motivated and do not need a nudge from the achievement-oriented leader. It is the leader's responsibility to assess followers' needs to determine when achievement-oriented leadership is indicated and for whom.

Audio Link 10.2
Listen to Greg Mortenson.

CASE STUDY

The following case describes the numerous challenges Greg Mortenson faced as he attempted to build schools in remote parts of Afghanistan and Pakistan. Questions are provided at the end that will help you analyze the case and explore how an effective leader can overcome obstacles.

Hard Lessons

For seven days in 1993, mountaineer Greg Mortenson was lost on the Baltoro glacier at the base of K2, the world's second highest mountain. On his way down the mountain after rescuing a critically ill fellow climber, Greg had become separated from his group and lost his way without food, water, or shelter.

Exhausted, weak, and disoriented, he stumbled into the remote, tiny village of Korphe, Pakistan. The villagers treated Greg as an honored guest, nursing him back to health. During his recuperation, he observed the village's children scratching school lessons in the dirt. After learning Korphe had no school and could not afford the $1-a-day salary for a teacher, Greg promised the village chief that he would return and build the village a school.

Fulfilling that promise presented Greg with a series of difficulties rivaling those he faced scaling K2. A former emergency trauma nurse, Greg had no clue where to start. He began by focusing on finding the $12,000 he estimated was needed to build the Korphe school. He wrote 580 letters to celebrities to ask for donations and received $100 in reply. He sold everything he owned, including the car in which he had been living and his prized climbing equipment. His mother, an elementary school principal, led a spontaneous "Pennies for Pakistan" drive at her school, which brought in $623.45.

Greg's big break came from a small article about his efforts that appeared in the American Himalayan Foundation's newsletter. Dr. Jean Hoerni, inventor of the silicon chip and a fellow climber, sent Greg $12,000 with a note that said, "Don't screw up."

Turns out that getting money may have been the easy part. Greg discovered he couldn't get the building materials to Korphe until he first constructed a 284-foot bridge 60 feet above the Braldu River. Villagers had used a basket on a cable over the chasm to get across, but it was unsuitable to ferry construction materials.

In Greg's search for somewhere to store the materials he had purchased while the bridge was built, his unfamiliarity with the culture and people led him to trust a shady businessman who offered to safekeep but then stole his construction supplies.

Back in Korphe, the village chief was forced to pay off a rival tribal leader with 12 rams—a precious commodity to the small village—when he threatened violence to keep the school from being built.

The missteps, delays, and obstacles frustrated the driven Greg, and his frustration spilled over onto the villagers and the project. But the wisdom of the Haji Ali, the village leader, taught him a life-altering lesson when he told Greg, "The mountains have been here a long time, and so have we."

"Americans think you have to accomplish everything quickly. . . . [He] taught me to slow down and make building relationships as important as building projects," says Greg. "He taught me that I had more to learn from the people I work with than I could ever hope to teach them" (Mortenson & Relin, 2006, p. 150).

As he proceeded, Greg found that it was important for him to gain the trust of Islamic religious leaders, military commanders, government officials, and tribal chiefs in Pakistan and Afghanistan. Among his most important allies, however, were the everyday men and women he encountered in taxis, gas stations, and the villages he visited. Attracted by Greg's determination and generosity, these individuals enabled him to succeed by arranging transportation, smoothing the way with political and religious leaders, or just making sure he understood the "right" way to address those he needed to approach for help.

It took three years for Greg and the villagers to finish the Korphe school, with Greg spending six months a year and untold money to travel back and forth to Pakistan from his home in Bozeman, Montana. During this time, he was encouraged to form the Central Asia Institute (CAI), a nonprofit organization with the mission to promote and support community-based education, especially for girls, in remote regions of Pakistan and Afghanistan. Greg became CAI's director, running it out of the basement of his home. Within three months of finishing the Korphe school, CAI built three new schools in other Pakistan villages.

Not everyone was enamored with Greg's efforts, however. He was abducted and held at gunpoint, had two fatwas declared against him by enraged Islamic mullahs, endured CIA investigations, and received death threats. The region was increasingly under the control of the Taliban, a fundamentalist religious and political movement known for its strong restrictions of women. Under Taliban rule, girls were no longer permitted to engage in any education, and Greg's insistence on providing education to girls drew the ire of those who adhered to the Taliban philosophy.

In addition, after attacks by al-Qaeda terrorists brought down the Twin Towers of the World Trade Center in New York City on September 11, 2001, Greg received hate mail and death threats from fellow Americans enraged that he would help Muslim children.

Greg continued undaunted. Taking a cue from his mother's spontaneous campaign years before, CAI began Pennies for Peace, an educational program for American schoolchildren combining curriculum about Afghanistan and Pakistan with "penny drives" to build and supply CAI schools. Greg engaged in a rigorous speaking schedule to bring more public attention to CAI's efforts and collaborated with journalist David Oliver Relin on a book chronicling his story and efforts of CAI. *Three Cups of Tea: One Man's Mission to Promote Peace . . . One School at a Time* hit the top of the bestseller list, selling more than 4 million copies, with a portion of the proceeds going to CAI.

(Continued)

Video Link 10.4

Watch Greg Mortenson.

(Continued)

Establishing a school requires an invitation from the local community and 2–4 years of preplanning with the village elders, tribal chiefs, military commanders, Islamic clerics, and government officials influential in the area. Each project involves local people in the planning and implementation, including providing land, labor, and local resources such as wood, stone, and sand. Once the school has been completed, furnished, and stocked with supplies, CAI continues to provide support until the village can sustain the school's costs on its own (Zimmerman, 2008).

As of 2010, CAI had established 145 schools in rural, and often volatile, regions of Afghanistan and Pakistan, providing education for more than 64,000 children, including 52,000 girls (Central Asia Institute, 2009).

The organization also supports scholarships for students to continue their education beyond their village school, hires teachers, develops clean drinking water and sanitation for villages, and establishes women's centers where village women can become empowered and learn a craft that will allow them to support their families.

Today, Greg continues his rigorous speaking schedule and has written a second book, *Stones into Schools: Promoting Peace with Books, Not Bombs, in Afghanistan and Pakistan,* which was released in 2009. That same year he was awarded Pakistan's highest civil honor, *Sitara-e-Pakistan ("Star of Pakistan"),* for his humanitarian effort to promote girls' education in rural areas.

Questions

1. In pursuing his goals, Greg faced momentous challenges. What were his strategies for overcoming those obstacles?

2. Which of the obstacles that hinder goal achievement discussed in the chapter do you think Greg faced?

3. Do you think Greg utilized path-goal leadership in his efforts? In what ways?

4. What styles of leadership did Greg show with the Pakistani people?

Summary

Challenges and difficulties will always be present for people in the workplace. A leader plays a critical role in helping people overcome these obstacles. Most important, effective leaders help individuals *define their goals* and the *paths* they wish to take to meet those goals. Based on expectancy theory, leaders can help others be *motivated* by helping them feel *competent,* to receive what they *expect* from their work, and to see the overall *value* of their work.

If the obstacle a person faces is a *complex task,* the leader should provide *directive leadership.* If the obstacle is a task that is too *simple or mundane,* however, the leader needs to give *supportive leadership.* Sometimes leaders have followers who are *uninvolved* in the group or organization; for these individuals, the leader should adopt a *participative leadership* style. At other times, for followers who are not *challenged,* the leader should incorporate an *achievement-oriented leadership* style.

Obstacles will always exist and present a challenge in all endeavors. The sign of a good leader is one who is willing to help individuals overcome these obstacles so that they can more effectively move toward and accomplish their goals.

 Go to **http://www.sagepub.com/northouseintro2e/** *for additional exercises and study resources. Select Chapter 10, Overcoming Obstacles, for chapter-specific activities.*

Glossary Terms

achievement-oriented   219

competent   214

directive   216

expectancy theory   214

obstacles   210

participative   218

path-goal leadership   209

supportive   217

References

Central Asia Institute. (2009). *Greg Mortenson*. Retrieved December 22, 2010, from http://www.gregmortenson.com/

Hart, B. (2005, June 10). GPS voice fine for some of life's roads but not for others. *Deseret News* (Salt Lake City, UT). Retrieved December 22, 2010, from http://findarticles.com/p/articles/mi_qn4188/is_20050610/ai_n14666409

Herzberg, F. (1968). *Work and the nature of man*. New York: World.

House, R. J. (1971). A path-goal theory of leader effectiveness. *Administrative Science Quarterly, 16,* 321–328.

House, R. J. (1996). Path-goal theory of leadership: Lessons, legacy, and a reformulated theory. *Leadership Quarterly, 7*(3), 323–352.

Maslow, A. H. (1954). *Motivation and personality*. New York: Harper & Row.

Mortenson, G. (2009). *Stones into schools: Promoting peace with books, not bombs, in Afghanistan and Pakistan*. New York: Penguin Group.

Mortenson, G., & Relin, D. O. (2006). *Three cups of tea: One man's mission to promote peace . . . one school at a time*. New York: Penguin Books.

Peck, M. S. (1978). *The road less traveled*. New York: Simon & Schuster.

Skinner, B. F. (1953). *Science and human behavior*. New York: Free Press.

Vroom, V. H. (1964). *Work and motivation*. New York: John Wiley & Sons.

Zimmerman, C. (2008, February 24). Three cups of tea. *Longview Daily News* (Washington). Retrieved December 22, 2010, from https://www.ikat.org/three-cups-of-tea/

10.1   Path-Goal Styles Questionnaire

   Visit **www.sagepub.com/northouseintro2e** for downloadable versions of these questionnaires

Purpose

1. To identify your path-goal styles of leadership
2. To examine how your use of each style relates to other styles of leadership

Directions

1. For each of the statements below, circle the number that indicates the frequency with which you engage in the expressed behavior.
2. Give your immediate impressions. There are no right or wrong answers.

When I am the leader. . . .	Never	Seldom	Sometimes	Often	Always
1. I give clear explanations of what is expected of others.	1	2	3	4	5
2. I show interest in subordinates' personal concerns.	1	2	3	4	5
3. I invite subordinates to participate in decision making.	1	2	3	4	5
4. I challenge subordinates to continuously improve their work performance.	1	2	3	4	5
5. I give subordinates explicit instructions for how to do their work.	1	2	3	4	5
6. I show concern for the personal well-being of my subordinates.	1	2	3	4	5
7. I solicit subordinates' suggestions before making a decision.	1	2	3	4	5
8. I encourage subordinates to consistently raise their own standards of performance.	1	2	3	4	5
9. I give clear directions to others for how to proceed on a project.	1	2	3	4	5
10. I listen to others and give them encouragement.	1	2	3	4	5
11. I am receptive to ideas and advice from others.	1	2	3	4	5
12. I expect subordinates to excel in all aspects of their work.	1	2	3	4	5

Scoring

1. Sum the responses on items 1, 5, and 9 (directive leadership).
2. Sum the responses on items 2, 6, and 10 (supportive leadership).
3. Sum the responses on items 3, 7, and 11 (participative leadership).
4. Sum the responses on items 4, 8, and 12 (achievement-oriented leadership).

Total Scores

Directive leadership: _____

Supportive leadership: _____

Participative leadership: _____

Achievement-oriented leadership: _____

Scoring Interpretation

This questionnaire is designed to measure four types of path-goal leadership: directive, supportive, participative, and achievement-oriented. By comparing your scores on each of the four styles, you can determine which style is your strongest and which is your weakest. For example, if your scores were directive leadership = 21, supportive leadership = 10, participative leadership – 19, and achievement-oriented leadership = 7, your strengths would be directive and participative leadership, and your weaknesses would be supportive and achievement-oriented leadership. While this questionnaire measures your dominant styles, it also indicates the styles you may want to strengthen or improve.

If your score is 13–15, you are in the high range.

If your score is 6–12, you are in the moderate range.

If your score is 3–5, you are in the low range.

10.2   Observational Exercise

 Visit www.sagepub.com/northouseintro2e for downloadable versions of these questionnaires

Obstacles

Purpose

1. To develop an understanding of the practical value of path-goal leadership as a strategy for helping followers reach their goals

2. To identify *obstacles* that limit group effectiveness

3. To investigate how a *leader's style* helps followers overcome *obstacles* to goal achievement

Directions

1. Observe a meeting, practice, or session of one the following groups (or a similar group): a sports team practice, a class project group meeting, a weekly staff meeting at work, a fraternity or sorority council meeting, or a planning meeting for a nonprofit organization.

2. Record what you observe at the meeting. Be specific in your descriptions.

   General observations of the meeting:

   Observations of the leader's behavior:

   Observations of group members' behaviors:

Questions

1. What are the *goals* of the individuals or group you observed? Are the goals clear?

2. What are the major obstacles confronting the individuals in the group?

3. What style of leadership did the leader exhibit? Was it appropriate for the group?

4. If you were leading the group, how would you lead to help group members?

10.3   Reflection and Action Worksheet

 Visit **www.sagepub.com/northouseintro2e** for downloadable versions of these questionnaires

Obstacles

Reflection

1. When it comes to helping people who are having problems, how do you view your own abilities? Are you comfortable with setting goals and giving directions to others?

2. One of the central responsibilities of a leader is to help his or her followers become motivated. This means helping them feel *competent,* helping them meet their *expectations,* and helping them *value* what they do. How would you apply these three principles in a leadership situation?

3. As you reflect on the *obstacles* discussed in the chapter, which obstacles would you be most and least effective at addressing? Why?

Action

1. To be an effective leader requires that you *clarify the goal* and *define the path* to the goal. What specific things could you do in an upcoming leadership situation to clarify the goal and define the path for others?

2. As you look at your results on the Path-Goal Styles Questionnaire, what scores would you like to change? Which styles would you like to strengthen? How can you make sure you exhibit the most effective style the next time you are leading a group?

3. People vary regarding their need to be helped. Some want a lot of assistance, and others like to be independent. Are you prepared to adapt your leadership to be helpful to those who need it? Discuss.

Before you begin reading . . .

Complete the *Core Values Questionnaire*, which you will find on p. 247. As you read the chapter, consider your results on the questionnaire.

Addressing Ethics in Leadership

11

Leadership has a moral dimension because leaders influence the lives of others. Because of this influential dimension, leadership carries with it an enormous ethical responsibility. Hand in hand with the authority to make decisions is the obligation a leader has to use his or her authority for the common good. Because the leader usually has more power and control than followers have, leaders have to be particularly sensitive to how their leadership affects the well-being of others.

In recent years, there have been an overwhelming number of scandals in the public and private sectors. Accounting and financial scandals have occurred at some of the largest companies in the world, including Adelphia, Enron, Tyco International, and WorldCom. In addition, there have been stories of sexual abuse in the Catholic church, accusations of child abuse perpetrated by polygamists, and a multitude of sexual scandals in the lives of public figures including governors, U.S. Senators, and mayors, to name but a few. As a result of such high-profile scandals, people are becoming suspicious of public figures and what they do. The public strongly seeks moral leadership.

Journal Link 11.1
Read more about ethics.

As mentioned in Chapter 1, "Being a Leader," the overriding purpose of this book is to answer the question, "What does it take to be an *effective* leader?" Closely related to this question, and perhaps even more important, is the question, "What does it take to be an *ethical* leader?" That query is the focus of this chapter.

Video Link 11.1
Watch more on ethics and leadership.

To begin, it is important to first define ethical leadership. In the simplest terms, **ethical leadership** is the influence of a moral person who moves others to do the right thing in the right way for the right reasons (Ciulla, 2003). Put another way, ethical leadership is a process by which a good person rightly influences others to accomplish a common good: to make the world better, fairer, and more humane. This chapter will discuss the nature of ethical leadership. Specifically, it will explore six factors that are related directly to ethical leadership (Figure 11.1) and will focus on how each of these factors plays a role in ethical leadership:

Video Link 13.2
Watch U. S.
President Obama speak
on ethics.

1. The *character* of the leader

2. The *actions* of the leader

3. The *goals* of the leader

4. The *honesty* of the leader

5. The *power* of the leader

6. The *values* of the leader

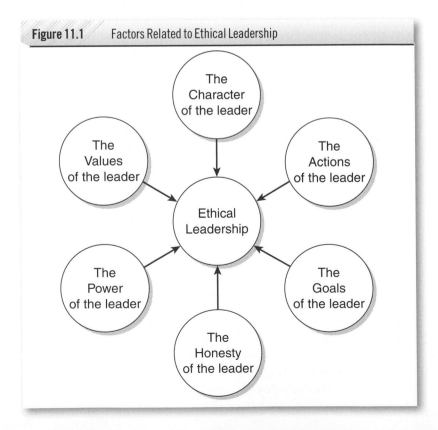

Figure 11.1   Factors Related to Ethical Leadership

ETHICAL LEADERSHIP IS ABOUT THE *CHARACTER* OF THE LEADER ◀

Character of the leader is a fundamental aspect of ethical leadership. When it is said that a leader has strong character, that leader is seen as a good and honorable human being. The leader's **character** refers to the qualities, disposition, and core values of the leader. More than 2,000 years ago, Aristotle argued that a moral person demonstrates the virtues of courage, generosity, self-control, honesty, sociability, modesty, fairness, and justice (Velasquez, 1992). Today, all these qualities still contribute to a strong character.

Character is something that is developed. In recent years, the nation's schools have seen a growing interest in character education. Misbehavior of public figures has led to mistrust of public figures, which has led to the public demanding that educators do a better job of training children to be good citizens. As a result, most schools today teach character education as part of their normal curriculum. A model for many of these programs was developed by the Josephson Institute (2008) in California, which frames instruction around six dimensions of character: *trustworthiness, respect, responsibility, fairness, caring, and citizenship* (see Table 11.1). Based on these and similar character dimensions, schools are emphasizing the importance of character and how core values influence an individual's ethical decision making.

Video Link 11.3
Watch more on the Six Pillars of Character

Although character is clearly at the core of *who you are* as a person, it is also something you can learn to strengthen and develop. A leader can learn good values. When practiced over time, from youth to adulthood, good values become habitual, and a part of people themselves. By telling the truth, people become truthful; by giving to the poor, people become charitable; and by being fair to others, people become just. Your virtues, and hence your character, are derived from your actions.

An example of a leader with strong character is Nobel Peace Prize winner Nelson Mandela (Chapter 2, "Recognizing Your Traits"). Mandela is a deeply moral man with a strong conscience. When fighting to abolish apartheid in South Africa, he was unyielding in his pursuit of justice and equality for all. When he was in prison and was offered the chance to leave early in exchange for denouncing his viewpoint, he chose to remain incarcerated rather than compromise his position. In addition to being deeply concerned for others, Mandela is a courageous, patient, humble, and compassionate man. He is an ethical leader who ardently believes in the common good.

Audio Link 11.1
Listen to more on ethical leadership.

Table 11.1   The Six Pillars of Character

Trustworthiness	
Trustworthiness is the most complicated of the six core ethical values and concerns a variety of qualities like honesty, integrity, reliability, and loyalty.	• Be honest • Be reliable: do what you say you'll do • Have the courage to do the right thing • Don't deceive, cheat, or steal • Build a good reputation
Respect	
While we have no ethical duty to hold all people in high esteem, we should treat everyone with respect.	• Be tolerant of differences • Use good manners • Be considerate of others • Work out disagreements
Responsibility	
Ethical people show responsibility by being accountable, pursuing excellence, and exercising self-restraint. They exhibit the ability to respond to expectations.	• Do your job • Persevere • Think before you act • Consider the consequences • Be accountable for your choices
Fairness	
Fairness implies adherence to a balanced standard of justice without relevance to one's own feelings or indications.	• Play by the rules • Be open-minded • Don't take advantage of others • Don't blame others
Caring	
Caring is the heart of ethics and ethical decision-making. It is scarcely possible to be truly ethical and yet unconcerned with the welfare of others. This is because ethics is ultimately about good relations with other people.	• Be kind • Be compassionate • Forgive others • Help people in need
Citizenship	
The good citizen gives more than she takes, doing more than her "fair" share to make society work, now and for future generations. Citizenship includes civic virtues and duties that prescribe how we ought to behave as part of a community.	• Share with your community • Get involved • Stay informed: vote • Respect authority • Protect the environment

Source: © 2008 Josephson Institute. The definitions of the Six Pillars of Character are reprinted with permission. www. charactercounts.org

Mandela clearly illustrates that character is an essential component of moral leadership. Character enables a leader to maintain his or her core ethical values even in times of immense adversity. Character forms the centerpiece of a person's values, and is fundamental to ethical leadership.

ETHICAL LEADERSHIP IS ABOUT THE *ACTIONS* OF THE LEADER ◄

In addition to being about a leader's character, ethical leadership is about the actions of a leader (see Figure 11.1). **Actions** refer to the ways a leader goes about accomplishing goals. Ethical leaders use moral means to achieve their goals. The way a leader goes about his or her work is a critical determinant of whether he or she is an ethical leader. We may all be familiar with the Machiavellian phrase "the ends justify the means," but an ethical leader keeps in mind a different version of this and turns it into a question: "Do the ends justify the means?" In other words, the actions a leader takes to accomplish a goal need to be ethical. They cannot be justified by the necessity or importance of the leader's goals. Ethical leadership involves using *morally appropriate actions* to achieve goals.

To illustrate the importance of ethical actions, consider what happened at the Abu Ghraib prison in Iraq in 2004. Because of the atrocities on 9/11, national security and intelligence gathering became a high priority. Rules and standards of interrogation were expanded and harsh interrogation methods were approved. The government's goal was to obtain information for purposes of national security.

Problems at the prison became evident when the media reported that prisoners were being sexually abused, humiliated, and tortured by prison personnel and civilian contract employees. Gruesome photographs of demeaning actions to prisoners appeared in the media and on the Internet. To obtain intelligence information, some Army soldiers used means that violated military regulations and internationally held rules on the humane treatment of prisoners of war established by the Geneva Convention in 1948.

In the case of the Abu Ghraib prison, the goal of maintaining national security and intelligence gathering was legitimate and worthwhile. However, the means that were used by some at the prison were considered by many to be unjustified and even ruled to be criminal. Many believe that the goals did not justify the means.

In everyday situations, a leader can act in many different ways to accomplish goals; each of these actions has ethical implications. For example, when a leader rewards some employees and not others, it raises questions of fairness. If a leader fails to take into consideration an employee's major health problems and instead demands that a job be completed on short notice, it raises questions about the leader's compassion for others. Even a simple task such as scheduling people's workload or continually giving more favorable assignments to one person over another reflects the ethics of the leader. In reality, almost everything a leader does has ethical overtones.

Handbook Link 11.1
Read more on ethics.

Given the importance of a leader's actions, what ethical principles should guide how a leader acts toward others? Ethical principles for leaders have been described by many scholars (Beauchamp & Bowie, 1988; Ciulla, 2003; Johnson, 2005; Kanungo, 2001; Kanungo & Mendonca, 1996). These writings highlight the importance of many ethical standards. In addition, there are three principles that have particular relevance to our discussion of the *actions* of ethical leaders. They are (1) showing respect, (2) serving others, and (3) showing justice.

1. *Showing respect.* To show respect means to treat others as unique human beings and never as means to an end. It requires treating others' decisions and values with respect. It also requires valuing others' ideas and affirming these individuals as unique human beings. When a leader shows respect to subordinates, subordinates become more confident and believe their contributions have value.

2. *Serving others.* Clearly, serving others is an example of altruism, an approach that suggests that actions are ethical if their primary purpose is to promote the best interest of others. From this perspective, a leader may be called on to act in the interest of others, even when it may run contrary to his or her self-interests (Bowie, 1991). In the workplace, serving others can be observed in activities such as mentoring, empowering others, team building, and citizenship behaviors (Kanungo & Mendonca, 1996). In practicing the principle of service, an ethical leader must be willing to be follower centered. That is, the leader tries to place others' interests foremost in his or her work, and act in ways that will benefit others.

3. *Showing justice.* Ethical leaders make it a top priority to treat all of their subordinates in an equal manner. Justice demands that a leader place the issue of fairness at the center of decision making. As a rule,

no one should receive special treatment or special consideration except when a particular situation demands it. When individuals are treated differently, the grounds for different treatment must be clear, reasonable, and based on sound moral values.

In addition, justice is concerned with the Golden Rule: Treat others as you would like to be treated. If you expect fair treatment from others, then you should treat others fairly. Issues of fairness become problematic because there is always a limit on goods and resources. As a result, there is often competition for scarce resources. Because of the real or perceived scarcity of resources, conflicts often occur between individuals about fair methods of distribution. It is important for a leader to establish clearly the rules for distributing rewards. The nature of these rules says a lot about the ethical underpinnings of the leader and the organization.

The challenge of treating everyone fairly is illustrated in what happened to Richard Lee when he coached his son's Little League baseball team. His son, Eric, was an outstanding pitcher with a lot of natural ability. During one of the games, Eric became frustrated with his performance and began acting very immaturely, throwing his bat and kicking helmets. When Richard saw Eric's inappropriate behavior, he immediately took his son out of the game and sat him on the bench. The player who replaced Eric in the lineup was not as good a pitcher, and the team lost the game.

After the game, Richard received a lot of criticism. In addition to Eric being mad at him, the parents of the other players were also very angry. Some of the parents came to Richard and told him that he should not have pulled his son out of the game because it caused the team to lose.

In this example, the other players' parents failed to recognize what Richard was doing as a coach. Richard made a strong effort to be fair to all the players by treating his son the way he would treat any player who acted out. He set a standard of good sportsmanship; when his own son violated the rules, he was disciplined. Richard's actions were ethical, but coaching the team as he did was not easy. He did the right thing, but there were repercussions.

This example underscores the importance of the *actions* of a leader. A leader's actions play a significant role in determining whether that leader is ethical or unethical.

► ETHICAL LEADERSHIP IS ABOUT THE *GOALS* OF THE LEADER

The **goals** that a leader establishes are the third factor related to ethical leadership. How a leader uses goals to influence others says a lot about the leader's ethics. For example, Adolf Hitler was able to convince millions of people that the eradication of the Jews was justified. It was an evil goal, and he was an immoral leader. The al-Qaeda terrorists' attack on targets in the United States was motivated by a goal to seek retribution for the United States' stance on Middle East affairs. On the positive side, Mother Teresa's goal to help the poor and disenfranchised was moral. Similarly, Habitat for Humanity's goal to build houses for the disadvantaged is moral. All of these examples highlight the significant role that goals play in determining whether leadership is ethical. The goals a leader selects are a reflection of the leader's ethics.

Identifying and pursuing just and worthy goals are the most important steps an ethical leader will undertake. In choosing goals, an ethical leader must assess the relative value and worth of his or her goals. In the process, it is important for the leader to take into account the interests of others in the group or organization and, in some cases, the interests of the community and larger culture in which he or she works. An ethical leader tries to establish goals on which all parties can mutually agree. An ethical leader with ethical goals will not impose his or her will on others.

Jacob Heckert, president of a regional health insurance company, is an example of a leader who used his leadership for worthwhile goals. Jacob believed in community service and advocated, but did not demand, that his employees engage in community service, as well. Because he had several friends with diabetes and two of his employees had died of end-stage renal disease, Jacob was particularly interested in supporting the National Kidney Foundation. To promote his cause, he urged his entire company of 4,000 employees to join him in raising money for the National Kidney Foundation's 5K. Each employee who signed up was responsible for raising $100. Everyone who participated received a free water bottle and T-shirt.

On the day of the rally, Jacob was surprised when more than 1,800 employees from his company showed up to participate. The rally was a great success, raising more than $180,000 for the National Kidney Foundation. The employees felt good about being able to contribute to a worthy cause, and they enjoyed the community spirit that surrounded the event. Jacob was extremely pleased that his goals had been realized.

ETHICAL LEADERSHIP IS ABOUT THE *HONESTY* OF THE LEADER ◄

Another major factor that contributes to ethical leadership is **honesty**. More than any other quality, people want their leaders to be honest. In fact, it could be said that being honest is synonymous with being ethical.

Audio Link 11.2
Listen to a story about ethics violations.

When we were children, we were frequently told by grown-ups to "never tell a lie." To be good meant telling the truth. For leaders, the lesson is the same. To be an ethical leader, a leader needs to be honest.

Dishonesty is a form of lying, a way of misrepresenting reality. Dishonesty may bring with it many negative outcomes, the foremost of which is that it creates distrust. When a leader is not honest, others come to see that leader as undependable and unreliable. They lose faith in what the leader says and stands for, and their respect for this individual is diminished. As a result, the leader's impact is compromised because others no longer trust and believe what he or she says.

Dishonesty also has a negative effect on a leader's interpersonal relationships. It puts a strain on how the leader and followers are connected to each other. When a leader lies to others, the leader in essence is saying that manipulation of others is acceptable. For example, when a boss does not come forth with a raise he promised, an employee will begin to distrust the boss. The long-term effect of this type of behavior, if ongoing, is a weakened relationship. Dishonesty, even when used with good intentions, contributes to the breakdown of relationships.

But being honest is not just about the leader telling the truth. It also has to do with being open with others and representing reality as fully and completely as possible. This is not an easy task because there are times when telling the complete truth can be destructive or counterproductive. The challenge for a leader is to strike a balance between being open and candid, and at the same time monitoring what is appropriate to disclose in a particular situation.

An example of this delicate balance can be seen in a story about Dan Johnson. Dan was hired to work as an executive with a large manufacturing company. The new job required Dan and his family to leave the small Michigan community they lived in, giving up jobs and friends, to move to Chicago. The family put its house on the market and began looking for a new home and jobs in Chicago. A few days after Dan started, his boss, Justin Godfrey, took him aside and told him that he should not sell his Michigan house at that time. Justin suggested that Dan postpone his move by using his wife's job as an excuse when people inquired why the family had not moved to Chicago. Justin could not tell him any more, but Dan knew something major was about to happen. It did. The company announced a merger a few months later, and Dan's job in Chicago was eliminated. Justin was required to keep the merger news quiet, but if he had not confided the little information that he did, members of Dan's family would have uprooted their lives only to have them uprooted again. They would have experienced not only financial losses, but emotional ones, as well.

This example illustrates that it is important for a leader to be authentic. At the same time, it is essential that leaders be sensitive to the attitudes and feelings of others. Honest leadership involves a wide set of behaviors, which includes being truthful in appropriate ways.

► ETHICAL LEADERSHIP IS ABOUT THE *POWER* OF THE LEADER

Another factor that plays a role in ethical leadership is power. **Power** is the capacity to influence or affect others. A leader has power because he or she has the ability to affect others' beliefs, attitudes, and courses of action. Religious leaders, managers, coaches, and teachers are all people who have the potential to influence others. When they use their potential, they are using their power as a resource to affect change in others.

Journal Link 11.2
Read more about power and ethics.

The most widely cited research on power is French and Raven's (1959) work on the bases of social power. French and Raven identified five common and important bases of power: referent power, expert power, legitimate power, reward power, and coercive power (see Table 11.2). Each of these types of power increases a leader's capacity to have an impact on others, and each has the potential to be abused.

Since power can be used in positive ways to benefit others or in destructive ways to hurt others, a leader needs to be aware of and sensitive to how he or she uses power. Power is not inherently bad, but it can be used in negative ways. How a leader uses power says a great deal about that leader's ethics.

Examples of unethical leaders who used power in negative ways include Adolf Hitler in Germany and Jim Jones in Guyana. Each of these leaders used power to influence others in horribly destructive

Table 11.2	Five Bases of Power	
1. Referent power	Based on followers' identification and liking for the leader	Example: A college professor who is highly admired by students
2. Expert power	Based on the followers' perceptions of the leader's competence	Example: A person with strong knowledge about a software program
3. Legitimate power	Associated with having status or formal job authority	Example: A judge who presides over a court case
4. Reward power	Derived from having the capacity to provide benefits to others	Example: A supervisor who can give bonuses to employees
5. Coercive power	Derived from being able to penalize or punish others	Example: A teacher who can lower a student's grade for missing class

Source: Based on French and Raven, 1959.

ways. As was mentioned earlier, Hitler was able to lead the killings of millions of Jews and other marginalized groups in Germany. Jones was an American who set up a religious cult in the country of Guyana, and who led more than 900 of his followers to commit suicide by drinking cyanide-laced punch. While these are extreme examples, power can also be abused in everyday leadership. For example, a supervisor who forces an employee to work every weekend by threatening to fire the worker if she or he does not comply is being unethical in the use of power. Another example is a high school cross-country track coach who is highly admired by his runners, but who requires them to take costly health food supplements even though the supplements are not proven effective by standard medical guidelines. There are many ways that power can be abused by a leader. From the smallest to the largest forms of influence, a leader needs to try to be fair and caring in his or her leadership.

The key to not misusing power is to be constantly vigilant and aware of the way one's leadership affects others. An ethical leader does not wield power or dominate, but instead takes into account the will of the subordinates, as well as the leader's own will. An ethical leader uses power to work with subordinates to accomplish their mutual goals.

► ETHICAL LEADERSHIP IS ABOUT THE *VALUES* OF THE LEADER

A final factor that contributes to understanding ethical leadership is *values*. **Values** are the ideas, beliefs, and modes of action that people find worthwhile or desirable. Some examples of values are peace, justice, integrity, fairness, and community. A leader's ethical values are demonstrated in everyday leadership.

Scholar James MacGregor Burns suggested that there are three kinds of leadership values: ethical values, such as kindness and altruism; modal values, such as responsibility and accountability; and end values, such as justice and community (Ciulla, 2003). **Ethical values** are similar to the notion of character discussed earlier in this chapter. **Modal values** are concerned with the means or actions a leader takes. **End values** describe the outcomes or goals a leader seeks to achieve. End values are present when a person addresses broad issues such as liberty and justice. These three kinds of values are interrelated in ethical leadership.

In leadership situations, both the leader and the follower have values, and these values are seldom the same. A leader brings his or her own unique values to leadership situations, and followers do the same. The challenge for the ethical leader is to be faithful to his or her own leadership values while being sensitive to the followers' values.

For example, a leader in an organization may value community and encourage his or her employees to work together and seek consensus in planning. However, the leader's subordinates may value individuality and self-expression. This creates a problem because these values are seemingly in conflict. In this situation, an ethical leader needs to find a way to advance his or her own interests in creating community without destroying the subordinates' interests in individuality. There is a tension between these different values; an ethical leader needs to negotiate through these differences to find the best outcome for everyone involved. While the list of possible conflicts of values is infinite, finding common ground between a leader and followers is usually possible, and is essential to ethical leadership.

In the social services sector, where there are often too few resources and too many people in need, leaders constantly struggle with decisions that test their values. Because resources are scarce, a leader has to decide where to allocate the resources; these decisions communicate a lot about the leader's values. For example, in mentoring programs such as Big Brothers Big Sisters, the list of children in need is often much longer than the list of available mentors. How do administrators decide which child is going to be assigned a mentor? They decide based on their values and the values of the people with whom they work. If they believe that children from single-parent households should have higher priority, then those children will be put at the top of the list. As this example illustrates, making ethical decisions is challenging for a leader, especially in situations where resources are scarce.

An important facet of dealing with values and leadership is to understand one's own values and integrate those values with others'. The Core Values Questionnaire that you completed prior to reading this chapter underscores the importance of a leader knowing his or her own values, having the courage to express them, and integrating these values with others' values in an effort to achieve a common goal.

An example of someone whose values are apparent in his leadership is Lance Armstrong, seven-time winner of the Tour de France (1999–2005) and cancer survivor (see Box 11.1). During his cancer treatment, Armstrong established the Lance Armstrong Foundation to empower cancer survivors to live life on their own terms and to raise awareness about cancer and funds to fight the disease. To date, his foundation has raised more than $250 million.

Video Link 11.4
Watch Lance Armstrong speak.

Box 11.1   Live Strong—Lance Armstrong's Story

At age 25, Lance Armstrong was one of the world's best cyclists and had won the World Championships, the Tour DuPont, and multiple Tour de France stages. Young and at the top of his game, Armstrong seemed invincible, with a limitless future.

Then he was told that he had testicular cancer. The most common cancer in men aged 15 to 35, the testicular cancer cure rate is a promising 90% if detected early. Like most young, healthy men, Armstrong ignored the warning signs and never imagined the seriousness of his condition. Going untreated, the cancer soon spread to Armstrong's abdomen, lungs, and brain. His chances dimmed. Next to the challenge he now faced, bike racing seemed insignificant.

Armstrong had a combination of physical conditioning, a strong support system, and his competitive spirit on his side. He educated himself about his disease and its treatment. Armed with this knowledge and confidence in medicine, he declared himself not a cancer victim but a cancer survivor, undergoing aggressive treatment and beating the disease.

(Continued)

(Continued)

During his treatment, before he even knew his own fate, he created the Lance Armstrong Foundation. This marked the beginning of Armstrong's life as an advocate for people living with cancer and for the cancer community. He created the signature yellow rubber wristband inscribed with the words *LiveStrong*. Millions of these bracelets have been sold to raise money for his foundation.

Remarkably, after recovering from treatment he returned to racing and won seven consecutive Tour de France titles. While Armstrong's victories in the 1999–2005 Tours de France were awe inspiring, his choice to turn adversity into becoming an advocate for those with cancer and those who will develop the disease is testament to a stronger will.

Lance Armstrong's story is very moving and powerful. The strength of his character and the outcomes of his

work are remarkable. Who would expect someone diagnosed with advanced cancer to beat the disease and then go on to win seven Tours de France? Who would have the courage to start a foundation to eradicate cancer before being treated for his own disease? Lance Armstrong has strong values. He is determined and courageous. He lives by his values and uses his values to advocate for the good of others.

The Lance Armstrong Foundation is making contributions to cancer care that benefit people throughout the world. As Armstrong says, "Without cancer, I never would have won a single Tour de France. Cancer taught me a plan for more purposeful living, and that, in turn, taught me how to train and to win more purposefully. It taught me that pain has a reason, and that sometimes the experience of losing things—whether health or a car or an old sense of self—has its own value in the scheme of life" (Armstrong, 2001, p. 64).

CASE STUDY

The following case describes the scandal involving the president of a small, conservative college. Questions are provided at the end of the case that will help you analyze the man's ethical behavior as a leader.

Scandal on a Conservative Campus

For nearly three decades George C. Roche III served as president of Hillsdale College, a small, private liberal arts school tucked away in a rural Michigan town 85 miles southeast of Detroit. Hillsdale, with roughly 1,200 students, may have been small, but it was well known and supported in conservative circles. Roche had transformed the institution from obscurity into a citadel espousing the values of family, faith, and freedom. He had gained notoriety by declaring that the college would be "independent" of any federal money, including student financial aid. He succeeded in rallying supporters to this cause, raising $325 million to make it a reality. He increased the college's endowment from $4 million to $184 million and provided student aid to any of Hillsdale's students who needed it (Ellis, 2000).

The college, advertising itself as a Christian institution that builds character in students, featured prominent conservatives such as Margaret Thatcher and William F. Buckley Jr. in its seminars and publications. Faculty members were attracted by the college's traditional curriculum centered on the "Great Books." The institution thrived, and Roche was a hero in the world of conservatives and a lord on his own campus. He hired his son to work at Hillsdale as a professor and his daughter-in-law, Lissa, to be editor of *Imprimis*, the college's monthly magazine that had nearly 1 million readers.

Then, on October 17, 1999, the 41-year-old Lissa took a gun from her husband's cabinet, went into the university's arboretum, and shot herself. This was hours after a confrontation in her father-in-law's hospital room, where Lissa confessed to her husband and her father-in-law's new wife that she and Roche had been having a sexual affair on and off for 19 years.

Ten days later, Lissa's husband and the president's son, George Roche IV, informed the college's board of trustees about the allegations. The elder Roche, who denied the affair, was placed on leave of absence.

Lissa's death, however, wasn't the first sign that things weren't what they ought to be in the president's office. As the college's success grew, few people, including the board, questioned Roche's increasingly centralized authority over all college operations. He traveled around the country, staying in luxurious accommodations, while proclaiming the college's values and virtues. He became one of the highest-paid college presidents in the United States, earning $524,000 in salary and benefits in 1998 (Van Der Werf, 1999).

On campus, Roche's authoritarian style didn't go over well with the faculty, who voted to form a grievance committee. He would not recognize the committee's existence, saying, "In my experience, faculty control leads to chaos." Many professors allege that those who spoke out were threatened with their jobs (Van Der Werf, 1999).

In 1988, the American Association of University Professors censured Hillsdale for "inadequate protection against an improper exercise of administrative power." One former employee described Roche's administration as "a rather Stalinish kind of environment" (Miller, 1999). Students claimed to have been expelled for speaking out or trying to get information on the administration's practices.

"They may talk about freedom, but they sure don't practice it," said one Hillsdale student (Van Der Werf, 1999).

In early 1999, Roche shocked Hillsdale by divorcing his wife of 44 years who was undergoing treatment for cancer. Rumors had circulated for years that he was unfaithful to the mother of his four children, and they were rekindled when he remarried five months later and just a month before Lissa's suicide.

It was these kinds of allegations and information that brought the college's board of trustees to hold an emergency meeting on November 10, six days after they had put the president on leave of absence. Roche flew back from Hawaii, where he was on his honeymoon. In that meeting, Ronald Trowbridge, a college vice president for external relations, said, "We will never know the truth. But the perception of the truth is what condemns President Roche. He cannot retrieve his credibility. There are only two people in the world who know for certain what happened—one is dead, and the other is denying everything" (Ellis, 2000).

After initially refusing to do so when the scandal broke, Roche retired as the college's president releasing a statement, saying, "I am nearly 65 years of age and have no wish to continue."

"We have proved that integrity, values and courage can still triumph in a corrupt world," he wrote in his resignation letter. "Hillsdale College is a monument to those beliefs" (Ellis, 2000).

Roche, who was believed to have left the college with a retirement package worth more than $1 million, moved to remote Ouray, Colorado. He died in 2006 in Louisville, Kentucky.

(Continued)

(Continued)

Questions

1. Using the factors related to ethical leadership discussed in the chapter, would you describe George Roche's III tenure as president ethical? In what ways?

2. Using the Six Pillars of Character as a basis, how did George Roche III's personal character affect his leadership?

3. Describe Roche's ethical leadership through the actions of showing respect, serving others, and showing justice.

4. Some would argue that Roche was a good leader given his ability to create a vision and succeed in achieving the goals of that vision. Should his actions in his personal life discredit that view?

5. Given that there is no way to substantiate whether or not George Roche III and Lissa had an affair, was he treated fairly by the board of trustees?

Summary

There is a strong demand for ethical leaders in our society today. This chapter answers the question "What does it take to be an ethical leader?" Ethical leadership is defined as a process in which a good person acts in the right ways to accomplish worthy goals. There are six factors related to ethical leadership.

First, *character* is fundamental to ethical leadership. A leader's character refers to whom the leader is as a person and his or her core values. The *Six Pillars of Character* are trustworthiness, respect, responsibility, fairness, caring, and citizenship.

Second, ethical leadership is explained by the *actions* of the leader—the means a leader uses to accomplish goals. An ethical leader engages in showing respect, serving others, and showing justice.

Third, ethical leadership is about the *goals* of the leader. The goals a leader selects reflect his or her values. Selecting goals that are meaningful and worthwhile is one of the most important decisions an ethical leader needs to make.

Fourth, ethical leadership is concerned with the *honesty* of the leader. Without honesty, a leader cannot be ethical. In telling the truth, a leader needs to strike a balance between openness and sensitivity to others.

Fifth, *power* plays a role in ethical leadership. A leader has an ethical obligation to use power for the influence of the common good of others. The interests of subordinates need to be taken into account, and the leader needs to work *with* subordinates to accomplish mutual ends.

Finally, ethical leadership is concerned with the *values* of the leader. An ethical leader has strong values and promotes positive values within his or her organization. Because leaders and followers often have conflicting values, a leader needs to be able to express his or her values and integrate these values with others' values.

In summary, ethical leadership has many dimensions. To be an ethical leader, you need to pay attention to whom you are, what you do, what goals you seek, your honesty, the way you use power, and your values.

 Go to **http://www.sagepub.com/northouseintro2e/** *for additional exercises and study resources. Select Chapter 11, Addressing Ethics in Leadership, for chapter-specific activities.*

Glossary Terms

actions 233	goals 236
character 231	honesty 237
end values 240	modal values 240
ethical leadership 230	power 238
ethical values 240	values 240

References

Armstrong, L. (2001, December 3). Back in the saddle. *Forbes, 168,* 64.

Beauchamp, T. L., & Bowie, N. E. (1988). *Ethical theory and business* (3rd ed.). Englewood Cliffs, NJ: Prentice Hall.

Bowie, N. E. (1991). Challenging the egoistic paradigm. *Business Ethics Quarterly, 1*(1), 1–21.

Ciulla, J. B. (2003). *The ethics of leadership.* Belmont, CA: Wadsworth/ Thomson Learning.

Ellis, J. (2000, January 19). Sex, lies and suicide. *Salon.* Retrieved December 22, 2010, from http://salon.com./books/it/2000/01/19/hillsdale

French, J. R., Jr., & Raven, B. (1959). The bases of social power. In D. Cartwright (Ed.), *Studies in social power* (pp. 150–167). Ann Arbor, MI: Institute for Social Research.

Johnson, C. R. (2005). *Meeting the ethical challenges of leadership* (2nd ed.). Thousand Oaks, CA: Sage.

Josephson Institute. (2008). *The pillars of character*. Los Angeles: Author.

Kanungo, R. N. (2001). Ethical values of transactional and transformational leaders. *Canadian Journal of Administrative Sciences, 18*(4), 257–265.

Kanungo, R. N., & Mendonca, M. (1996). *Ethical dimensions of leadership*. Thousand Oaks, CA: Sage.

Miller, J. J. (1999, November 12). Horror at Hillsdale: A conservative citadel, rocked by scandal. *National Review Online*. Retrieved December 22, 2010, from http://www.nationalreview.com/articles/220720/horror-hillsdale/john-j-miller

Van Der Werf, M. (1999, November 19). A scandal and a suicide leave a college reeling: Hillsdale president quits amid rumors of affair with his daughter-in-law, who killed herself. *Chronicle of Higher Education*. Retrieved December 22, 2010, from http://chronicle.com/article/A-Scandala-Suicide-Leave/18281

Velasquez, M. G. (1992). *Business ethics: Concepts and cases* (3rd ed.). Englewood Cliffs, NJ: Prentice Hall.

11.1   Core Values Questionnaire

 Visit www.sagepub.com/northouseintro2e for downloadable versions of these questionnaires

Purpose

1. To identify the core values most important to you

2. To reinforce core values and their role in ethical leadership

Directions

1. Review the values listed below. Use the blank lines at the bottom to add any values that are important to you that are not listed.

2. Put a star next to all the values that are important to you, including any you may have added. This will become your personal set of values.

3. Take 2 to 3 minutes to narrow the starred values to your top eight values by crossing off the values that are less important to you and circling the more important values.

4. Next, narrow the list to five important values, using the same process.

5. Narrow that list of five to three important values.

6. From these three values, choose your top two core values.

Core Values		
Peace	Authenticity	Love
Wealth	Power	Recognition
Happiness	Influence	Family
Success	Justice	Truth
Friendship	Integrity	Wisdom
Fame	Joy	Status
_____	_____	_____
_____	_____	_____

Source: Adapted from the "Self-Guided Core Values Assessment," Center for Ethical Leadership, www.ethicalleadership.org. Used with permission.

Scoring Interpretation

This exercise is designed to identify your core values. Ethical leadership includes knowing what your core values are and having the courage to integrate them with your actions, being mindful of the common good.

•   Value words are packed with meaning. You likely went through a process of "bundling"—embedding one value in another and counting two or more values as one. This is a natural process. By narrowing your lists, you did not throw away any values; rather, you clarified what you mean by these words.

•   Your two core values are easy to remember. Imagine putting them in your pocket when you leave home each day. These two values represent your larger set of values.

•   Your core values can help you make difficult decisions as a leader. They can help you find common ground with others.

11.2 Observational Exercise

 Visit www.sagepub.com/northouseintro2e for downloadable versions of these questionnaires

Ethical Leadership

Purpose

1. To become aware of the dimensions of ethical leadership
2. To assess how actual leaders exhibit ethical leadership

Directions

1. For this exercise, you must observe a public presentation of a leader in your community. This can be a pastor, a college president, a mayor, a city commissioner, the head of a social service agency, or some other community leader.

2. Record what you observe about the leader's ethics in the categories that follow. Try to be thorough in your descriptions of the leader's presentation.

Leader's name: _____ Leader's title: _____
Occasion: _____

The *character* of the leader: What was the leader like? What kind of person was the leader? What were the leader's strengths and weaknesses?

Comments:

The *actions* of the leader: How does this leader go about accomplishing goals? Where does the leader stand on (1) showing respect, (2) serving others, and (3) showing justice?

Comments:

The *goals* of the leader: What were the leader's main goals? Were the leader's goals clear to you and others in the audience? How would you assess the value and worth of those goals?

Comments:

The *honesty* of the leader: What did you observe about this leader's honesty? Was the leader open and forthright? How authentic did you find this leader to be?

Comments:

The *power* of the leader: Based on French and Raven's (1959) types of power, what kind of power did this leader exhibit? What did you observe about how this leader would use his or her power with others?

Comments:

The *values* of the leader: Based on the presentation, what do you think this leader values? What is important to this leader? What values did this leader promote in his or her presentation?

Comments:

Questions

1. What is your overall assessment of this leader's ethics?

2. What specific examples in the leader's presentation were particularly revealing of the leader's ethics?

3. Which factors of ethical leadership (character, actions, goals, honesty, power, and values) were most apparent in the leader's presentation? Discuss.

4. On a scale from 1 to 10, how would you describe this speaker's ethical leadership? Defend your answer.

11.3   Reflection and Action Worksheet

 Visit **www.sagepub.com/northouseintro2e** for downloadable versions of these questionnaires

Ethical Leadership

Reflection

1. This chapter suggests that leadership has a *moral dimension* and that leaders have a responsibility to use their authority for the common good. Do you agree? Discuss.

2. When you consider the *character of a leader* and *what a leader does* (the leader's actions), which of these two factors is more important with regard to ethical leadership? Can a person with bad character be an ethical leader? Discuss your answers.

3. In this chapter, the circumstances at Abu Ghraib prison are used as an example of unethical leadership. Do you agree with this assessment? How do you view what happened at Abu Ghraib? What factors explain the leadership ethics in this situation?

4. This chapter includes a story about Richard Lee, the father who coached his son's Little League baseball team. What was your reaction to the story? Do you think Richard was an ethical leader? How would you have responded in this situation?

Action

1. Based on your responses to the Core Values Questionnaire, what are your core values? Do you think other people know your core values? Are you comfortable talking about these values with others? In your planning for the future (e.g., next five years), how will your values influence what you do? Discuss.

2. *Character* is a fundamental aspect of ethical leadership. What are your character strengths and weaknesses? List three specific actions you could take to strengthen your character.

3. In the Observational Exercise, you observed and analyzed the ethical leadership of a specific leader. If you were to apply the same analysis to your own leadership, how would you describe yourself? What factors best explain the ethics of your own leadership? If you were to try to become a more ethical leader, what specific changes should you make in your leadership? Discuss.

Glossary

ability   a natural or acquired capacity to perform a particular activity

accommodation   an unassertive but cooperative conflict style that requires individuals to attend very closely to the needs of others and ignore their own needs

achievement-oriented leader   a leader who challenges individuals to perform at the highest level possible, establishes a high standard of excellence, and seeks continuous improvement

actions   the ways one goes about accomplishing goals

administrative skills   competencies a leader needs to run an organization in order to carry out the organization's purposes and goals

authentic leadership   an emerging leadership approach that looks at the authenticity of leaders and their leadership

authoritarian leadership   a style of leadership in which leaders perceive subordinates as needing direction and need to control subordinates and what they do

avoidance   a conflict style that is both unassertive and uncooperative, and characterized by individuals being passive and ignoring conflict situations rather than confronting them directly

behavior approach   an approach to leadership research that focuses on behavior and examines what leaders do and how they act

challenge   to stimulate people to commit themselves to change

change   a move toward something different; a shift away from the way things currently are

character   one's qualities, disposition, and core values

charisma   magnetic charm and appeal; a special personality characteristic that gives people the capacity to do extraordinary things

cohesiveness   a sense of "we-ness;" the cement that holds a group together, or the esprit de corps that exists within a group

collaboration   a conflict style that requires both assertiveness and cooperation and occurs when both parties agree to a positive settlement to the conflict and attend fully to the other's concerns while not sacrificing or suppressing their own

competent   a leader who presents himself in a way that suggests to others (and himself) that he knows what he is doing

competition   a conflict style of individuals who are highly assertive about pursuing their own goals but uncooperative in assisting others to reach their goals

compromise   a conflict style that involves both a degree of assertiveness and a degree of cooperativeness

conceptual skills   capabilities that involve working with concepts and ideas, the thinking or cognitive aspects of leadership

concern for people   refers to how a leader attends to the people in the organization who are trying to achieve its goals

concern for production   refers to how a leader is concerned with achieving organizational goals

confidence   feeling positive about oneself and one's ability to succeed

conflict   a felt struggle between two or more interdependent individuals over perceived incompatible differences in beliefs, values, and goals, or over differences in desires for esteem, control, and connectedness

conflict style   a patterned response or behavior that people use when approaching conflict

consideration behavior   a relationship leadership behavior in which the leader creates camaraderie, respect, trust, and regard with followers

content conflicts   involve struggles between leaders and others who differ on issues such as policies and procedures

content dimension   involves the objective, observable aspects of communication

contingency theory   a leadership theory that focuses on the match between the leader's style and specific situational variables

democratic leadership style   a style of leadership in which leaders treat subordinates as fully capable of doing work on their own and work with subordinates, trying hard to treat everyone fairly, without putting themselves above subordinates

determination   being focused and attentive to tasks; showing initiative, persistence, and drive

differentiation   an interaction process that occurs in the early phase of conflict that helps participants define the nature of the conflict and clarify their positions with regard to each other

directive leader   a leader who sets clear standards of performance and makes rules and regulations clear for others

emotional intelligence   concerned with a person's ability to understand his or her own and others' emotions, and then to apply this understanding to life's tasks; the ability to perceive and express emotions, to use emotions to facilitate thinking, to understand and reason with emotions, and to manage emotions effectively within oneself and in relationships with others

empathy   a process in which an individual suspends his or her own feelings in an effort to fully understand the feelings of another individual

employee orientation   a relationship leadership behavior in which the leader takes an interest in workers as human beings, values their uniqueness, and gives special attention to their personal needs

end values   the outcomes or goals a leader seeks to achieve

ethical leadership   a process by which a good person rightly influences others to accomplish a common good

ethical values   concerned with the character or virtuousness of the leader

expectancy theory   people will be more highly motivated when they are capable of performing their work, the effort they put into a task leads to an expected outcome, and they value the outcome

face saving   communicative attempts to establish or maintain one's self-image or another's self-image in response to threat

fractionation   the technique of breaking down large conflicts into smaller, more manageable pieces

goals   the aims or outcomes an individual seeks to achieve

"Great Man" theories   early trait theories of leadership that focused on identifying the innate qualities and characteristics possessed by great social, political, and military leaders (see also trait approach)

honesty   telling the truth and representing reality as fully and completely as possible

initiating structure   task leadership in which the leader organizes work, defines role responsibilities, and schedules work activities

integrity   adhering to a strong set of principles and taking responsibility for one's actions; being honest and trustworthy

intelligence   having good language skills, perceptual skills, and reasoning ability

interpersonal skills   people skills; those abilities that help a leader to work effectively with subordinates, peers, and superiors to accomplish the organization's goals

laissez-faire leadership style   a style of leadership, sometimes labeled nonleadership, in which leaders ignore workers and their work motivations and engage in minimal influence

leader-member exchange (LMX) theory conceptualizes leadership as a process that is centered on the interactions between leaders and followers

leadership   a process whereby an individual influences a group of individuals to achieve a common goal

leadership style   the behaviors of leaders, focusing on what leaders do and how they act

listening   paying attention to what people say while being attentive to what people mean

map   a laid-out path to follow to direct people toward their short- and long-term goals

mission   the goal toward which a group is working, which provides organization to the rest of its activities

modal values   concerned with the means or actions a leader takes

norms   the rules of behavior that are established and shared by group members

obstacle   a problem that hinders group productivity

out-group   individuals in a group or an organization who do not identify themselves as part of the larger group, and who are disconnected and not fully engaged in working toward the goals of the group

participative leader   a leader who invites others to share in the ways and means of getting things done

path-goal leadership   leadership in which a leader should choose a style that best fits the needs of individual group members and the task they are doing

path-goal theory   a leadership theory that examines how leaders use employee motivation to enhance performance and satisfaction

personal style   unique habits regarding work and play, which have been ingrained over many years and influence one's current style

philosophy of leadership   a unique set of beliefs and attitudes about the nature of people and the nature of work that have a significant impact on an individual's leadership style

picture   an ideal image of where a group or an organization should be going

power   the capacity to influence or affect others

principled negotiation   an approach to conflict that decides issues on their merits rather than through competitive haggling or through excessive accommodation

problem-solving skills   one's cognitive ability to take corrective action in a problem situation in order to meet desired objectives

process behaviors   behaviors used by leaders to help group members feel comfortable with each other and at ease in the situations in which they find themselves

production orientation   task leadership in which the leader stresses the production and technical aspects of the job

relational approach   an approach to leadership research that examines the nature of relations between leaders and followers

relationship behaviors   behaviors used by leaders that help subordinates feel comfortable with themselves, with each other, and with the situation they find themselves in

relational conflicts   refer to the differences we feel between ourselves and others concerning how we relate to each other

relationship dimension   refers to the participants' perceptions of their connection to one another

relationship-oriented leadership   leadership that is focused primarily on the well-being of subordinates, how they relate to each other, and the atmosphere in which they work

servant leadership   an emerging leadership approach that emphasizes the "caring principle" with leaders as "servants" who focus on their followers' needs in order to help these followers become more autonomous, knowledgeable, and like servants themselves

situational approach   an approach to leadership research based on the premise that different situations demand different kinds of leadership

skill   a competency developed to accomplish a task effectively

sociability   capable of establishing pleasant social relationships; being sensitive to others' needs and concerned for their well-being

social identity theory   explains why and how individuals identify with particular social groups and how these identifications affect their behavior

social perceptiveness   having insight into and awareness of what is important to others, how they are motivated, the problems they face, and how they react to change

spiritual leadership   an emerging leadership approach that examines how leaders use values, a sense of "calling," and membership to motivate followers

standards of excellence   the expressed and implied expectations for performance that exist within a group or an organization

status quo   the current situation; the way things are now

strategic planning   a conceptual skill, the cognitive ability to think and consider ideas to develop effective strategies for a group or an organization

structure   a blueprint for the work of a particular group that gives form and meaning to the purposes of its activities

supportive   a leader who provides what is missing—the human connection—by encouraging others when they are engaged in tasks that are boring and unchallenging; offers a sense of human touch for those engaged in mundane mechanical activity

synergy   the group energy created from two or more people working together, which creates an outcome that is different from and better than the sum of the individual contributions

task behaviors   behaviors used by leaders to get the job done

task-oriented leadership   leadership that is focused predominantly on procedures, activities, and goal accomplishments

technical competence   having specialized knowledge about the work we do or ask others to do

Theory X   a general theory created by Douglas McGregor in which leaders assume that people dislike work, that they need to be directed and controlled, and that they want security—not responsibility

Theory Y   a general theory created by Douglas McGregor in which leaders assume that people like work, that they are self-motivated, and that they accept and seek responsibility

trait   a distinguishing personal quality that is often inherited (e.g., intelligence, confidence, charisma, determination, sociability, and integrity)

trait approach   an approach to leadership research that focuses on identifying the innate qualities and characteristics possessed by individuals (see also Great Man theories)

transformational leadership theory   a theory that describes leadership as a process that changes people and organizations

values   the ideas, beliefs, and modes of action that people find worthwhile or desirable

vision   a mental model of an ideal future state

Photo Credits

CHAPTER 1

Chapter Opening Photo: © iStockphoto.
com/kali9.

CHAPTER 2

Chapter Opening Photo: Digital Vision/
Thinkstock

Photo 2.1: The Frick Collection,
New York.

Photo 2.2: © Getty Images/Photos.com/
Thinkstock.

Photo 2.3: Library of Congress.

Photo 2.4: British Imperial War Museum.

Photo 2.5: © Bettmann/Corbis.

Photo 2.6: South Africa The Good News/
www.sagoodnews.co.za.

Photo 2.7: © Haruyoshi Yamaguchi/Corbis.

Photo 2.8: © Pace Gregory/Corbis Sygma.

CHAPTER 3

Chapter Opening Photo: © iStockphoto.
com/Niko Guido.

Photo 3.1: © Buena Vista/courtesy Everett
Collection.

Photo 3.2: © Warner Bros./Courtesy Everett
Collection.

Photo 3.3: © Corbis Sygma.

CHAPTER 4

Chapter Opening Photo: © Christopher
Robbins/Valueline/Thinkstock.

CHAPTER 5

Chapter Opening Photo: © iStockphoto.
com/Jacob Wackerhausen.

CHAPTER 6

Chapter Opening Photo: Ciaran Griffin/
Lifesize/Thinkstock.

Photo 6.1: The National Archives.

Photo 6.2: Photograph by Ian Muttoo.

CHAPTER 7

Chapter Opening Photo: © istockphoto.com/
laflor.

CHAPTER 8

Chapter Opening Photo:
© Jupiterimages/photos.com/
Thinkstock.

CHAPTER 9

Chapter Opening Photo: Jupiterimages/
Photos.com/Thinkstock.

CHAPTER 10

Chapter Opening Photo: © iStockphoto
.com/Mark Rose.

CHAPTER 11

Chapter Opening Photo: © iStockphoto
.com/Karen Struthers.

Photo 11.1: © Elizabeth Kreutz/Corbis.

Index

Tear-Out Questionnaries

1.1 Conceptualizing Leadership Questionnaire

 Visit www.sagepub.com/northouseintro2e for downloadable versions of these questionnaires

Purpose

1. To identify how you view leadership
2. To explore your perceptions of different aspects of leadership

Directions

1. Consider for a moment your own impressions of the word *leadership*. Based on your experiences with leaders in your lifetime, what is leadership?
2. Using the scale below, indicate the extent to which you agree or disagree with the following statements about leadership.

Statement	Strongly disagree	Disagree	Neutral	Agree	Strongly agree
1. When I think of leadership, I think of a person with special personality traits.	1	2	3	4	5
2. Much like playing the piano or tennis, leadership is a learned ability.	1	2	3	4	5
3. Leadership requires knowledge and know-how.	1	2	3	4	5
4. Leadership is about what people do rather than who they are.	1	2	3	4	5
5. Followers can influence the leadership process as much as leaders.	1	2	3	4	5
6. Leadership is about the process of influencing others.	1	2	3	4	5
7. Some people are born to be leaders.	1	2	3	4	5
8. Some people have the natural ability to be leaders.	1	2	3	4	5
9. The key to successful leadership is having the right skills.	1	2	3	4	5
10. Leadership is best described by what leaders do.	1	2	3	4	5
11. Leaders and followers share in the leadership process.	1	2	3	4	5
12. Leadership is a series of actions directed toward positive ends.	1	2	3	4	5
13. A person needs to have certain traits to be an effective leader.	1	2	3	4	5
14. Everyone has the capacity to be a leader.	1	2	3	4	5
15. Effective leaders are competent in their roles.	1	2	3	4	5
16. The essence of leadership is performing tasks and dealing with people.	1	2	3	4	5

Statement	Strongly disagree	Disagree	Neutral	Agree	Strongly agree
17. Leadership is about the common purposes of leaders and followers.	1	2	3	4	5
18. Leadership does not rely on the leader alone but is a process involving the leader, followers, and the situation.	1	2	3	4	5
19. People become great leaders because of their traits.	1	2	3	4	5
20. People can develop the ability to lead.	1	2	3	4	5
21. Effective leaders have competence and knowledge.	1	2	3	4	5
22. Leadership is about how leaders work with people to accomplish goals.	1	2	3	4	5
23. Effective leadership is best explained by the leader-follower relationship.	1	2	3	4	5
24. Leaders influence and are influenced by followers.	1	2	3	4	5

Scoring

1. Sum scores on items 1, 7, 13, and 19 (trait emphasis)

2. Sum scores on items 2, 8, 14, and 20 (ability emphasis)

3. Sum scores on items 3, 9, 15, and 21 (skill emphasis)

4. Sum scores on items 4, 10, 16, and 22 (behavior emphasis)

5. Sum scores on items 5, 11, 17, and 23 (relationship emphasis)

6. Sum scores on items 6, 12, 18, and 24 (process emphasis)

Total Scores

1. Trait emphasis: _____

2. Ability emphasis: _____

3. Skill emphasis: _____

4. Behavior emphasis: _____

5. Relationship emphasis: _____

6. Process emphasis: _____

Scoring Interpretation

The scores you received on this questionnaire provide information about how you define and view leadership. The emphasis you give to the various dimensions of leadership has implications for how you approach the leadership process. For example, if your highest score is *trait emphasis*, it suggests that you emphasize the role of the leader and the leader's special gifts in the leadership process. However, if your highest score is *process emphasis*, it indicates that you think leadership is centered on the communication between leaders and followers, rather than on the unique qualities of the leader. By comparing your scores, you can gain an understanding of the aspects of leadership that you find most important and least important. The way you think about leadership will influence how you practice leadership.

2.1 Leadership Traits Questionnaire

 Visit www.sagepub.com/northouseintro2e for downloadable versions of these questionnaires

Purpose

1. To gain an understanding of how traits are used in leadership assessment
2. To obtain an assessment of your own leadership traits

Directions

1. Make five copies of this questionnaire. This questionnaire should be completed by you and *five people* you know (e.g., roommates, coworkers, relatives, friends).
2. Using the following scale, have each individual indicate the degree to which he or she agrees or disagrees with each of the 14 statements below regarding your leadership traits. Do not forget to complete this exercise for yourself.

_____ (name) is

Statements	Strongly disagree	Disagree	Neutral	Agree	Strongly agree
1. Articulate: Communicates effectively with others	1	2	3	4	5
2. Perceptive: Discerning and insightful	1	2	3	4	5
3. Self-confident: Believes in oneself and one's ability	1	2	3	4	5
4. Self-assured: Secure with self, free of doubts	1	2	3	4	5
5. Persistent: Stays fixed on the goals, despite interference	1	2	3	4	5
6. Determined: Takes a firm stand, acts with certainty	1	2	3	4	5
7. Trustworthy: Is authentic, inspires confidence	1	2	3	4	5
8. Dependable: Is consistent and reliable	1	2	3	4	5
9. Friendly: Shows kindness and warmth	1	2	3	4	5
10. Outgoing: Talks freely, gets along well with others	1	2	3	4	5
11. Conscientious: Is thorough, organized, and careful	1	2	3	4	5
12. Diligent: Is industrious, hardworking	1	2	3	4	5
13. Sensitive: Shows tolerance, is tactful and sympathetic	1	2	3	4	5
14. Empathic: Understands others, identifies with others	1	2	3	4	5

Scoring

1. Enter the responses for Raters 1, 2, 3, 4, and 5 in the appropriate columns on the scoring sheet on this page. An example of a completed chart is provided on page 41.

2. For each of the 14 items, compute the average for the five raters and place that number in the "average rating" column.

3. Place your own scores in the "self-rating" column.

Leadership Traits Questionnaire Chart

	Rater 1	Rater 2	Rater 3	Rater 4	Rater 5	Average rating	Self-rating
1. Articulate							
2. Perceptive							
3. Self-confident							
4. Self-assured							
5. Persistent							
6. Determined							
7. Trustworthy							
8. Dependable							
9. Friendly							
10. Outgoing							
11. Conscientious							
12. Diligent							
13. Sensitive							
14. Empathic							

Summary and interpretation:

Scoring Interpretation

The scores you received on this questionnaire provide information about how you see yourself and how others see you as a leader. The chart allows you to see where your perceptions are the same as those of others and where they differ. There are no "perfect" scores for this questionnaire. The purpose of the instrument is to provide a way to assess your strengths and weaknesses and to evaluate areas where your perceptions are similar to or different from those of others. While it is confirming when others see you in the same way as you see yourself, it is also beneficial to know when they see you differently. This assessment can help you understand your assets as well as areas in which you may seek to improve.

Example 2.1 Leadership Traits Questionnaire Ratings

		Rater 1	Rater 2	Rater 3	Rater 4	Rater 5	Average rating	Self-rating
1.	Articulate	4	4	3	2	4	3.4	4
2.	Perceptive	2	5	3	4	4	3.6	5
3.	Self-confident	4	4	5	5	4	4.4	4
4.	Self-assured	5	5	5	5	5	5	5
5.	Persistent	4	4	3	3	3	3.4	3
6.	Determined	4	4	4	4	4	4	4
7.	Trustworthy	5	5	5	5	5	5	5
8.	Dependable	4	5	4	5	4	4.4	4
9.	Friendly	5	5	5	5	5	5	5
10.	Outgoing	5	4	5	4	5	4.6	4
11.	Conscientious	2	3	2	3	3	2.6	4
12.	Diligent	3	3	3	3	3	3	4
13.	Sensitive	4	4	5	5	5	4.6	3
14.	Empathic	5	5	4	5	4	4.6	3

Summary and interpretation: The scorer's self-ratings are higher than the average ratings of others on *articulate, perceptive, conscientious,* and *diligent.* The scorer's self-ratings are lower than the average ratings of others on *self-confident, persistent, dependable, outgoing, sensitive,* and *empathic.* The scorer's self-ratings on *self-assured, determined, trustworthy,* and *friendly* are the same as the average ratings of others.

3.1 Leadership Styles Questionnaire

 Visit www.sagepub.com/northouseintro2e for downloadable versions of these questionnaires

Purpose

1. To identify your style of leadership
2. To examine how your leadership style relates to other styles of leadership

Directions

1. For each of the statements below, circle the number that indicates the degree to which you agree or disagree.
2. Give your immediate impressions. There are no right or wrong answers.

Statements	Strongly disagree	Disagree	Neutral	Agree	Strongly agree
1. Employees need to be supervised closely, or they are not likely to do their work.	1	2	3	4	5
2. Employees want to be a part of the decision-making process.	1	2	3	4	5
3. In complex situations, leaders should let subordinates work problems out on their own.	1	2	3	4	5
4. It is fair to say that most employees in the general population are lazy.	1	2	3	4	5
5. Providing guidance without pressure is the key to being a good leader.	1	2	3	4	5
6. Leadership requires staying out of the way of subordinates as they do their work.	1	2	3	4	5
7. As a rule, employees must be given rewards or punishments in order to motivate them to achieve organizational objectives.	1	2	3	4	5
8. Most workers want frequent and supportive communication from their leaders.	1	2	3	4	5
9. As a rule, leaders should allow subordinates to appraise their own work.	1	2	3	4	5
10. Most employees feel insecure about their work and need direction.	1	2	3	4	5
11. Leaders need to help subordinates accept responsibility for completing their work.	1	2	3	4	5
12. Leaders should give subordinates complete freedom to solve problems on their own.	1	2	3	4	5
13. The leader is the chief judge of the achievements of the members of the group.	1	2	3	4	5

Statements	Strongly disagree	Disagree	Neutral	Agree	Strongly agree
14. It is the leader's job to help subordinates find their "passion."	1	2	3	4	5
15. In most situations, workers prefer little input from the leader.	1	2	3	4	5
16. Effective leaders give orders and clarify procedures.	1	2	3	4	5
17. People are basically competent and if given a task will do a good job.	1	2	3	4	5
18. In general, it is best to leave subordinates alone.	1	2	3	4	5

Scoring

1. Sum the responses on items 1, 4, 7, 10, 13, and 16 (authoritarian leadership).

2. Sum the responses on items 2, 5, 8, 11, 14, and 17 (democratic leadership).

3. Sum the responses on items 3, 6, 9, 12, 15, and 18 (laissez-faire leadership).

Total Scores

Authoritarian Leadership _____

Democratic Leadership _____

Laissez-Faire Leadership _____

Scoring Interpretation

This questionnaire is designed to measure three common styles of leadership: authoritarian, democratic, and laissez-faire. By comparing your scores, you can determine which styles are most dominant and least dominant in your own style of leadership.

If your score is 26–30, you are in the very high range.

If your score is 21–25, you are in the high range.

If your score is 16–20, you are in the moderate range.

If your score is 11–15, you are in the low range.

If your score is 6–10, you are in the very low range.

4.1 Task and Relationship Questionnaire

 Visit www.sagepub.com/northouseintro2e for downloadable versions of these questionnaires

Purpose

1. To identify how much you emphasize task and relationship behaviors in your life
2. To explore how your task behavior is related to your relationship behavior

Directions

For each item below, indicate on the scale the extent to which you engage in the described behavior. Move through the items quickly. Do not try to categorize yourself in one area or another.

Statements	Never	Rarely	Sometimes	Often	Always
1. Make a "to do" list of the things that need to be done.	1	2	3	4	5
2. Try to make the work fun for others.	1	2	3	4	5
3. Urge others to concentrate on the work at hand.	1	2	3	4	5
4. Show concern for the personal well-being of others.	1	2	3	4	5
5. Set timelines for when the job needs to be done.	1	2	3	4	5
6. Help group members get along.	1	2	3	4	5
7. Keep a checklist of what has been accomplished.	1	2	3	4	5
8. Listen to the special needs of each group member.	1	2	3	4	5
9. Stress to others the rules and requirements for the project.	1	2	3	4	5
10. Spend time exploring other people's ideas for the project.	1	2	3	4	5

Scoring

1. Sum scores for the odd-numbered statements (task score).
2. Sum scores for the even-numbered statements (relationship score).

Total Scores

Task score: _____

Relationship score: _____

Scoring Interpretation

This questionnaire is designed to measure your task-oriented and relationship-oriented leadership behavior. By comparing your scores, you can determine which style is more dominant in your own style of leadership. If your task score is higher than your relationship score, you tend to give more attention to goal accomplishment and somewhat less attention to people-related matters. If your relationship score is higher than your task score, your primary concern tends to be dealing with people, and your secondary concern is directed more toward tasks. If your scores are very similar to each other, it suggests that your leadership is balanced and includes an equal amount of both behaviors.

If your score is 20–25, you are in the high range.

If your score is 15–19, you are in the high moderate range.

If your score is 10–14, you are in the low moderate range.

If your score is 5–9, you are in the low range.

5.1 Leadership Skills Questionnaire

 Visit www.sagepub.com/northouseintro2e for downloadable versions of these questionnaires

Purpose

1. To identify your leadership skills
2. To provide a profile of your leadership skills showing your strengths and weaknesses

Directions

1. Place yourself in the role of a leader when responding to this questionnaire.
2. For each of the statements below, circle the number that indicates the degree to which you feel the statement is true.

Statements	Not true	Seldom true	Occasionally true	Somewhat true	Very true
1. I am effective with the detailed aspects of my work.	1	2	3	4	5
2. I usually know ahead of time how people will respond to a new idea or proposal.	1	2	3	4	5
3. I am effective at problem solving.	1	2	3	4	5
4. Filling out forms and working with details comes easily for me.	1	2	3	4	5
5. Understanding the social fabric of the organization is important to me.	1	2	3	4	5
6. When problems arise, I immediately address them.	1	2	3	4	5
7. Managing people and resources is one of my strengths.	1	2	3	4	5
8. I am able to sense the emotional undercurrents in my group.	1	2	3	4	5
9. Seeing the big picture comes easily for me.	1	2	3	4	5
10. In my work, I enjoy responding to people's requests and concerns.	1	2	3	4	5
11. I use my emotional energy to motivate others.	1	2	3	4	5
12. Making strategic plans for my company appeals to me.	1	2	3	4	5
13. Obtaining and allocating resources is a challenging aspect of my job.	1	2	3	4	5

Statements	Not true	Seldom true	Occasionally true	Somewhat true	Very true
14. The key to successful conflict resolution is respecting my opponent.	1	2	3	4	5
15. I enjoy discussing organizational values and philosophy.	1	2	3	4	5
16. I am effective at obtaining resources to support our programs.	1	2	3	4	5
17. I work hard to find consensus in conflict situations.	1	2	3	4	5
18. I am flexible about making changes in our organization.	1	2	3	4	5

Scoring

1. Sum the responses on items 1, 4, 7, 10, 13, and 16 (administrative skill score).

2. Sum the responses on items 2, 5, 8, 11, 14, and 17 (interpersonal skill score).

3. Sum the responses on items 3, 6, 9, 12, 15, and 18 (conceptual skill score).

Total Scores

Administrative skill: _____

Interpersonal skill: _____

Conceptual skill: _____

Scoring Interpretation

The Leadership Skills Questionnaire is designed to measure three broad types of leadership skills: administrative, interpersonal, and conceptual. By comparing your scores, you can determine where you have leadership strengths and where you have leadership weaknesses.

If your score is 26–30, you are in the very high range.

If your score is 21–25, you are in the high range.

If your score is 16–20, you are in the moderate range.

If your score is 11–15, you are in the low range.

If your score is 6–10, you are in the very low range.

6.1 Leadership Vision Questionnaire

 Visit www.sagepub.com/northouseintro2e for downloadable versions of these questionnaires

Purpose

1. To assess your ability to create a vision for a group or an organization
2. To help you understand how visions are formed

Directions

1. Think for a moment of a work, school, social, religious, musical, or athletic organization of which you are a member. Now, think what you would do if you were the leader and you had to create a vision for the group or organization. Keep this vision in mind as you complete the exercise.
2. Using the following scale, circle the number that indicates the degree to which you agree or disagree with each statement.

Statements	Strongly disagree	Disagree	Neutral	Agree	Strongly agree
1. I have a mental picture of what would make our group better.	1	2	3	4	5
2. I can imagine several changes that would improve our group.	1	2	3	4	5
3. I have a vision for what would make our organization stronger.	1	2	3	4	5
4. I know how we could change the status quo to make things better.	1	2	3	4	5
5. It is clear to me what steps we need to take to improve our organization.	1	2	3	4	5
6. I have a clear picture of what needs to be done in our organization to achieve a higher standard of excellence.					
7. I have a clear picture in my mind of what this organization should look like in the future.	1	2	3	4	5
8. It is clear to me what core values, if emphasized, would improve our organization.	1	2	3	4	5
9. I can identify challenging goals that should be emphasized in my group.	1	2	3	4	5
10. I can imagine several things that would inspire my group to perform better.	1	2	3	4	5

Scoring

Sum the numbers you circled on the questionnaire (visioning ability skill).

Total Scores

Visioning ability skill: _____

Scoring Interpretation

The Leadership Vision Questionnaire is designed to measure your ability to create a vision as a leader.

If your score is 41–50, you are in the very high range.

If your score is 31–40, you are in the high range.

If your score is 21–30, you are in the moderate range.

If your score is 10–20, you are in the low range.

7.1 Setting the Tone Questionnaire

 Visit www.sagepub.com/northouseintro2e for downloadable versions of these questionnaires

Purpose

1. To develop an understanding of how your leadership affects others
2. To help you understand your strengths and weaknesses in establishing the tone for a group or an organization

Directions

1. For each of the statements below, indicate the frequency with which you engage in the behavior listed.
2. Give your immediate impressions. There are no right or wrong answers.

When I am the leader . . .	Never	Seldom	Sometimes	Often	Always
1. I give clear assignments to group members.	1	2	3	4	5
2. I emphasize starting and ending group meetings on time.	1	2	3	4	5
3. I encourage group members to appreciate the value of the overall group.	1	2	3	4	5
4. I encourage group members to work to the best of their abilities.	1	2	3	4	5
5. I make the goals of the group clear to everyone.	1	2	3	4	5
6. I model group norms for group members.	1	2	3	4	5
7. I encourage group members to listen and to respect each other.	1	2	3	4	5
8. I make a point of recognizing people when they do a good job.	1	2	3	4	5
9. I emphasize the overall purpose of the group assignment to group members.	1	2	3	4	5
10. I demonstrate effective communication to group members.	1	2	3	4	5
11. I encourage group members to respect each other's differences.	1	2	3	4	5
12. I promote standards of excellence.	1	2	3	4	5
13. I help group members understand their purpose for being in the group.	1	2	3	4	5
14. I encourage group members to agree on the rules for the group.	1	2	3	4	5
15. I encourage group members to accept each other as unique individuals.	1	2	3	4	5

When I am the leader . . .	Never	Seldom	Sometimes	Often	Always
16. I give group members honest feedback about their work.	1	2	3	4	5
17. I help group members understand their roles in the group.	1	2	3	4	5
18. I expect group members to listen when another group member is talking.	1	2	3	4	5
19. I help group members build camaraderie with each other.	1	2	3	4	5
20. I show group members who are not performing well how to improve the quality of their work.	1	2	3	4	5

Scoring

1. Sum the responses on items 1, 5, 9, 13, and 17 (providing structure).

2. Sum the responses on items 2, 6, 10, 14, and 18 (clarifying norms).

3. Sum the responses on items 3, 7, 11, 15, and 19 (building cohesiveness).

4. Sum the responses on items 4, 8, 12, 16, and 20 (promoting standards of excellence).

Total Scores

Providing structure: _____

Clarifying norms: _____

Building cohesiveness: _____

Promoting standards of excellence: _____

Scoring Interpretation

This questionnaire is designed to measure four factors related to setting the tone: providing structure, clarifying norms, building cohesiveness, and promoting standards of excellence. By comparing your scores, you can determine your strengths and weaknesses in setting the tone as a leader.

If your score is 20–25, you are in the high range.

If your score is 15–19, you are in the high moderate range.

If your score is 10–14, you are in the low moderate range.

If your score is 5–9, you are in the low range.

8.1   Responding to Members of the Out-Group Questionnaire

 Visit www.sagepub.com/northouseintro2e for downloadable versions of these questionnaires

Purpose

1. To identify your attitudes toward out-group members
2. To explore how you, as a leader, respond to members of the out-group

Directions

1. Place yourself in the role of a leader when responding to this questionnaire.
2. For each of the statements below, circle the number that indicates the degree to which you agree or disagree.

Statements	Strongly disagree	Disagree	Neutral	Agree	Strongly agree
1. If some group members do not fit in with the rest of the group, I usually try to include them.	1	2	3	4	5
2. I become irritated when some group members act stubborn (or obstinate) with the majority of the group.	1	2	3	4	5
3. Building a sense of group unity with people who think differently than I is essential to what I do as a leader.	1	2	3	4	5
4. I am bothered when some individuals in the group bring up unusual ideas that hinder or block the progress of the rest of the group.	1	2	3	4	5
5. If some group members cannot agree with the majority of the group, I usually give them special attention.	1	2	3	4	5
6. Sometimes I ignore individuals who show little interest in group meetings.	1	2	3	4	5
7. When making a group decision, I always try to include the interests of members who have different points of view.	1	2	3	4	5
8. Trying to reach consensus (complete agreement) with out-group members is often a waste of time.	1	2	3	4	5
9. I place a high priority on encouraging everyone in the group to listen to the minority point of view.	1	2	3	4	5
10. When differences exist between group members, I usually call for a vote to keep the group moving forward.	1	2	3	4	5
11. Listening to individuals with extreme (or radical) ideas is valuable to my leadership.	1	2	3	4	5

Statements	Strongly disagree	Disagree	Neutral	Agree	Strongly agree
12. When a group member feels left out, it is usually his or her own fault.	1	2	3	4	5
13. I give special attention to out-group members (i.e., individuals who feel left out of the group).	1	2	3	4	5
14. I find certain group members frustrating when they bring up issues that conflict with what the rest of the group wants to do.	1	2	3	4	5

Scoring

1. Sum the even-numbered items, but reverse the score value of your responses (i.e., change 1 to 5, 2 to 4, 4 to 2, and 5 to 1, with 3 remaining unchanged).

2. Sum the responses of the odd-numbered items and the converted values of the even-numbered items. This total is your leadership out-group score.

Total Score

Out-group score: _____

Scoring Interpretation

This questionnaire is designed to measure your response to out-group members.

- A high score on the questionnaire indicates that you try to help out-group members feel included and become a part of the whole group. You are likely to listen to people with different points of view and to know that hearing a minority position is often valuable in effective group work.

- An average score on the questionnaire indicates that you are moderately interested in including out-group members in the group. Although interested in including them, you do not make out-group members' concerns a priority in your leadership. You may think of out-group members as having brought their out-group behavior on themselves. If they seek you out, you probably will work with them when you can.

- A low score on the questionnaire indicates you most likely have little interest in helping out-group members become a part of the larger group. You may become irritated and bothered when out-group members' behaviors hinder the majority or progress of the larger group. Because you see helping the out-group members as an ineffective use of your time, you are likely to ignore them and make decisions to move the group forward without their input.

    If your score is 57–70, you are in the very high range.

    If your score is 50–56, you are in the high range.

    If your score is 45–49, you are in the average range.

    If your score is 38–44, you are in the low range.

    If your score is 10–37, you are in the very low range.

9.1 Conflict Style Questionnaire

 Visit www.sagepub.com/northouseintro2e for downloadable versions of these questionnaires

Purpose

1. To identify your conflict style
2. To examine how your conflict style varies in different contexts or relationships

Directions

1. Think of two different situations (A and B) where you have a conflict, a disagreement, an argument, or a disappointment with someone, such as a roommate or a work associate. Write the name of the person for each situation below.

2. According to the scale below, fill in your scores for Situation A and Situation B. For each question, you will have two scores. For example, on Question 1 the scoring might look like this: 1. 2 | 4

3. Write the name of each person for the two situations here:

Person A _____   Person B _____

1 = never	2 = seldom	3 = sometimes	4 = often	5 = always

	Person A | Person B	
1.	___ | ___	I avoid being "put on the spot"; I keep conflicts to myself.
2.	___ | ___	I use my influence to get my ideas accepted.
3.	___ | ___	I usually try to "split the difference" in order to resolve an issue.
4.	___ | ___	I generally try to satisfy the other's needs.
5.	___ | ___	I try to investigate an issue to find a solution acceptable to both of us.
6.	___ | ___	I usually avoid open discussion of my differences with the other.
7.	___ | ___	I use my authority to make a decision in my favor.
8.	___ | ___	I try to find a middle course to resolve an impasse.
9.	___ | ___	I usually accommodate the other's wishes.
10.	___ | ___	I try to integrate my ideas with the other's to come up with a decision jointly.
11.	___ | ___	I try to stay away from disagreement with the other.
12.	___ | ___	I use my expertise to make a decision that favors me.
13.	___ | ___	I propose a middle ground for breaking deadlocks.

Person A	Person B	
14.	___|___	I give in to the other's wishes.
15.	___|___	I try to work with the other to find solutions that satisfy both our expectations.
16.	___|___	I try to keep my disagreement to myself in order to avoid hard feelings.
17.	___|___	I generally pursue my side of an issue.
18.	___|___	I negotiate with the other to reach a compromise.
19.	___|___	I often go with the other's suggestions.
20.	___|___	I exchange accurate information with the other so we can solve a problem together.
21.	___|___	I try to avoid unpleasant exchanges with the other.
22.	___|___	I sometimes use my power to win.
23.	___|___	I use "give and take" so that a compromise can be made.
24.	___|___	I try to satisfy the other's expectations.
25.	___|___	I try to bring all our concerns out in the open so that the issues can be resolved.

Source: Adapted from "Confirmatory Factor Analysis of the Styles of Handling Interpersonal Conflict: First-Order Factor Model and Its Invariance Across Groups," by M. A. Rahim and N. R. Magner, 1995, *Journal of Applied Psychology, 80*(1), 122–132. In W. Wilmot and J. Hocker (2011), *Interpersonal Conflict* (pp. 146–148). New York: McGraw-Hill. Used with permission of publisher.

Scoring: Add up your scores on the following questions:

A|B	A|B	A|B	A|B	A|B
1. __|__	2. __|__	3. __|__	4. __|__	5. __|__
6. __|__	7. __|__	8. __|__	9. __|__	10. __|__
11. __|__	12. __|__	13. __|__	14. __|__	15. __|__
16. __|__	17. __|__	18. __|__	19. __|__	20. __|__
21. __|__	22. __|__	23. __|__	24. __|__	25. __|__
__|__ A|B **Avoidance Totals**	__|__ A|B **Competition Totals**	__|__ A|B **Compromise Totals**	__|__ A|B **Accommodation Totals**	__|__ A|B **Collaboration Totals**

Scoring Interpretation

This questionnaire is designed to *identify* your conflict style and *examine* how it varies in different contexts or relationships. By comparing your total scores for the different styles you can discover which conflict style you rely most heavily upon and which style you use least. Furthermore, by comparing your scores for Person A and Person B, you can determine how your style varies or stays the same in different relationships. Your scores are on this questionnaire are indicative of how you responded to a particular conflict at a specific time and therefore might change if you selected a different conflict or a different conflict period. The Conflict Style Questionnaire is not a personality test that labels or categorizes you; rather, it attempts to give you a sense of your more dominant and less dominant conflict styles.

Scores from 21 to 25 are representative of a very strong style.

Scores from 15 to 20 are representative of a strong style.

Scores from 11 to 15 are representative of an average style.

Scores from 6 to 10 are representative of a weak style.

Scores from 0 to 5 are representative of a very weak style.

10.1   Path-Goal Styles Questionnaire

 Visit www.sagepub.com/northouseintro2e for downloadable versions of these questionnaires

Purpose

1. To identify your path-goal styles of leadership
2. To examine how your use of each style relates to other styles of leadership

Directions

1. For each of the statements below, circle the number that indicates the frequency with which you engage in the expressed behavior.
2. Give your immediate impressions. There are no right or wrong answers.

When I am the leader. . . .	Never	Seldom	Sometimes	Often	Always
1. I give clear explanations of what is expected of others.	1	2	3	4	5
2. I show interest in subordinates' personal concerns.	1	2	3	4	5
3. I invite subordinates to participate in decision making.	1	2	3	4	5
4. I challenge subordinates to continuously improve their work performance.	1	2	3	4	5
5. I give subordinates explicit instructions for how to do their work.	1	2	3	4	5
6. I show concern for the personal well-being of my subordinates.	1	2	3	4	5
7. I solicit subordinates' suggestions before making a decision.	1	2	3	4	5
8. I encourage subordinates to consistently raise their own standards of performance.	1	2	3	4	5
9. I give clear directions to others for how to proceed on a project.	1	2	3	4	5
10. I listen to others and give them encouragement.	1	2	3	4	5
11. I am receptive to ideas and advice from others.	1	2	3	4	5
12. I expect subordinates to excel in all aspects of their work.	1	2	3	4	5

Scoring

1. Sum the responses on items 1, 5, and 9 (directive leadership).
2. Sum the responses on items 2, 6, and 10 (supportive leadership).
3. Sum the responses on items 3, 7, and 11 (participative leadership).
4. Sum the responses on items 4, 8, and 12 (achievement-oriented leadership).

Total Scores

Directive leadership: _____

Supportive leadership: _____

Participative leadership: _____

Achievement-oriented leadership: _____

Scoring Interpretation

This questionnaire is designed to measure four types of path-goal leadership: directive, supportive, participative, and achievement-oriented. By comparing your scores on each of the four styles, you can determine which style is your strongest and which is your weakest. For example, if your scores were directive leadership = 21, supportive leadership = 10, participative leadership – 19, and achievement-oriented leadership = 7, your strengths would be directive and participative leadership, and your weaknesses would be supportive and achievement-oriented leadership. While this questionnaire measures your dominant styles, it also indicates the styles you may want to strengthen or improve.

If your score is 13–15, you are in the high range.

If your score is 6–12, you are in the moderate range.

If your score is 3–5, you are in the low range.

11.1 Core Values Questionnaire

 Visit www.sagepub.com/northouseintro2e for downloadable versions of these questionnaires

Purpose

1. To identify the core values most important to you
2. To reinforce core values and their role in ethical leadership

Directions

1. Review the values listed below. Use the blank lines at the bottom to add any values that are important to you that are not listed.
2. Put a star next to all the values that are important to you, including any you may have added. This will become your personal set of values.
3. Take 2 to 3 minutes to narrow the starred values to your top eight values by crossing off the values that are less important to you and circling the more important values.
4. Next, narrow the list to five important values, using the same process.
5. Narrow that list of five to three important values.
6. From these three values, choose your top two core values.

Core Values		
Peace	Authenticity	Love
Wealth	Power	Recognition
Happiness	Influence	Family
Success	Justice	Truth
Friendship	Integrity	Wisdom
Fame	Joy	Status
_____	_____	_____
_____	_____	_____

Source: Adapted from the "Self-Guided Core Values Assessment," Center for Ethical Leadership, www.ethicalleadership.org. Used with permission.

Scoring Interpretation

This exercise is designed to identify your core values. Ethical leadership includes knowing what your core values are and having the courage to integrate them with your actions, being mindful of the common good.

- Value words are packed with meaning. You likely went through a process of "bundling"—embedding one value in another and counting two or more values as one. This is a natural process. By narrowing your lists, you did not throw away any values; rather, you clarified what you mean by these words.

- Your two core values are easy to remember. Imagine putting them in your pocket when you leave home each day. These two values represent your larger set of values.

- Your core values can help you make difficult decisions as a leader. They can help you find common ground with others.